What Grandmother Said

ALIX MEYNELL
with some of the diaries

What Grandmother Said

The Life of Alice Dowson 1844-1927
based on her diaries
by her granddaughter

ALIX MEYNELL DBE

COLT BOOKS
Cambridge

COLT BOOKS
9 Clarendon Road
Cambridge CB2 2BH
tel: 01223 357047   fax: 01223 365866

First published by Colt Books in 1998

ISBN 0 905899 76 8

Printed in Great Britain by
Biddles Limited, Guildford and King's Lynn

To the late Phoebe David my friend,
researcher and collaborator, without
whose help and inspiration, this book
would have been an altogether lesser
enterprise

Contents

Illustrations

Acknowledgements

My CHIEF debt is to my friend, the late Mrs Phoebe David, to whom I have dedicated this book. I have greatly missed her enthusiasm and informed advice these last months. On this account, the contribution of my editor, Elfreda Powell, has been invaluable, not only as a highly professional editor but in being someone with whom I could mull over the subject and who was interested enough to do some research herself.

I owe a big debt of gratitude to my friend John Commander for his encouragement generally and for his help in bringing the book to publication; and to his wife, Yvonne Skargon, for taking the photographs which illustrates so well the basic material from which I have made this book. I am also much indebted to my relatives Ditta and Jimmie Kerr, for their support and belief in my ambitious enterprise.

Next, my thanks go to David Doughan (Reference Librarian at the Fawcett Library) for his unstinted and patient help with my enquiries on all Alice's political causes, especially Women's Suffrage and the Contagious Diseases controversy. I am grateful to the Fawcett Library, London Guildhall University, for permission to print the flysheet from their Newsletter No. 24.

I am also extremely grateful to Adam Daber, Curator of the Quarry Bank Mill Trust (and Carol O'Mahoney, formerly Archivist there) for untold help with my researches about the Gregs' early influence in the cotton industry and I thank the Trust for lending me the miniature of Hannah Greg (née Lightbody) included in this book. I also owe a big thank you to Mrs Jacks (née Greg) and her daughter the late Mrs Edward, for giving up so much of their time to show me over the Mill and, afterwards, to answer my queries about it and its relationship to Alice's family.

Baroness David and my friend Susan Hicklin searched out early information for me on the Contagious Diseases Acts and, on medical matters generally, I have had help from the B.M.A., Claire Nutt of the Wellcome Institute Library for the History of Medicine, Dr Sonnex (consultant dermatologist) and Dr Speake (general practitioner). On dental matters, dental surgeon Mr John Sharp has been most patient in giving me the information I asked for.

Huw Yardley and James Rhys at the Journal of the House of Commons, have taken endless trouble to supply me with information as also has Adrian Henstock, Principal Archivist of the Nottinghamshire Archives. Roy Jenkins has allowed me to make use of (and quote from) his recently published book on Gladstone and I am grateful for prompt and helpful answers to my enquiries from the Josephine Butler Society, The Galton Institute (formerly the Eugenics Society), Cambridge University Library, the Local Studies Library of the Derbyshire City Council and my own public library in Suffolk. Mr S. H. G. Twining, a director of Twinings, gave me information on the price of tea in the 1860's. Martha Westwater, whose book *The Wilson Sisters*, a study of Upper-class Victorian Life, is out of print, kindly gave me one of her copies.

The two paintings by John Opie R.A. are reproduced by kind permission of Ben Dowson, eldest surviving grandchild of Alice and Ben. The portrait of Ben by Arnsby Brown is reproduced by kind permission of Sir Philip Dowson, the youngest grandchild of Alice and Ben. The flysheet opposing the Contagious Diseases Acts is reproduced by permission of the Fawcett Library.

Finally, I have to thank my patient secretary, Anne Springall and a number of friends and relatives, especially Maggie Bishop who prepared the index with me, Betty Hopkins who helped to analyse the letters to and from Bonn, Jacqueline Watson, Peg Leask and Claude L. Clifford and my relatives, Elizabeth Joy, Rhona Dowson, Balbir Law and Benedict Meynell.

Preface

THIS IS the story of my grandmother Alice, who was born in 1844 and lived until 1927. It had to be written, not because my grandmother was anybody special, except to her family, but because she left a remarkable and uniquely complete contemporary account of middle-class life in Victorian England in the form of diaries, letters and other records.

Born in Prestbury, in Cheshire, Alice (Greg) spent her childhood in the village of Bollington but her married life was spent in Nottingham and in the village of Upper Broughton on the Nottinghamshire/Leicestershire border. Her husband (Ben Dowson) came from Geldeston in Norfolk where he was born in 1836. He moved to Nottingham to join his uncles' law firm there in 1853, and died in 1918. They had ten children, eight boys and two girls; all were born in Nottingham and lived into old age.

My grandmother's diaries begin two years before her marriage in 1863 and all except one of the fifty-three daily diaries that she kept from then until her death have survived. My grandfather also wrote a fairly full account of the various branches of his family, from 1795 (the year of his grandfather's marriage) until 1882. I have called it the Family Record. Some of his accounts survive in the Nottingham archive.

The family were frequent and prolific letter writers and some 300 of these have survived, mostly those written in the 1880s to and from Bonn where the two daughters were at school for a while. There is also a batch of letters written from India by the elder daughter who went there in 1897 to nurse the victims of the plague in Bombay.

The two families were inextricably linked by four Unitarian families – the Dowsons of Norfolk, the Gregs of Cheshire and the Enfields and Needhams of Nottingham. The Unitarians, who in those days were socially and politically influential, have been described by Claire Tomalin as 'rational dissenters' who:

represented the critical and sceptical tradition of protestantism without its black insistence on guilt. They had thrown out the doctrine of the Trinity, the idea of original sin and the concept of eternal punishment, explaining them all as purely poetic myths. [They] breathed the spirit of prudent optimism.

Now in my ninety-fifth year, I look back to my childhood and I vividly remember my grandmother. For various reasons, her house was more home to me than any other house; indeed I lived there during two short periods of my life, at the age of two and of seventeen, when I spent some months there instead of at school working for my Oxford entrance. She died when I was twenty-four.

It is in her old age that I remember her. I loved her and I respected her both for the strength of her opinions and for the fact that they were accompanied by a refreshing tolerance of the opinions of others. She emerges from the pages of her diaries first and foremost as the devoted wife and mother of a large Victorian family but, in the course of researching her life, I have discovered a larger person: I was right about her convictions and her tolerance but I have found, as well, a determined and active liberal politician and early feminist.

ALIX MEYNELL
Lavenham, 1997

Alice's and Ben's Family Trees

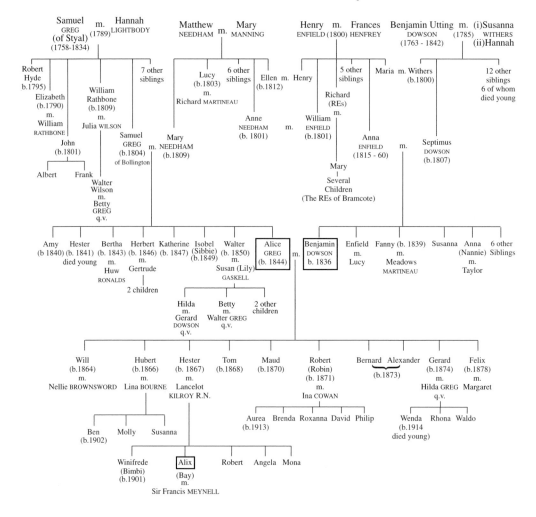

CHAPTER 1

Alice

'When you go out with gentlemen, never take wine.
It's quite exciting enough without.'

WHEN MY grandmother Alice gave me this advice, I was a wholly inexperienced sixteen-year-old and she an elderly widow. Sixty years further back in time, in August 1860, Alice had been about the same age as I was then.

It was a fine summer day and a young man – tall, handsome, fair-haired – was paying an afternoon call with his uncle at a house called The Mount in the village of Bollington, near Macclesfield, the home of Samuel and Mary Greg, Alice's parents.

The young man, Ben Dowson, would become my grandfather. The uncle, William Enfield, was not only his, but also Alice's, for he was married to her aunt Anne.

While on 12 August, Alice would be just sixteen, Ben was twenty-three and a very new clerk in his uncle's law office in Nottingham. Alice and Ben had never met before and for him it was love at first sight. Years later, this is how Ben described that first meeting:

> It is a date that has always remained fixed in my mind... in the after-noon we called at Mr Samuel Greg's house. It was only a visit of a few minutes, but it sufficed to give me a picture of that sweet home as it then was. The girls, scarcely more than children, rushed me down the terrace to get a peep at the lovely view over the hills to Buxton. Amy and Bertha I already knew and loved, but this was my first sight of Alice, then nearly 16, but looking so slight and young.

By an extraordinary chance, photographs exist both of Alice and Ben from about this time. The date of Alice's is recorded on the back: February 1862, and an entry in Alice's diary describes her going to Manchester with her mother and younger sister Katherine, 'to have our photos taken *carte-de-visite*. Amy, Herbert

1

ALICE, AGED 18

and Walter have been done and Bertha was [done] last year in London.' The photograph shows a very formal and solemn girl in a full long skirt and shoulder cloak, her hand resting on an open book on a most unlikely pillar. It is visiting-card size and mounted on a piece of board and, after 135 years, in a pale sepia and white, so there is nothing to relieve the solemnity. Fortunately, a word portrait exists to colour and lighten this picture in a letter written by my grandfather on the morning of their Golden Wedding:

Let me give you some idea of my dear Alice when I married her fifty

2

BEN, C 1860

years ago – outwardly, a sweet slim girl, just out of childhood, with beautiful red gold hair and deep telling eyes, inwardly so much more than this, a treasure that I only learnt the true loveliness of, as our life together went forward, She always had a brave, as well as a loving heart; and great nobility of mind...

Photographs were rare in those days. The next that has survived of Alice dates from about six years later. In this (page 69) she is seen seated with her third child on her knee. The first picture we have of Ben shows him in informal dress, with a very young handsome face.

Alice's father, Samuel, was the fourth son of the Samuel Greg

(Senior) who, in 1784, had founded a cotton spinning empire. Alice's mother was Mary Needham, one of a family of eight who lived at Lenton, then a village just outside Nottingham.

Samuel Greg (Junior) managed the company's cotton mill at Bollington, a village not far from Styal and within walking distance of Macclesfield. The Mount was a large comfortable family house with a big garden and ample grounds, overlooking Bollington village.

The visit to Alice's home, so momentous for the young people, must also have been very poignant for their elders, because Ben's mother, Anna Dowson, had died just two months earlier. Not only was she Uncle William's young sister, she had also been Alice's mother's life-long friend. The Enfield and Needham families had known each other all their lives, both living in and around Nottingham and both Unitarian.

The links between the Gregs and Needhams were almost as close: the elder Samuel Greg had sent his sons to Mr Taylor's Unitarian school in Nottingham from the age of seven, and the boys at the school were made welcome at the Needham's home, Lenton House.

Though Mary Greg (Alice's mother) and Anna Dowson (Ben's mother) had been special friends since childhood, they had probably seen little of one another since marriage: one had gone to live in Cheshire, the other in Norfolk. Both marriages had taken place in the mid-1830s, a decade before the era of railway travel when a journey across England could take two or three days with several coach changes. A journey that the Needham family made from Nottingham to Norwich, for example, was recorded as having taken three days.

Frequent letter-writing had kept the two mothers' friendship alive, as well as the exchange of visits by their children. There had indeed been such a visit that same year, 1860, when Alice's two elder sisters, Amy and Bertha, had been Easter guests in Anna and Septimus Dowson's Southtown house on the outskirts of Yarmouth: 'the last time,' Ben wrote, 'that we were ever to meet as a united family in the old home. How little we guessed the great change so close upon us!'

It is quite time for Alice's voice to be heard. That it can be heard as early as January 1862 is due to the chance discovery long after my grandmother's death of her private diary for 1862 and 1863. I found it hidden amongst a lot of old photograph albums that came to me when her home was sold on the death of the last of my uncles. It is written in a school exercise book, inscribed at the front in a careful copy-book hand: ALICE GREG. PRIVATE, 1862, and signed at the end ALICE DOWSON. It may well have lain unopened from that day 135 years ago to the day I found it.

When she begins her diary, she is already deep in love:

> It was a year last Monday since I first saw Ben – to speak of at least. (3 February) Mo and Puppy [her parents] came home from seeing Ben this very day at 5 o'clock. I couldn't get to hear much about him, for I daren't ask mother somehow, If *only* I could go and see him, tho' its wrong to be discontented! (6 February)
> This day last year I first felt that Ben cared for me. (9 March)

This last entry was only nine months after their first meeting in the garden of her home, so it may have been 'love at first sight' for her too.

What kind of person was Alice at seventeen, as she emerges from her diary? Quite clearly a girl of great sweetness and gentleness, with strong inherited religious beliefs, liberal opinions and an enquiring mind, whether about the eclipse of the moon or the rights and wrongs of hunting. She emerges as a naturally happy girl who enjoyed walking, bathing and croquet, and painting. She appears devoted to all her family in apparently equal measure, except perhaps her eldest sister, Amy – the sunbeam of the house Alice calls her – who seems to have been *prima inter pares*.

We know nothing about Alice's education because her diary did not begin until she was seventeen. However, there is nothing in what she says about her young sisters' education, or in my grand-father's account of his forebear's education, to suggest that the Gregs departed from the norm for the middle classes: they had a governess to take charge of the children (both boys and girls) as they left the nursery, after which the boys were sent away to school sometime between the ages of seven and ten.

Middle-class girls most commonly stayed at home with a gov-erness throughout their education, but this was not the case in Alice's circle of families. Her mother, Mary Needham, went to Mrs Turner's school in Nottingham which 'was something very differ-ent from the ordinary schools for young ladies'. Here the girls were taught not only the usual subjects but also botany, history and philosophy; they learnt to speak French, to take an interest in public affairs, to think for themselves and 'have an earnest purpose in life'.

It is clear from Alice's diary that her young sisters were part governess and part school educated and probably the same was true of Alice. She often refers to her school friends, and there is a chance remark that while in London she went to visit 'Miss Boon poor thing. She has so few pupils now.' So we can assume she went to a boarding school in or near London.

As to the type of school, there is only the fact that letters written to her daughters in later life show that she is critical of it; she writes more than once that she hopes her daughters will have a better education than she had.

In Alice's mother's day, there were of course fewer schools in England for girls than for boys; those that there were would usually have been small family schools. The era of Miss Buss and Miss Beale, of Cheltenham Ladies College (founded 1854) and Roedean, still lay then well in the mists of the future. My grandfather's Family Record mentions two girls' boarding schools, which had been run by members of his family: one at Worksop, in the late eighteenth century, kept by Mrs Henfrey, his maternal grandmother; and one at Clapham Common, started in the begin-ning of the nineteenth century by Mrs Hannah Dowson, his step-grandmother on his father's side. Alice seems to have gone to a family-type school of this kind in London, her sisters to one in Brighton.

When we meet Alice on the first page of her diary in 1862, she is taking lessons from a governess by the name of Miss Ronalds, who is there primarily for Alice's younger sisters, Katie and Isobel ('Sibbie'). Alice still feels young enough to write (23 January 1862): 'We children went to tea with...' but old enough to be feeling the constraint of the schoolroom:

> Things are not going on very smoothly with Miss Ronalds now, especially lessons. (2 March)
> Mo had a talk with Miss Ronalds) and so brought things to a crisis and there were little explosions, especially about the sewing class, but all was comfortably settled at last. (6 March)

Like other girls of her time and social circle, Alice would have been instructed in music, painting, sewing, and duty to the 'lower classes'. Diary entries refer to her or her sisters taking Sunday school and –

> We began a sewing class and reading aloud for the girls, down in the schoolroom. We made clothes for the poor people. 34 girls there. Very successful. (4 February)

Those attending the class would probably have been millgirls from Bollington.

Alice was perhaps over serious and a bit of a prig at this age. She shows something of this in her criticism of '*dear* Fanny' – one of her friends – for being 'a *little* touched by gaiety and admiration... the poor girl has had 2 proposals already though she is only 18'. She is scathing about 'flirting' and when she comments on the engagement of this same Fannny, she writes: 'I am very glad... for it will take her out of the flirting Bury set.'

She may not have received a proposal herself but, reading between the lines, she appears to have had at least one devoted admirer and knew it. He was Albert, her uncle John Greg's son and he came often to the house: 'I had dreamt a *horrid* dream about A,' Alice wrote. 'That he was found stone dead near the back hall door.' Perhaps she was feeling guilty, knowing that her heart was wholly committed to Ben and had not – could not, given the conventions of the day – tell him so.

She is also very ready to examine her own faults and to receive criticism too from the older generation:

> Mo told me I was getting supercilious and uncharitable – in my letters chiefly. Of course it grieved me but I daresay its true and it is as well I should know it (7 Jan).

An early diary entry is about a visit to Manchester to buy ball dresses for a dance which she is attending with her seventeen-year-old sister Bertha, with whom she usually paired off for functions and visits. She doesn't describe the dresses at all, however. Indeed, throughout this young diary she appears very little interested in clothes or in what she or her friends look like or wear. This may be due to puritanism, so much a part of her upbringing – but surely, in the first pages of this specially private diary, she would have felt able to let herself go? Of the dance itself, she says only that it was 'pretty nice. Albert was there and Frank and Edmund Schwabe. Of course it was nothing like the Nottingham dances. I thought Bertha the prettiest in the room.'

How much was Alice influenced by her forebears and family traditions? Her grandfather, Samuel Greg (Senior), had been an enlightened employer in the cotton industry at the end of the eighteenth century and early years of the nineteenth, who had treated his workpeople with a humanity unusual in those days, when the terrible conditions described later with such force in Dickens' *Hard Times*, Disraeli's *Two Nations* and Mrs Gaskell's *Mary Barton* were endured by working people in the north of

England. Samuel opened his first mill in 1784 in Cheshire, at Quarry Bank, near Styal.

Because Styal was an isolated country hamlet, Samuel had to import most of his labour and he drew it mainly from the poorest of the poor in the workhouses of the growing industrial towns. To begin with, many were child apprentices for whom he signed indentures with their previous parishes undertaking to 'find provide and allow unto the said Apprentice meet, competent and sufficient Meat, Drink, Apparel, Lodging, Washing, and other things necessary and fit'.

In the early 1800s as many as a hundred boys and girls were looked after in his Apprentice House, one of whom would later comment that:

> the rooms were very clean, the floors frequently washed... Our beds were good, we slept two to a bed and had clean sheets once a month, new clothes for Sundays once in two years and new working jackets when those had worn out...

Some twenty years later, when the business expanded, Samuel built a model village alongside Quarry Bank Mill with houses for the millworkers, a chapel and a school for the apprentices and the children of the adult workforce.

Samuel and later his son Robert Hyde Greg have been described as 'both diligent in their duties' and going frequently far beyond the provisions of the law'. Engels cites Robert Hyde Greg as one of three paternalistic employers, whose ideas he dismisses as basically self-serving and tending to enslave the workers. It is not known whether he met Robert or visited Styal but the description he gives of the comfortable cottages and social conditions could certainly have applied to the workpeople at Quarry Bank Mill.

The influence of Samuel's wife, Hannah (Alice's grandmother) must have been all important. A Unitarian, she had grown up in Liverpool where she was a close friend of the influential Quakers, William and Hannah Rathbone. She has been described as 'a highly intelligent woman'; she had been brought up in an intellectual and progressive atmosphere, about which she would later write that 'one evening at Liverpool... went farther in education, in forming the heart and taste of the youthful listener, than years of the common routine of instructions'. She named her youngest son, William Rathbone, which I see as a recognition of her debt to her Rathbone friends.

Hannah is known to have interested herself in the welfare and education of the apprentices when Samuel established his home at Quarry Bank in 1796. She was said to have believed in education for its own sake and her influence must surely also be seen in the fact that, as early as 1788, Samuel made himself responsible for the education of those of his workforce who were children, paying a teacher and buying the necessary books for them to learn the basic skills of reading, writing and arithmetic and even engaging a music teacher for them. Later she would open a school for the mill workers' children. So she was something of a pioneer as regards the education of the working classes at that time.

It is said that once the Apprentice House was built it played a special part in the life of the whole Greg family. Hannah was no doubt responsible, too, for starting up a 'Female Society', a 'Sick Club' and a debating society for the benefit of the workers and she took an active interest in medical provision for the apprentices and adult workforce. Indeed, we are told that Samuel was prepared to leave to 'the ladies' all social concerns such as the cost of building and equipping the school. He was first and foremost a man of business; his wife must have been the leading influence in the firm's liberal attitude to its workforce.

Inevitably, Hannah had also had a big influence on her own children's upbringing. Her daughters were educated as well as her sons and all 'were trained from childhood to take an active and intelligent interest in the work of the world'. Both sons and daughters did some of the teaching at the Styal village school.

The sons – including Alice's father Samuel (Junior) were all sent away to good Unitarian schools at seven years old and went on to university in Edinburgh. Samuel (Senior) himself had had the opportunity to travel before settling down to regular work and he arranged that his sons should all have a Continental Tour before starting work at Styal. He expected this tour to be primarily directed to making foreign contacts useful for the firm's business but Hannah insisted that it must be as much an opportunity for them to study European culture.

The eldest daughter, Elizabeth, who married William Rathbone (Hannah's friends' son) would become a well-known educationalist. In 1870, at the age of eighty, she had a considerable influence on the Foster Education Act, sending Mr Foster a string of memoranda on the bill (based on her own experience) – 'the most useful hints of their kind that he had received'. 'Aunt Rathbone', as Alice called her, must also have had an influence on the adolescent Alice and her sisters.

The Greg grandparents had lived at Quarry Bank House, overlooking the River Bollin which supplied power for the mill and, to this day, runs through the garden of the still beautiful bow-fronted house. In Samuel (Senior)'s day Quarry Bank House was noted 'for its cultured atmosphere' and 'visitors were impressed with its simplicity and the family's obvious contentment'. Alice never knew that atmosphere because both her grandparents had died before she was born, but her diary contains frequent entries about later happy family gatherings there and, in her old age, I have heard her talk of it with affection – and a little awe, perhaps retained from those days of childhood and early youth, when it was the home of her uncle Robert, then head of the Greg family and business and for a time MP for Manchester.

However much or little Alice may have been affected by the family tradition of liberalism, established by her grandparents she never knew, the living influence of her parents in the same direction must have been strong. Her father was only thirty and full of socialist idealism when the management of the company fell to him and his brothers on Samuel (Senior)'s death in 1834. Liberalism was quite as strong in his wife's family, the Needhams of Lenton, but in their case it took the form of supporting the national liberation

HANNAH GREG (NÉE LIGHTBODY)
wife of Samuel Greg (Senior), Alice's grandmother

movements on the Continent. Both Garibaldi and Kossuth, the exiled Hungarian patriot, received their public support and their large house at Lenton was open to Italian patriots sheltering in England. In her 1910 diary Alice would comment on an illustration of the new Kossuth Mausoleum at Budapest' that:

> This appeared in the *Sphere* just 53 years since Kossuth visited my parents at The Mount, (an exile, v. poor, – lecturing here and there for his living,) March 18th 1857. I remember it so very well.

SAMUEL GREG (JUNIOR)
Alice's father

When young Samuel took over Lowerhouse Mill at Bollington, he planned a Utopian community there on strictly ideological lines. Mrs Gaskell, the author – and another Unitarian – was a friend of Samuel and his wife and she often stayed with them at The Mount. (Later, her niece, Lilly, would marry one of Alice's brothers.) It is easy to imagine the long and comfortable talks they must have had together about young Samuel's plans to replace at Bollington the horrors that Mrs Gaskell would later describe in her books.

Alice's father has been described as seeing in Bollington 'a chance to create Utopia to his own design'; as seeking to change the relationship between master and men, making his employees 'virtuous, sensible, well informed and well-bred men (and women)', and when his plans matured, calling together 'a few of his trusted workmen to discuss how to put them into execution'. He built a village hall and school and rebuilt the workmen's cottages, with gardens and allotments and even paid gardeners to look after them if the workers had insufficient time!

In fact, Samuel Junior became more interested in pursuing his Utopian dream than in ensuring a healthy profit margin. By 1847, he was £32,000 in debt – a spectacular amount for those days – the modern-day equivalent of which would be around £1.6 million. Lowerhouse Mill had to be rescued by his brothers, and in a final blow, even his favoured workpeople went on strike because they thought some new machinery he had installed would cost them jobs. It is said that this broke his heart and that he never went down to the mill again.

All this happened when Alice was only three years old and there is no means of knowing whether, or if, she was in any way directly influenced by the story. Her father called her 'his strawberry' so we can assume a special relationship on his side and it is easy to imagine that his small daughter would have been a great comfort in those grim days of failure in 1847. However, in Alice's diaries of the 1860s and 1870s, he is a much loved and honoured father, often mentioned as giving lectures or preaching, but now elderly and already very much prone to illness. On his death, his wife and daughter Amy (but mainly Amy according to Alice) put together his writings and life story in a book called *A Layman's Legacy*, in which his lifelong piety from the age of seven emerges very clearly. It was in this atmosphere that Alice grew up.

Alice's diaries for 1862 and 1863 cover the same period and often the same events as Ben's Family Record, but have little in common with it. Ben's account was intended for general reading by his

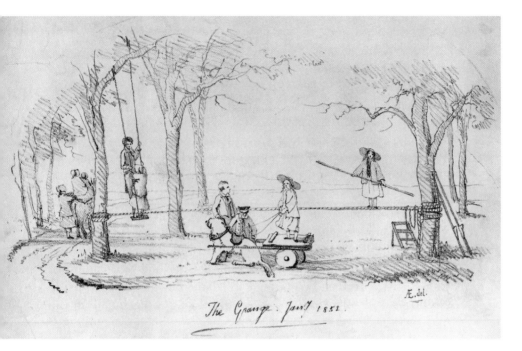

The Grange. Jan 7 1852.

Æ.del.

CHILDREN PLAYING AT BRAMCOTE
home of Alice's uncle, Richard Enfield. One of the children
may well have been Alice.

descendants; Alice's is the private diary of a young girl in love.

It is time to tell Ben's story up to his arrival at Bollington in August 1860, and to cover for them both the fateful year 1861, which appears, in Alice's words, only in the form of 'this time last year'.

CHAPTER 2

Ben

'Young for my age and altogether innocent.'

WE KNOW a good deal more about Ben's upbringing and early life, than we do about Alice's. He was the first child of Anna and Septimus Dowson, and was born in 1836 in a small house called The Farm, in the village of Geldeston, three miles from Beccles on the Norfolk/Suffolk border. Christened 'Benjamin', he was always known as 'Ben'.

His father was the youngest son of Benjamin Utting and Susanna Dowson who lived at The Old House in Geldeston (it is still so called) which he made the centre of the family malting and corn merchanting business. His mother was one of a family of Enfields who lived at The Grange in Bramcote village, just outside Nottingham. Enfield relatives were still living at Bramcote in the mid-1930s.

When Ben was two, the family moved to Yarmouth on Septimus being appointed manager of the Yarmouth end of the business. Benjamin Utting died four years later, but Ben and his younger brother Enfield continued to be always welcome at The Old House, sometimes staying there with their grandmother for weeks at a time.

Benjamin Utting (or B.U.D. as he was known) was a man of strong personality and high principles. A noted liberal all his life, he had been one of the Young Whigs to welcome the French Revolution in its early days. He was a practising Unitarian and the devoted father of a very numerous family. Fortunately in the circumstances, he was also an extremely successful businessman.

Left at the age of twenty-five on the death of his father, with a business in confusion and encumbered with debts, he had suddenly to provide a home for his widowed stepmother, for a sister still living at home, and for his own young wife and growing family. He immediately left Mutford Hall where they had lived with his father in ease and considerable comfort, and moved to Geldeston village where, for £3,200, he bought two malt-houses, the local public house and some cottages and land as well as The Old House for the family to live in.

Being in the midst of fine barley-growing land and linked by the river Waveney and the plentiful waterways of East Anglia to the towns of the eastern counties as well as to London and the Continent, Geldeston was eminently suitable as a centre of the business that Benjamin Utting now set about establishing. Earlier Dowsons had been linen drapers in Yarmouth, and farmers in Mutford; under B. U. D. they became a large and highly respected firm of maltsters, corn merchants and shippers. So quickly successful was he, that by the end of the eighteenth century (only twelve years after his father's death) the company had premises in Norwich, Beccles, Gorleston and Yarmouth. Early progress made with paying off his father's debts had established confidence in him in the local business community.

In Benjamin Utting's day, before the coming of the railway, there was a large amount of traffic by water between Yarmouth and Norwich. The firm even became builders of small boats and Ben's grandfather owned a cabin boat in which he travelled about the area; it was called *The Zephyr* and this would be the name that his grandson would give to the yacht he had built, upwards of a century later.

Fortunately, B.U.D. was not alone in his task. He had the ready help of his widowed stepmother and 'they were a great mutual support to one another'. She was a woman of high principles and liberal views (she refused to eat sugar because of its connection with the slave trade) and no doubt she had a continuing influence on her young stepson and his family. They kept in touch with her by visits and letters throughout her life.

So, in 1800, B.U.D. was a man of position and substance; he could afford the luxury of having his and his wife's portraits painted by Opie. Their grandson pronounced both portraits to be 'most lifelike and excellent'. Susanna was then still a beautiful

BENJAMIN UTTING DOWSON
painted by John Opie R.A., 1800, Ben's grandfather

woman with auburn hair and reddish-brown eyes. She was in the habit of writing rather bad verse on all family occasions and had this to say about the portrait, which, if not poetry, at least shows that she was pleased with it!

> When low in earth this faded form shall lie,
> Thanks to thy genius Opie, I shall live.

Sadly, there followed a decade of family tragedy. Her three eldest children, all daughters died one year after another, 'on the verge of

SUSANNA DOWSON
painted by John Opie R.A., 1800, Ben's grandmother

womanhood'. Doctors were called but hope of recovery seems to have been given up as the disease struck. The unfolding tragedy is very movingly described in the diaries of Ben's uncle Withers, then a young schoolboy, who watched his three older sisters die, some quickly, some slowly, but all with remarkable courage, resignation and even cheerfulness, at least in front of their young brothers. These years were not all tragedy, however; during them, the four youngest children were born, Septimus (Ben's father) the thirteenth (despite his name), and last, in 1807.

* * *

The house to which Septimus moved his family when he became manager of the Yarmouth branch was on the outskirts of the town. It had a big garden within which an area of rough ground was set aside for the children to play in. From here the two boys could see the harbour at Yarmouth, watch the weekly passenger steamers arrive from London and Bristol and the comings and goings on the river. 'I well remember', Ben wrote,

> the constant delight it was to me as a lad to push along the riverside, through the long line of wharfs, and ship and boat-building yards, and watch from point after point all the different operations going on in the port. The place even then had all the air of an old, continental town, and yet was alive with mercantile life; often there would be as many as a hundred ships loading or unloading in the port at the same time...
>
> The herring boats as they came up the river on their return from their fishing journeys, were followed by boys, running along as near to the river as they could, shouting and singing... The takes of these boats were sometimes enormous, a single boat bringing in more than ten lasts of fish, each last being about 12,000 fish... A last would be worth from about £8 to £20 at that time.

The coming of the railways was a special excitement in the boys' childhood. Ben describes a journey to Nottingham for a family wedding in 1840 when he was four years old, and part of the journey was by train 'for the embryo Midland Railway was just opened and consisted of a line from Derby to Nottingham'. And some time in 1843 or 1844 he and his brother were taken to see the new railway line being built from Yarmouth to Norwich: 'it was the first bit of railway made in either Norfolk or Suffolk and it created interest throughout the neighbourhood'.

Septimus concerned himself closely with the upbringing of his elder children and thought that they should learn something of the family business as early as possible. Their house was less than a mile from the wharf and granary belonging to B.U. Dowson & Sons, so the boys were anyhow brought up in the midst of the business. Ben describes how it was always a treat to be taken over the malthouses and granary by his father, to talk to the workmen, to learn about the different processes, see the heavily laden wherries coming down with the tide and watch the corn being unloaded, and loaded into the ships for foreign parts.

When the boys went to stay at The Old House they could see the Geldeston end of the business and identify with it in a special way. In autumn and winter the farmers would bring their corn to be loaded on to the wherries for transfer by the river Waveney to Beccles and beyond. This is how Ben was to describe it:

> Many waggon loads of corn would arrive during the day, some of them with splendid teams of horses. Amongst the better class of farmers there was quite a rivalry in the turnout of their teams... Often the Staithe [a wharf with a dyke or short canal communicating with the river] would be full of waggons, and a file as well, waiting in the road outside. There was a long shed capable of holding from 40 to 50 horses, where the waggoners could stall their horses and give them a feed and a rest.

From Ben's account, it appears that Benjamin Utting became very much of a hero to him. It is easy to see how a romantic admiration for what his grandfather had achieved would have become part of the young boy's delight in the land and the water-ways of his childhood, and in the processes of the business with which they were so closely involved. As the eldest grandson – the fourth Benjamin, he proudly claimed – he could well have pictured himself as one day being its head.

Ben's parents were always interested in public affairs and they discussed them in the presence of their children. Ben remembered listening to them talk and having political and national events explained to him as a child: he was told of the Khyber Pass disaster in 1840 when he was four (this was when the British garrison had withdrawn from Khabul, and a whole regiment had been wiped out by Afghan tribesmen: Gladstone had called it a signal disaster); and at ten in 1846 he had the Repeal of the Corn Laws (which had protected British corn producers from foreign imports) explained to him as being 'right, though it would almost certainly injure our business and make us poorer'.

Both parents appear to have been committed Liberals, as were most Unitarians, and Ben wrote that the boys found the elections at Yarmouth – 'very exciting; we used to shout lustily for our colour which was blue; the Tories were red'.

Their father had a happy, enjoying nature when they were children; he took them on expeditions, taught them about birds and read aloud to them: Ben remembered hearing him read *Dombey and Son* as it came out in monthly parts. But later his father 'lost his brightness and love of fun' and became 'anxious, quick-tempered and unwilling to brook contradiction'.

In the Family Record this change in Septimus is put down to 'business worries and the poor health of his wife'. Anna indeed died young, but there were also painful differences between the parents over religion. The Unitarians did not believe in the Trinity, so when his wife said (as Ben quotes) that 'she now felt that she must pray to Christ', Septimus must have known that she was moving away from their shared faith. In later years, he too left the Unitarian faith, but at the time his wife's change of belief was a serious blow.

Fortunately, the family could always look to their uncle Withers and aunt Maria for support and light-hearted enjoyment. They lived in Norwich and the family ties with them could not have been stronger: uncle Withers was their father's elder brother, and aunt Maria was their mother's sister, for Withers and Septimus had married Enfield sisters. At the time of his marriage, so it is recorded, Withers held a farewell party in London for his eleven bachelor friends at which '1 doz of Port wine was purchased and almost all consumed on the premises'. As elder brother, Withers had always had a special concern for Septimus who for a time had lived with him and had served his lawyer's articles in his office in Norwich.

Uncle Withers and aunt Maria had no children of their own, and so it is not surprising that a deep and lasting affection grew up between the two families: their uncle, wrote Ben, 'invariably brought sunshine into the house', bathed with the children and took them on expeditions; and aunt Maria was 'a second mother' to them all, paying frequent visits to the house in Yarmouth and sometimes staying for weeks at a time. And, of course, she very much took their mother Anna's place when, at forty-five, she died after the birth of her eleventh child.

At Christmas, there was a great distribution of Christmas dinners from the Yarmouth house to the men employed by B.U.D. & Sons and then the children were allowed into the kitchen to help in the preparations. The caring relationship that Septimus maintained with his workpeople is shown in Ben's description of Christmas present-giving:

> The amounts given to each family were carefully apportioned by my father. One or two of the largest families received 10 lbs of beef 4 lbs of currants, a shilling for tea and tickets for a liberal supply of flour and beer; this distribution was quite an event, and made us know something of most of the families. When we handed the parcels to the family, we children used to accompany the gift with some special good wishes such as 'a pocket full of money and a cellar full of wine'.

Ben tells us in his Family Record, 'At the time of my grandfather's death I was 6 years old; from this period my memories are very clear and I shall be speaking almost entirely from my own knowledge.'

His record of his schooldays in Brighton and London has the vividness and detail of a contemporary account, suggesting a diary was kept. And sure enough – I find that his diary for 1843 to 1854 (from the ages of seven to eighteen) is held in Norwich library. Interesting examples quoted from it are these descriptions – of arriving in London in 1851:

> One realised that something special was going on as soon as London

was reached. The Exhibition held the field, and all the dwellers in the great city were under its spell. It seemed to pressage to all the opening of an era of universal peace, the talk of it was in everyone's mouth.

and of attending the Duke of Wellington's funeral:

> We had to take up our station at about 4 o'clock in the morning, and could not stir again until about 5 o'clock in the afternoon. The funeral procession began about 12.00 o'clock and it seemed to take hours to pass. The funeral car was most gorgeous and the bright colours of the trappings contrasted strongly with the 20 black dray horses that drew the car. When it got light you could realise the enormous numbers of people pressed into the spaces from which anything could be seen... Some fearful scenes took place through women fainting... The only way they could be got out was by passing them over the heads of the crowd... there were however only one or two fatal accidents on this day, though 7 persons were killed at the Duke's lying in state at Westminster.

Ben was sent to boarding school in Brighton at the age of ten. Before this he and his brother and sister Fanny had been taught at home by a Swiss governess, who was in general charge of their lives as well as their education, taking them for walks and joining in their life after lessons. She was charming and vivacious and Ben was fond of her and tried to please her. There was also a male tutor engaged to teach them English and arithmetic – 'a big stiff pompous man', writes Ben, who was 'inclined to favour Fanny and never ceased to enlarge on her virtues and my wickedness and inattention'. He makes the very human admission here that it 'rather annoyed' him that his sister, three years younger and a very forward child 'always did her best'.

Boarding school was a considerable shock to the young Ben. He describes himself at this age as being 'young for my age and altogether innocent':

> I had no idea of the wickedness of ordinary school life... There was

24

no little bullying. I could bear a bit of pain and illusage without its troubling me but some boys had bad times to pass through.

Bullying is also mentioned in his uncle Withers' diary as a fact of school life.

After Brighton, Ben was sent to London University school where discipline was much more relaxed and friendly: corporal punishment was forbidden and 'one could go about naturally and without fear'. Lords cricket ground (the old one) was used for school matches and Ben, a keen and good cricketer, was a member of the first eleven and so played several times at Lords, once even as captain. Amongst his schoolmates at Brighton were a Martineau, a Courtauld and a Needham, all families with which Ben's family already had ties and with which his and Alice's lives would be linked in the future: his sister Fanny married a Martineau, Alice's mother was a Needham, and her sister Lucy had married a Martineau too, and Sarah Courtauld was one of her greatest friends.

At eighteen Ben went on to London University, joining University Hall in Gordon Square. He explains that:

Few dissenters (Unitarian or other) went to Oxford or Cambridge. University Hall was designed by its founders, mostly leading Unitarians, as a place for those who were not willing to conform to the national Church and so could reap some of the benefits of university life.

His fees were paid by his mother's brother Edward, who thus 'enabled my father to do more for his children than would otherwise have been possible' (a happy family practice that has continued through the generations, my own university fees and those of my sisters having been paid for by two of my uncles).

Ben did not, however, complete his university course because his uncles, William and Richard Enfield, offered a place in their law office in Nottingham either to Ben or to his brother, Enfield. A good opening like this could not be refused and Enfield, having spent a year in Germany to learn German had already, at the wish of his father, entered the family office at Geldeston. He had wanted to study for the priesthood but his father had refused to provide the money for that training.

'I well remember wishing his lot of entering the family business had fallen to me,' Ben writes sadly. He does not say why, as the eldest son, his wishes did not prevail, but I judge from what he says and does not say, that his uncles preferred him to his brother. He says too that it was his mother's wish that he should join his uncles – 'She... felt that with them I should be sure of a healthful and improving life.'

So, for whatever reason, this was the end of any childhood dreams Ben may have had of following his grandfather into the family business. He abandoned his university studies (which as he describes them, were far from arduous and allowed plenty of time for the very considerable pleasures of London with much theatre-going), and went to work in Nottingham for a few trial months before finally committing himself. When, after this period, he began his articles, it was still 'without having developed any love for the law. I thought the life beareable, no more.' It is easy to read between the lines of this unemotional statement and picture the young man's inner struggle before he accepted his uncles' offer.

In July 1856, a year after he had taken this important step in life, Ben and his brother Enfield were given a holiday together in Switzerland. Ben was twenty, his brother nineteen. Enfield's expenses were paid by one of his uncles, and their parents made what Ben describes as a 'considerable sacrifice', giving him £30 which he was 'to make go as far as possible'. What he made it go to was a four-week holiday, half of which was spent on a walking tour in Switzerland.

Where today's tourists reach for their cameras, Ben and Enfield reached for their sketchbooks and during the journey up the Rhine they were 'mainly in the bow of the steamer, sketch book in hand, trying to catch each castle or special view as we rapidly passed on our way'. Their greatest excitement was their first sight of the Swiss Alps from their hotel on the north shore of Lake Constance, 'shining in the sun, crested with snow, gleaming with an intense brilliancy – a memory for life'.

In Switzerland, they embarked on a walking tour of what I can only describe as 'Olympic' proportions. It took them in a zig-zag route across Switzerland, from Lake Constance to Chamonix, in fourteen days – some 400 miles of foot-slogging which included most of the major passes with glaciers to manoeuvre, and thousands of feet of climbing and descent. Though excited and jubilant about their achievement, both – not surprisingly – were completely exhausted at the end of the fortnight.

There followed, for Ben, three years working under his uncles in Nottingham, and a year in London with a law firm largely engaged in Court work, after which he passed his finals early in 1860: 'I was placed 13th and might have been higher,' he reports. 'I simply aimed at passing.' And on 1 May, he began work as a salaried clerk in his uncles' office, only to be summoned home within weeks to be at his mother's deathbed.

So, on that August afternoon in 1860, his emotions must have been very near the surface, his grief over the death of his mother was only weeks old and his disappointment about having to become a lawyer probably lingering still. In contrast, the Greg sisters were happy and carefree and Alice was young and beautiful. No wonder he fell in love.

CHAPTER 3

The Engagement

'God stopped the rain.'

THE MEETINGS between Alice and Ben over the next three years, described in detail in Alice's private diary, were not – could not be – frequent, if only because she lived in Cheshire, Ben in Nottingham. And when they did meet, privacy was hard to come by. In their day, it was not proper for young people of opposite sex to be alone together unless married or engaged or (as described by Jane Austen) when 'arranged' for a proposal by the parents. Their best hope of achieving a degree of privacy was on the dance floor or on a walk when pairing-off could be managed. And then, of course, the *weather* could be all important. Fortunately for Alice, at a crucial moment – 'God stopped the rain'.

But that is to anticipate. Between then and Ben's first visit to Bollington two years earlier in August 1860, many heart-stopping meetings, many anxieties, hopes and fears are recorded by Alice in her diary, or are referred to in it as 'this time last year'.

Ben had lived with his uncle William and aunt Anne while serving his three years of articles in Nottingham. Having no children of their own, they had treated him very much as a son of the house. Now, in the summer of 1860, so soon after his mother's death, they must have been anxious to distract and comfort him – and were probably aware of the impression made on their favourite nephew by the Bollington visit. And since they were aunt and uncle to Alice as well as to Ben, it is not surprising to learn that Alice (accompanied by one of her sisters) was given an early invitation to stay with them in Nottingham.

The visit took place the following spring and it proved fateful for both. This is Ben's account of it:

my aunt rejoiced to see her nephews & nieces enjoy themselves and she gave me leave to come in as often as I liked. I was constantly at the house, often to lunch, and then again in the evening. We read aloud Trollope's *Framley Parsonage* and played cards. There were several dances ... Aunt Anne got both Bertha & Alice new dresses; they looked a very sweet pair of girls, and quite smart, which was unusual.

This was not the only time he would refer to his beloved as less than smart. Did he consider that the social status of the Greg family – being 'in trade' and living in the industrial north – was less than that of his own or of the chief families of Nottingham? Or did the fact that his uncle William was Town Clerk of Nottingham perhaps carry a special status?

There was a further visit in the autumn, by which time Ben had moved to rooms not shared with other clerks and had 'made his first investments in furniture'. Here he dared to invite his aunt and the two Greg sisters to tea:

I had the honour of entertaining aunt Anne, Bertha & Alice to tea, and making Alice sit for the first time in the rocking chair, partly wicker, which she still uses in our Dining Room in the Park.

(Often and often, I, his granddaughter, have sat in that chair in the home of their old age at Broughton.)

When one comes to the events of 1862, there is no shortage of detail from Alice:

I got a letter from aunt Anne to ask me to go for 3 weeks at the end of June to go picnics & sketch ... It made me so happy. Ben has always wanted us to go in the summer so that we can row on the river ... Though it is a long time off, yet it is pretty well certain. (22 February)

The visit did eventually take place, but an even more exciting invitation intervened; this was from Henry Enfield's family (another uncle) for Alice and Bertha to spend a fortnight in April with them in London and go to a ball at University Hall (Ben's old college) to which Ben, most likely, was also going. 'It is just

29

possible we may go, though not at all likely', Alice writes with her usual caution about anything really badly wanted. But, two days later, 'We *are* going to London after all!!!'

Then came the news in a letter from Ben to Alice's mother – which Alice was allowed to see but not to keep – that Ben was actually to be staying at the Henry Enfields while the sisters were there. 'Oh,' Alice wrote, 'things seem going to be *too* happy for me,' and again with her determination not to exaggerate or overstate, came the defensive word – 'almost'. However, as the party left for London, she was full of solemn thoughts, hoping/expecting that this visit would provide the opportunity for Ben to propose to her and wondering about what would follow: 'It seemed like a very leaving of home ... either a greater hope or a crushing disappointment.'

Tantalisingly, she would have to wait almost two weeks to find out whether it was to be hope or disappointment because Ben was only to come to London on the actual day of the ball. It had been a full six months since they had met and very likely they would not have been able even to write to each other during that time. It must have seemed a very long six months indeed.

Alice's anxiety and excitement steadily mounted as she went through the visits and entertainments provided for the sisters in London: she 'can't help not much liking Mr. S because he once thought Ben conceited, of all people in the world!!!'; at a dance given by the Martineaus (Ben's sister Fanny and brother-in-law Meadows), a partner's 'reddish whiskers' remind her 'the least little bit of Ben'; there is a continuing fear that her aunt Camilla who is old and very ill may die before 30 May and make it impossible for her relatives (including Alice of course) to go to the ball; she realises that 'this time next week I shall most likely [again the careful reservation] be at the Hall Ball with him'; and then, 'I had a headache from getting so excited about tomorrow'.

She has drawn a line down the two and a half closely written pages about Ben's arrival, and the days of his stay. When it was learned that he would arrive at about four o'clock, Alice 'got into such a dreadful state' that all she could do in the afternoon was stay lying down while the rest of the house party went out for a drive. And this is how she describes his arrival:

> a ring at the door a little before 4.00; we looked out & found it was him; went down to the door in such a state I could hardly stand; his face had almost gone out of my memory & I watched at the garden door to see him come in – & in a moment the *dear* face appeared – *just* the same as ever ... We sat in the drawing room talking – at least the others talked ...I hope they did not notice me.

And this is how Ben describes the same occasion:

> how well I remember my arrival, & the feeling of excited satisfaction at being again under the same roof with Alice; she had on such a pretty dress, blue silk, which made her look quite smart.

Again the criticism of Alice's style of dress! She was probably most carefully outfitted for this great London visit but she makes no mention of the preparations and even when she is describing the dances and other events of the visit, she says nothing of what she or anyone else was wearing. Reading her diary, I find nothing of the coquette in her. With her combination of charm and overwhelming innocence, I find myself likening her, at this age, to Jane Austen's Catherine Morland but with, of course, more intelligence and independence of mind.

What she liked and looked for was what she called 'serious talk'. She records with obvious approval the fact that during the ball (when they danced four out of nine dances together, including the supper dance) Ben told her that 'he only cared for dancing for the opportunity for talking'. Out on a walk, she was glad to find time for 'a nice talk about in what way it was necessary (?) for lawyers to be dishonest or at least self-deceiving'.

Alice's description of the ball itself shows in its very shortness that she had only one thought and eyes for only one man:

> As Ben took me down to the carriage he asked me for the first dance

31

... I think I *never* enjoyed an evening more ... We came away about 3.30, Ben, Enfield, Bertha & I together.

Alice does not say what kind of dances they danced, or who her other partners were, or anything about the supper, or the grandeur of the surroundings for this, her first big ball.

The following day, Ben went off to play in a cricket match between the old and new men of University Hall, and Alice had to be content with seeing him when the family party went to watch the match in the afternoon. Since he was not 'in' when they arrived, she was able to sit by him for a time, and 'it was so delightful watching'. However, in the evening there was a change of mood: 'Ben seemed quite different and I went very sad somehow' – another girl was there who was 'very lovely', and whom Ben and Enfield said they liked very much. 'So did I at first,' she writes; and then there are some words written over so closely that they can't be read but their meaning can be guessed!

All was well again next day which they spent together, much of the day at the Exhibition where she stuck 'as close to Ben as I dared always, and he took hold of my hand once or twice to lead me to the pictures'. There followed two blank days while Ben was away visiting his sister Fanny and her husband Meadows Martineau, in Esher, and, on 4 June, going with them to the Derby. Alice had to be satisfied with the company of Ben's brother Enfield, which she enjoyed because he alternately made her laugh and talked of Ben or of serious matters, especially of religion – a favourite subject with her and also with him, as he had now been granted his wish and was studying for the priesthood.

When Ben returned, it was 'before we had done breakfast' and 'his presence was like the sunshine'. His early arrival was no doubt due to the fact that he was no longer staying in the house and that this was the last day of his holiday; the following day he would return to work and Nottingham. In spite of which, however, he found time for another cricket match. But Alice was happy because he gave her his watch to hold, and they spent the rest of the day together. 'Often my hand was in his as we went along.' But there was still no proposal.

However, she knew that she would see him again very soon because the planned visit to aunt Anne in Nottingham was to be at the beginning of July, in only a fortnight's time. Moreover, as Ben helped her into the cab after a dance that evening 'he held my hand *very* tight while he said "we shall soon see each other again". I could say nothing – but oh, I *am* happy'.

This is Ben's own account of these packed days:

> We had a wonderful time, visits to the Exhibition, dances, a cricket match & Alice & I were more to each other than we had ever been before ... [When] I bad Alice goodbye I knew it was but a short parting as she was coming again to Nottingham & it was a very happy farewell, we had grown so close together.

Alice and Bertha stayed on in London for the intervening fortnight, thus avoiding, for Alice, a journey back to Cheshire and then south again. For the first time, aunt Anne's invitation to Nottingham had been to Alice only.

Each event of the second London fortnight is carefully recorded by Alice. They went again to the Exhibition where she managed 'to keep pretty well to myself where Ben and I had been together'; there were private dances and public duties like taking Sunday school, even once 'two hours at hospital, singing to the patients'; there were serious lectures and, on Sundays, both chapel and church with sermons at each. She was far from resenting these. Comments in her diary on both sermons and lectures show her to be devout, but also to be thinking for herself in matters of religion:

> Went to hear Mr. Spergeon. He was very interesting and very peculiar. His talk about original sin was very offensive to me, but *some* things were very nice. 'Let no man think that because he is doing no positive evil he shall escape. It is a *positive evil* to do no good ...
> [The emphases are hers.]

Her comment on her 'dear' Fanny, criticised at the beginning of her diary for being over-influenced by the 'flirting Bury set', whose wedding took place while she was in London, is another glimpse of the young and slightly censorious righteousness that brings Catherine Morland to my mind:

> I do hope she may be happy ... I am sure she loves him truly – & I think is improved since her engagement ... May he be worthy of her & lead her nearer to the Father!

The only unhappy interruption to all the activities of the fortnight occurs when her parents forbid a proposed visit to the theatre. Cousin Frank, Albert's younger brother, had suggested taking the girls and their aunt and had booked the tickets when a 'telegraph' arrived from home saying that 'we mustn't make any more engagements', followed by –

> a letter from Mo [her mother] to say they *do not wish us* to go with Frank tonight or make *any other* engagement while we are here! So we are in a fix ... Frank told us he had heard from Puppy [her father] to forbid our going so he has given the tickets away – *poor* fellow! He looked quite knocked down ... I am afraid Puppy's letter must have been very severe.

She adds – obviously after seeing the letter – 'No, it wasn't but still F was hurt.' Alice doesn't argue or express surprise at her parents' veto or say anything about the reason for it. It is tantalising not to know. Alice would surely have known if her father had religious objections. Did her parents share the view quite widely held in those days that actors and actresses – and so the theatre itself – were not respectable? If so, they would surely have warned her before she went to London. Did they then think that, in going to the theatre with her unmarried cousin, Alice was having altogether too free a time? We shall never know since the diary doesn't return to the subject.

*   *   *

The routine during the Nottingham visit was for Alice and her aunt to go sketching together each morning, mainly at or near the Castle. Judging from Ben's references to Nottingham in his Family Record and from a simple map which I found between the pages of Alice's diary, the town consisted at this time of little more than the Castle, the old market place, the Midland Railway station and Trent Bridge cricket ground. It is quite usual for Ben to run down to the Trent to bathe before breakfast; the Park had not yet been developed; and large families occupied town houses that nowadays are public buildings or offices.

Though Ben was no longer on holiday, he was given a good deal of time off to spend with Alice during her visit. One 'most delightful day' was spent together when they went in a party of eleven on an expedition to Dovedale, not returning till eight or nine at night:

> I was with Ben *all* day. He never left me. I can't give a full account of it here but it was a beautiful day & Ben took care of me & helped me about ... We had a good deal of nice talk about the Bible & atonement & his mother & Enfield ... He asked for my photo – I had one to spare but I didn't say anything.

However, though they had all these times of relative privacy together, there was still no proposal, and when Ben came to dinner the following evening and 'Ben and I sat *close* together for a long time – his arm round mine and I was very happy', there was again no proposal.

It is easy to imagine uncle William and aunt Anne waiting with exasperation and wondering how to bring the young man to the point. He had been given every sign of family approval with the partnership, and every opportunity to declare himself during the London visit, and now during this one, to Nottingham. To Alice's surprise – but probably to no one else's – her aunt took an opportunity next day while they were sketching together, to 'say she knew about it and how glad she should be etc. I was quite startled at her knowing it and talking about it,' Alice writes, 'but she was very nice'.

After this, as her visit neared its end, Alice must have been on daily, hourly tenterhooks for the actual proposal. At last, Saturday of her last weekend arrived but it rained so hard all day that no one could pretend to want to go for a walk. The only hope of privacy was that it would be fine enough for them to walk back from a family dinner party that evening. It was and this is how Alice describes 'the most eventful day' of her life:

> I was *so* afraid it would rain too much for us to walk home – but God stopped the rain. Ben made me take his arm directly we got out. (Enfield and Herbert [her brother] were behind). We walked a long way without speaking. Then he began – as if he could hardly speak – & asked if he might write to my father. My breath seemed to be quite gone and I was in a dream but I told him I knew I *did* love him. He said he had loved me ever since that first spring we knew each other ... We parted at the door and I behaved just as usual, only I lay awake a *long* time *thinking*. (5 July 1862)

Ben's account says simply:

> Alice and I came to an understanding; it all seemed so simple and easy and yet so momentous ... and how delighted all my people were, especially my father and aunt Maria [whose approval he would have felt to be in place of his dead mother's].

The next morning was Sunday. Alice got up early to write to her mother and go to chapel where she saw Ben; she even stays on after this to teach at Sunday school. It falls to Ben to tell aunt Anne their news and the two are then left alone together for the first time: 'I went close to Ben. "Give me a kiss, Alice," he said, and he gave me that kiss that I have longed for ever since that first Spring.' (So, when she wrote that the previous evening she had 'behaved just as usual,' she meant just that: they had not even kissed.)

On Monday, before she left for home, the engaged couple were left alone in the drawing room 'for I should think 1½ hours', wrote Alice.

> We were *so* cosy together till at last he said he ought to go to the office.

Then we sat up and he looked at me with *such* a bright, *happy, heavenly* smile. I never saw anything so beautiful. He gave me his photo, a very bad one but better than nothing.

She arrived home at Bollington to find that 'everybody is delighted ... I slept with Amy. Oh how we did talk.' There is plenty of evidence in Alice's diaries and in letters of the time that it was quite usual for sisters and young female friends to share a bed and Alice clearly regarded this as an occasion for intimate talk.

Ben had written to Alice's mother at once and his formal letter to her father arrived the day after Alice herself. This was followed by a letter from her father to Ben, telling him that he may tell his father – 'uncle Sep' to Alice. It was arranged for Alice to meet him at the William Enfields in Nottingham to receive his blessing on the engagement – 'I was in such a *dreadful* fright before he came in,' she writes, 'he is very nice and kind but so grave and sad'. Aunt Anne who had done so much to bring the couple together was, however, strangely displeased. Alice confides in her diary:

I was *very* glad to have seen uncle Sep. Aunt Anne too got to understand things better I think, and perhaps got more reconciled? But we think she will be *very* difficult sometimes to get on with when I am married.

Alice's parents decided that the wedding would not be for two years, that meantime the couple might write once a fortnight and that Ben would be welcome at Bollington as often as he could find time. The welcome was limited, in Alice's account, by the words 'only not too often', but Ben wrote that he was at once made to feel one of the family and was always welcomed there. The restriction about the number of letters was felt by both to be hard, but neither Alice nor Ben makes any comment about the long engagement. It will surprise today's readers that there is nowhere any mention of an engagement ring.

In the first six months of her engagement, Alice spent a happy carefree time at home with frequent visits from Ben, local dances (where she mentions dancing with 'dear old Albert'), visits to friends and evening parties at Quarry Bank with games of whist and amateur theatricals – '*so* well done'. They were all 'learning the new waltz' and she was learning to cook.

Of course, with Alice, there were also plenty of activities and talk of a serious nature: ' a very nice talk with Frank about shooting. He can't make up his mind whether its wrong or not ...' and in the ethos of the time, there was also a good sprinkling of preaching and lectures by her father – 'Puppy gave a *very* nice lecture on Garibaldi' – and of sewing classes and other good works:

> Sale at sewing class, which was *very* tiring. Ber & I were on our legs 5 hours. Eclipse of the moon but it was too cloudy to see anything, so we slept instead. (6 December)

On one of Ben's weekends, they went on a Monday to 'a sort of dinner party' at Quarry Bank. There were ten of them and it was hosted by uncle Robert Hyde Greg:

> We had to sing but it was rather jolly on the whole ... we went up to the observatory & saw Mars & the moon. So jolly. The gentlemen were shooting all day.

Two of Ben's visits are picked out for mention in his Family Record: his first when Alice met him alone at Macclesfield station and insisted that they get out of the carriage and walk the last part of the way 'so as to make sure that he would see her home to best advantage'; and a visit in early October when they and Alice's young sisters go for a picnic and 'all of us were young and in high spirits'.

Perhaps not surprisingly after these carefree happy months, the time came when, as Ben puts it, 'Alice began to have doubts and questioned herself closely as to whether she loved me well enough to leave her home for my sake.' Shared with Ben who says that he too had had doubts soon after they were engaged, she was at first able, within a day or two, to tell her diary that she was 'so happy' with her doubts gone. But a month or two later they recurred – this time more seriously as Ben's account makes very clear:

> My visits to Bollington were unsettling & she generally had to pay for them with a bad headache. For a time it seemed best that I should keep away as much as possible, & not write. There was a Black Monday when all seemed dark; & when the shadow lifted, we were in a serious rather than a joyous mood for the rest of our engagement.

A careful reading of Alice's diary shows that, starting from their first meeting, when she was a child and Ben a grown man, Alice had put him on such a high pedestal that she hardly saw him or their engagement as part of real life, and when she did, it frightened her: on her arrival in Nottingham, her diary note had been – 'It is so delightful to see his dear face again, only I feel how *far* below him I am'; and about her family's approval of her engagement, she says, 'Everybody delighted – only I am so *far* below him that I feel nobody ought to be quite satisfied.'

So, when she woke to reality, the prospect of marriage to such a paragon, and the very strength of his love and of his trust in her combined to make it all more alarming. Today's readers need perhaps to be reminded that the conception of 'teenagers' as a period of life with problems distinct from childhood was only recognised after the Second World War. Marriage was frightening enough to young, early Victorian girls without the complication that Alice had made for herself: again and again when she notes in her diary that someone's wedding day is at hand, she adds – 'poor thing'! At this time the commitment of marriage meant 'for life' in a way difficult to realise in today's atmosphere of divorce. Until the Matrimonial Causes Act of 1857, it had required an Act of Parliament to secure an *individual* divorce!

Alice was also being torn apart by her home ties; her mother was clearly very dependent on her and didn't always have easy relations with the younger children: this Christmas there had been an angry argument about whether the young ones need go to chapel and

Alice writes that – 'Poor Mo did so cry when they were gone. At such sort of times I do think that poor Mummy will miss me when I am gone.'

Her doubts this second time seem to have been triggered off by the arrival of her first wedding present – very much ahead of time – while she was on a happy visit to her so lately married friend Fanny Bibby putting her into a panic: 'I am *so* frightened sometimes when I look forward', she tells her diary on 9 February.

And by 18 February, during a short visit from Ben, she was 'very wretched because I was afraid I didn't care enough for Ben and as if I never *could* do such a dreadful irrevocable thing and as if I couldn't leave Mummy; and I felt as if *whatever* I did, I must be so wretched that I quite *longed* to die'.

She was now so unhappy that she could not keep it to herself and confided in her mother who said that

> she felt perfectly *sure* that I was meant to marry him & that I *really did* love him enough to marry him & I believe I *do* only these queer feelings *will* come.

Her mother too now realised that this was serious and that to postpone the wedding for so long was a mistake. She suggested that it be brought forward to that autumn. 'It did so frighten me,' Alice wrote, 'and yet I almost agree, for then my doubts will be over.' And next day, she talked to her father and wrote to Ben to tell him 'all about it'.

It must have been this letter, written on Sunday 22 February that caused the 'black Monday' that Ben refers to. Letters were also exchanged between both parents and Ben, and it was agreed to bring forward the wedding to that September, 1863. The storm, which had clearly been serious, blew over almost as quickly as it had started and by 26 February, Alice was able to tell her diary that 'things are getting more settled now between us, & I feel to love him again as much as ever'.

According to my reading, what there was of Catherine Morland in Alice disappeared during that February and Alice Greg grew up.

CHAPTER 4

The Wedding

'I had expected to be rather (if not very) wretched & miserable when I first married, knowing how so many people are ...'

IT IS no wonder, perhaps, that both these intelligent young people should have suffered more or less serious pre-wedding doubts. Although it was nearly two years since their first short meeting, there had been very little time for them to learn more about each other than to know that they were in love. There had been Alice's two visits to the William Enfields (in the spring and autumn of 1861); there had then been a gap of six months when they would not have been able even to write to each other; there had been the exciting London house party with the Henry Enfields in May/June 1862 when they were fellow house-guests for less than a week, though packed with dances and other entertainment. And that was literally all until the Nottingham visit in July which ended with their engagement.

Were Ben's delays in proposing to Alice due, in any way, to his feeling that they knew each other too little? He admitted to her that he had been the first to have doubts. That his doubts were more easily dismissed than Alice's does not necessarily show a greater love on his part; the love for a mother and the 'pull' of family sur-roundings that added fuel to Alice's doubts were absent in Ben whose mother had recently died and who, when he first met Alice, had already left his home to live alone in Nottingham.

Once the doubts of both were acknowledged and stilled, they lost no time in finding out about each other. Alice writes that 'they had some satisfying talks' and that, on Easter Sunday, 'Ben and I were walking about in the Rookery most of the day talking'.

This, however, was a month later. So far from the two having an immediate chance to discuss the new plan for an earlier wedding, it had been agreed that Ben should stay away from Bollington for a full month. In fact he did not come again until the Easter weekend at the beginning of April.

Fortunately for Alice's spirits, a national event had occurred in early March which involved much local activity. This was the marriage of the Prince of Wales and Princess Alexandra of Denmark, which appears to have been received with wide national enthusiasm. The arrival of the Princess, her meeting with the Prince of Wales at Gravesend and the procession through London were witnessed and described by their friends the Sharpes. Alice's younger sister Sibbie and five friends came from school for a few days for the celebrations in Bollington.

This is Alice's excited description of the day of the royal wedding:

> There was a holiday all over the kingdom & *great* rejoicings; flags & processions in every village; illuminations, bonfires, fireworks, dinners & teaparties *everywhere*. It is *very grand* to see a *whole* nation so pour out their hearts in love & enthusiasm for their Queen & her family ... We went to see the procession in Bollington. Of course we all wore favours all day. In the evening Albert's great bonfire on White Nancy [a local hill] was lighted & about 8 or 9 on the other hills.

Alice and one of her sisters also went with their parents that evening to a mayoral ball in Macclesfield. She writes that there was excitement beforehand about what her mother should wear and that 'dear Puppy and Mummy enjoyed it and I was so glad it answered for them'. For herself, she reports only that she had 'a jolly waltz with Albert' whose affection for her is clearly still a worry: 'I am so sorry for him. He does so need someone to pet him & take care of him. I wish he would marry.'

During the difficult days of doubt, Ben seems to have shown considerable maturity and sensitivity. None of his letters has survived but Alice's diary shows that they always gave comfort and reduced tension. And when he came to Bollington for Easter after the prescribed month's absence, he seems to have known just the moment and the way to break through Alice's shyness (she called it fear) and to ask for the private talk that she had been avoiding since his arrival: 'I was dreadfully scared,' she wrote. 'We didn't get any talk that night [of his arrival] as I was very tired and went to bed.' (2 April)

Alice again avoided being alone with Ben:

> Bertha, Ben & I went to Quarry Bank for the day ... we had a delightful day all together ... As the moon shone in my face coming home, Ben thought I looked unhappy & asked for a talk. He was trembling so, poor fellow. We had it all out & were all right & better than we've ever been before ... Ben *is* a *good* man & I must be thankful for him ... everything seems happy again now, so comfortable & peaceful – not the excitement it was before. (3 April)

In Ben's account he uses very similar words: 'For the rest of our engagement, we were in a serious rather than a joyous mood.'

It is noticeable too that Alice can now treat Ben as a real person and even think that there can be matters on which he might be open to criticism or she might be right and he wrong: 'Letter from Ben. He likes the 2nd verse of the National Anthem which I am *very* sorry for. But I *hope* he only fancies he does.' Alice was by no means alone in her opinion. Only the first of the three verses is normally sung, the tendentious second verse, 'Confound their politics, Frustrate their knavish tricks', being thus avoided. She doesn't say whether she convinced him but this is hardly surprising, for now all is bustle because it has been decided that Alice and her sister Amy are to join their parents on a two-month Continental tour to Italy, starting almost immediately.

According to Ben's account, it was known among Alice's father's siblings and nephews that he longed for another journey on the Continent but could not afford it; so they got up a fund to enable him to take such a journey in comfort. Alice writes that his sister Agnes and youngest brother, William Rathbone 'are so kind in giving money' and that 'the nephews have made a subscription of £200 for us' – about £10,000 by today's standards and revealing a remarkable degree of family solidarity in any age. Her father must indeed have been a much loved man but it cannot, surely, have been a coincidence that the holiday was made possible at a time when there had been trouble over Alice's engagement.

Their destination was the Riviera and Italy but they started with a week in Paris at the Hotel Meurice, visited the Louvre, drove up and down the boulevards and in the Bois de Boulogne where 'it was lovely. The trees just come & coming out ... lots of carriages ... The Emperor passed us. We dined at Table D'hote which was "tremenjiously" swell and will cost no end we fear.' But by the time they left, 'Amy and I had had quite enough of gay glaring Paris'.

Their longest stay in Italy was a fortnight in Florence, but they also spent a few days each at Genoa, Turin, the Italian Lakes and Milan. Victor Emmanuele II had only recently (in 1861) proclaimed himself King of All Italy, with the help of Alice's hero, Garibaldi, and Italy's struggle for independence was still continuing – Venetia and Rome would not become part of Italy until 1866. One of her father's objectives in concentrating the holiday in Italy had been his wish to visit and to show his wife and daughters some of the places of interest in the struggle for Italian independence, of which, through the Needhams, he had become a lifelong supporter.

Of course the tour was fully written up by Alice but, tempting as it is to follow her through her description of that remarkable holiday, the most interesting things about it today must be the many differences between such a tour then and now – not least, of course, the method of travel.

Travelling south from Paris, they stayed a night each at Dijon, Lyons and Avignon, from which I conclude that they probably went by road. At Cannes, they hired a private carriage to take them all the way to Genoa but transferred to the train in Italy – 'to avoid the shaking. I was glad to get to Genoa. So was Puppy,' she writes. From Genoa they travelled to Leghorn by ship and thence to

Florence by train, via Pisa (where, at least, there was the similarity with today of the beautiful echo in the Baptistry).

On the way home, they took the train from Florence to Sarzana where they transferred to a *vetturino* to get to Spezia and round the coast to Sestri. To cross the Alps by the Simplon, they hired a private carriage with six horses: 'We did a good deal of walking. The view from the top was splendid ... the road seemed cut into a precipice almost. In one place we went under a waterfall.'

The generosity of the family had made it possible for the party to engage a private courier and at her first mention of the tour, Alice had written, without comment as to fact or gender, that they had 'engaged a female courier'. They called her simply 'Marsch' (probably her surname) and she is mentioned often, particularly for her care of the ailing Mr Greg. Given the rarity, as well as the difficulties, of foreign travel then, and the number and variety of methods of travel and places visited, it is easy to imagine that such a tour needed a private courier – another difference between then and now.

Alice found a very different Riviera from the one we visit today: her first pleasure in the beauties of the blue Mediterranean was dimmed for her in Toulon by seeing 'poor chained prisoners working on the vessels' and her description of Cannes shows how complety it has changed. It must still have been a small coastal village:

> The place Cannes is *so* lovely with the sound & look of the blue Mediterranean & the doves & birds. In the evening the tree frogs made *such* a noise & the orange blossom smelt *so* sweet. Far the best thing we've had yet.

Other places were less romantic: all she said of 'Mentone' was that it was 'a very dirty town' and the same of San Remo; and, in Alassio, they stayed at 'the very oldest darkest dirtiest queerest hotel I ever was in. Full of smells & dirt & high rooms with old pictures round them.'

There are no such complaints about the big towns in Italy – Genoa, Florence and Turin – and Spezia, which must then have been quite a small place, gets high praise, 'a *lovely* place ... Amy and I bathed at 6 a.m. *So* jolly.' However, on the drive round the coast from there to Sestri, it was another matter: though 'the whole drive was most lovely' in places there are 'swarms of beggars all along the road' and 'Sestri might be beautiful if it wasn't so *horribly* dirty ... had a bad night with fleas and bugs'.

Another big difference between then and now is the fact that there were colonies of English ex-patriots in the most visited cities. They were taken about by friends in Genoa, and in Florence the English colony included a Needham uncle and aunt and there was much family entertainment, including a visit to 'the new open-air theatre' to see Donizetti's *Lucia di Lammermoor*.

Owing to these 'colonies', the visitors also had the advantage of being introduced to interesting local people: in Turin, Alice and her sister visited the Parliament buildings where they met 'the Prime Minister and so many great men'; and in Genoa they talked to the Hungarian patriot, Lajos Kossuth – 'he was so dignified and gentle and talked so interestingly,' Alice wrote.

It is clear from the diary, however, that what Alice enjoyed most in Italy were the mountain views and walks, bathing and sketching. At Bellagio, they were 'up before 4.0 am to sketch the mountains at sunrise. A cup of coffee at 6.0 & then up the hill, Papa carried most of the way in a chair. The views past describing; the ferns and flowers too; it was the loveliest thing we've seen.' Rising at six, for example, to bathe at Spezia, seems to be normal.

She also takes a very thorough and serious interest in sightseeing, both artistic and historical – in Nice they visited the place where Napoleon landed from Elba 'and the olive tree under which he slept'. In Genoa they saw 'the rock from which Garibaldi embarked for Sicily', which he had conquered in spectacular fashion with his volunteer army of red-shirts, and, in Spezia, the fortress of Varignano where he had been taken prisoner, and the bed there where he had lain after he had been shot in the ankle and thigh, only the year before, in 1862.

A separate note enclosed in the diary and signed 'Alice Greg. Florence. May 1863' lists her 'favourite pictures'; in the Uffizi and

Pitti galleries, there are Raphaels, Carlo Dolcis, many Del Sartos, but no Giottos, Piero della Francescas, Botticellis, or Fra Angelicos. Perhaps the accepted taste of the time was as different then from now, as were the methods of travel.

They spent some days in Geneva on the way home where, as usual, there were parties among the ex-patriots and even a dance. But by now it was mid-June and Alice was thinking only how 'delicious' it will be to get home. 'We are not intending to *see* anything more,' she writes and, on arrival at Dover, she is '*so* glad to step off foreign soil and on English again!'

Surprisingly, she made no demur when the returning party spent some days with family and friends in London before going north. Indeed she didn't even get a letter from Ben until she arrived home in Bollington, and when it was to say that he couldn't get away to see her for nearly a month because he was needed at the office in Nottingham, her only comment was 'I am *so* sorry'. She does not say that her doubts had returned whilst she had been away but she was certainly very solemn and restrained about her approaching marriage. 'I long to make my time stand still *a bit*. It is *so great* a change,' she wrote.

Again and again, she recorded bravely, 'I am not frightened'. But quite clearly she was. And, given the circumstances, she had ample reason for doubts and anxieties. In the first place, there is plenty of evidence in her diary that she had a basic fear of marriage as such; whenever she noted that someone was getting married, her comment was 'poor thing'. And then, the step she was taking was indeed huge – from a carefree, sheltered childhood, surrounded by a close extended family of loving parents, sisters, brothers and cousins, to the adult responsibilities of marriage for life, away from them all, in another part of the country. Add to this that she had been separated for two months from the physical presence of the man for whom she was taking this mighty step.

The word 'sex', of course, does not appear anywhere but on the day before the wedding, she dared to put her fear into words: 'I had been afraid lest I should get a horror of Ben at last'.

Fortunately, she was still in love and was able to add – in the same breath, as it were – 'but I didn't a bit. He was the greatest comfort to me after Mummy, I think.'

Ben's description of his own feelings and his conception of hers at this time shows that he was quite unaware of her mood. – 'Alice seemed to have parted with her doubts and to be quietly confident' he wrote in his Family Record. The period of her tour had been 'a long one' for him, and his spirits unlike hers had risen as the wedding drew near.

Being the serious character that she was, Alice was also full of solemn and religious thoughts: 'When I think how many long years I may have to live, I wonder if I shall be able to walk always worthily of the vocation whereto we are called.' This kind of sure faith was basic to her parents and relatives and to all their acquaintances, as well as to her husband-to-be and his family. Everything in the diary suggests that it was also sincerely hers.

During the intervening month before Ben's visit, there had been plenty of pleasant social activity to distract her, notably her parents' silver wedding which was celebrated with a large family picnic: 'We all went, aunt Agnes & Puppy & Miss Ronalds & all. Albert provided the grub which was most grand and altogether it was jolly' (26 June).

Albert (and usually Frank too) was ever present on social and family occasions and Alice's old affection for him and his obvious love for her were certainly strands pulling at her from her old life: on the day before her wedding he sent her a *dear* goodbye letter which, for the first time, she referred to as coming from 'my dear old *brother*, Albert' (the italics are mine).

Meantime, the preparations for the wedding had been proceeding apace: 'writing *lots* of letters of thanks' for presents; inspecting the chapel where they are to be married; visiting 'our old folks' in the village to say goodbye; trying on the wedding ring brought by Ben on his final visit; choosing bonnets for the bridesmaids and preparing her trousseau – 'We have lots of workwomen in the house, but we are coming to the end of sewing at last ... we are quite tired of dress and arrangements'. Alice's mother and sister Katie went to Nottingham to join Ben in choosing a house – 'They have decided upon a nice little house overlooking the park', Alice reported. There seems to have been no question of her going too.

As for the wedding celebrations, a dance was to be held in the evening of the day itself, and a party for the village. The family were much looked up to and the first wedding was clearly a great local occasion. Alice reported that most of the village had flags out and that people had been very busy putting up arches of evergreens and flags down the drive.

As the day grew really closer, she was always noting – 'last this', 'last that', 'last drive with Puppy', 'last Sunday as Alice Greg' (when she didn't go to chapel but 'stayed at home and wrote and thought'), and halfway through the day before the wedding, she broke off to say goodbye to her old life:

> I shall write the rest of this after we are married. So Goodbye to this old diary from Alice Greg. God give me strength to go through it all. (8 September)

The day before the wedding seems to have been regarded, in Alice's family at any rate, as the day for saying goodbye to her home, a day for being sad. As soon as Ben arrived that evening, he asked to see her alone:

> so he came up into the day nursery which was dark & filled with flowers & we sat together for 5 minutes. I was so sad but not nearly so sad as he expected ...
> When he was gone I dried up my tears & then went with Mummy to where they were all at tea in the drawing room & said how do you do to them all & gradually I got all right & merry again & was so all evening.

Ben's father (he remained 'uncle Sep' to Alice even after the wedding) and two of his young brothers had come with Ben from Nottingham, as well as their uncle William and aunt Anne. Ben's favourite brother Enfield had arrived earlier. Alice's school friend, Sarah Sharpe, was the only non-family member of the evening party for the two families; 'family' of course included Albert and Frank.

'After tea' that evening – there is no mention of there being any other meal – they looked at the wedding presents, Amy and Alice sang a little and they talked and 'were quite merry', except for an interruption for Alice to 'sign papers and things which was rather formidable'. Saying goodnight, Alice distributed lockets to her four sisters and to her friend Sarah Sharpe and one other girl called 'Carrie' (presumably her six bridesmaids) and uncle Sep gave her a delicate gold brooch in the shape of a double bow (which I still have in its original box).

In the days just before her marriage, Alice had been careful to sleep with each sister in turn. On the night before her wedding, she slept alone but in the same room as her two younger sisters, and she comforted herself in the early morning of her wedding day, by getting into bed with them:

> I woke in the night with my heart beating ever so. It seemed as if I could not believe it ... About 6.30 I heard Amy & Ber in the day nursery & soon Katie & Sibbie woke & I got into bed with them.

The fateful morning had arrived! There was what Alice called a 'stand up' breakfast, and by eight-thirty all the carriages were waiting.

> Mother & I were in her dressing room & that was the worst part of the whole day. I was dressed in white muslin & veil & wreath of orange flowers & white Myrtle & the other girls were dressed in white muslin & white cloaks and bonnets.

Alice and her mother and sister Katie set off in the last carriage. Her father met her at the chapel door 'and rather hurried me in before everybody was seated' and before Ben was ready, because he was engaged with the registrar who had arrived late. So

> I sat down in one of the little pews for two or three minutes ... I believe the Chapel was very full but I didn't see ... I wasn't frightened or inclined to draw back at all.
> So then we were married. It was not a particularly nice service – long & tedious. I had hold of Ben's hand all the time.

Ben's account is equally short and to the point – 'Mr Taylor who married us was very sympathetic and nice, but gave a longer address than we were prepared to take in just then.' In addition to the two fathers, the signatories to the marriage were William Enfield, and Alice's eldest sister Amy. Ben's father signed himself 'merchant'. Alice's father, retired of course from business, describes himself simply as 'gentleman'.

Alice goes on to describe how happy she was on the way home in the carriage with Ben; how, when they reached the drive to the house, some of the mill-people took out the horse and themselves dragged the carriage up to the front door with much cheering and laughing, 'and we laughed too for it was so funny'; how they went into the library 'for a kiss' and then out at once 'to receive all the others'; how 'Ben kissed all his new sisters'; and how they had to go out and bow to their charioteers, who wouldn't go away until Ben had given them some money, 'which they spent in "The Cock". Horrid things!'

Though Alice doesn't say so anywhere, it can be assumed that the family was teetotal, for the only drink at the wedding breakfast seems to have been tea. 'The breakfast was very unconventional. No champagne', is Ben's comment. Perhaps because tea-pouring is traditionally a woman's job, the three tables were headed and the tea poured by the senior women of the family – at one table, Alice with Ben on one side and her father on the other, her mother and eldest sister at either end of the big table and Bertha, the second eldest, at the head of the third.

The absence of alcohol may explain there being no toasts; certainly none are mentioned and, in another departure from today's customs, Alice left the table to go and dress before the speeches: 'While I was putting my feet in hot water,' she writes, 'someone came to tell me that Ben had made a *wonderful* little speech in reply to Mr Taylor's and then,' she continues, 'I went down to hear Puppy's speech about uncle Enfield'.

She does not say why her father should make a speech about William Enfield, though he was uncle to both Alice and Ben, and having no children of his own, had always treated Ben as a son. He was, too, senior partner of the law firm on which the couple's future depended and was also Town Clerk of Nottingham.

The speech ended the proceedings for bride and groom, who had a long journey before them – part by road, part by railway. Alice records, however, that after they had gone, the rest of the party went for a walk and 'had a most successful dance in the evening' and 'the poor people all had dancing or a tea party on the Saturday afternoon which they went down from our house to see'.

The going away was not so dreadful as Alice had expected: there were kisses all round, for her family and her new brothers; and as Alice and Ben set off in their carriage to Buxton 'over the hills with the lovely flitting sunshine' over them, they kept looking back at 'the dear home' as far as they could make it out. At Buxton, they took a train to Hassop (where they shared a carriage with a man from Nottingham known to Ben but 'were so circumspect that he did not guess who I was'). The last part of the journey was again by road, to the village of Baslow, 'a dear little place in Derbyshire where we spent our first two nights'.

Alice's account of the honeymoon is in two parts. The first was written in January 1864, the other, in February 1868.

The first account is on one page only and the sole reference to the wedding tour – she doesn't use the word 'honeymoon' – is in a half sentence: 'our tour was most happy', which is followed by the words – 'I am still *very* happy & we love each other more and more. Ben is the best husband in the world.' Again her religious faith is strongly in evidence for the remaining two thirds of the page are taken up with prayers and a quotation from the Bible.

The second account was written four and a half years later, by which time she already had three children, and it is packed with happiness. Of the four closely packed pages, three describe the week spent at Cromer, the only part of the tour which they had to themselves, the remaining two weeks being taken up with visiting relations – Ben's much-loved uncle Withers and his wife Maria in Norwich, his father in Southgate, other Dowsons at Geldeston, and Ben's sister Fanny and husband Meadows Martineau in Esher.

At Baslow they stayed at the Peacock Inn – 'a dear little place', where their rooms overlooked the village bowling green. They walked through the fields to Chatsworth and drove to Bakewell to buy painting things for Ben. At the end of the two days, they hired 'a queer littly tiny old brougham' to drive them over the hills 'all the way to Sheffield' from where they took the train to Peterborough.

Next day, they travelled by rail to Norwich and covered the last twenty miles to Cromer in 'a fly and pair'. Here rooms had been arranged for them by aunt Maria, in a boarding house on the cliffs above Cromer, 'and very cosy it was', says Alice. Aunt Maria had not attended the wedding, because she had been with Ben's motherless sister Fanny, who was having her first baby.

This second account provides us with a most charming glimpse of an idyll of happiness enjoyed, when the reverse had been expected. 'We were beginning to be most perfectly happy together,' Alice wrote as they arrived at Cromer. It was 'most delicious' warm weather all the time; they bathed several times and they hired 'a little old basket vehicle and pony' in which they drove about the country, and the pony was so nice and quiet that they could get out and walk whenever they liked. 'I never can express what a happy week it was,' she writes.

I had expected to be rather (if not very) wretched & miserable when first I married, knowing how so many people are, so I suppose the surprise of being happy made me all the happier. We used to laugh nearly all day ... We never wanted anything but each other's company. We had taken books, a novel & a solid, but we found that no novel was half so interesting as our chat and laughter.

Though they had no wish to read books, they spent the greater part of each morning in writing letters and 'could not wait for our letters till they came after breakfast, so Ben used to rush to the P.O. in the middle of breakfast to get them.'

For those who used the post, it seems to have been much swifter and more reliable than it is today and it enabled them to keep in touch on an almost daily basis; a letter even reached them from home on their first morning at Baslow and they seemed in no way surprised.

Signed 'Alice Dowson, February 1868', this touching account of their wedding tour closes with the following lines:

We got home on Tuesday September 29th. Aunt Anne & Bertha were there to welcome us and show us the *dear cosy* little house ... Ben always thinks he enjoyed the arriving at home almost the most of anything – I think it was very delightful but nothing could *quite* come up to the time at Cromer!

Though Alice's daily diary for February 1868 makes no mention of her writing this account of the wedding tour, she does describe

A most spring-like soft warm day. Ben & I had the most delicious walk that could be imagined ... sun shining, birds singing etc ... The children went a walk in the meadows to get crocuses.

So her account was of happiness, remembered in happiness.

CHAPTER 5

Young Marrieds

'... and we enjoyed ourselves most immensely.*'*

A YEAR and a few days after they were married, Alice and Ben's first child, a son, was born on 26 September 1869. They called him William Enfield after their mutual uncle: a natural and obvious 'thank you'. The first mention that a baby was on the way had been only a month before his birth: 'If all goes well we shall go home at Xmas, with our baby'. (Home was still Bollington, not yet Nottingham.)

Alice expressed no fear or anxiety. She seems, on the contrary, to have been entirely relaxed: it was not until a few days before the expected date of the baby's arrival that they even decided to engage a monthly nurse and then only 'as everybody thought it *very* desirable'. And on (as it happens) the very day before the baby was born, it being a Sunday and 'a lovely day', she and Ben went for a walk in the park and, in the evening, while Ben was at church, 'we others sat out of doors talking till he got back'. Not only was there no anxiety, there was also no question of hiding her 'condition' – the park in Nottingham was a perfectly public place.

Her family were not taking things as calmly as she was: her mother and father had come from Bollington to be present and aunt Maria had come from Norwich, a fortnight early – no doubt to be sure of being in time. Moreover, there was never any question of the monthly nurse managing alone, for 'Bar', Alice's childhood nanny, was there to help her 'little queen' (as she had called Alice in the days of her engagement) with her first baby. Alice's comments about the birth are strictly factual:

> Baby born at 6.o'clock. We had Mr White [the family doctor] & the monthly nurse. Ben had been up all night & at 6.30 he went to tell the 3 houses. Papa went home. He just saw the Baby before he went. Aunt Maria just saw him too before she went back to Norwich. Ben was very tired in evening. I slept all day nearly. It was v. nice to have mother.

But a picture can be seen that is very clear and alive: the loving elders gathered beforehand to support the young couple and greet the first grandchild; an all-night struggle for Alice with her old nanny and her mother supporting her; Ben up all night, excluded from the bedroom (no doubt joined by Alice's father and aunt Maria) and reduced to anxious waiting until he has the job of going to fetch the doctor; and then setting out on foot in the early dawn, full of excitement and pride, to wake 'the 3 houses' with his news. These '3 houses' would have been those belonging to the three Enfield uncles.

The next day, Alice has made no entry in her diary but the next, reporting that 'I went on perfectly well all the while', she adds – rather surprisingly – 'had hair done and ate a mutton chop'! After this, there are six completely blank days from which and from the short entries during the next week, it is clear that she became less well: 'Last day that I was at all bad' (14 October); and 'tried to walk for the first time and got dressed. It was such a funny feeling and quite an event' (15 October).

Right up to the end of the year, Alice's entries about her baby remain strictly factual and unemotional – stark even. Most of the pages are blank but we do learn: that 'Ben and I went in a hansom to the Registrar to get Baby registered'(19 October); that mother left and sister Katie came instead and *was delighted* with Baby' (22 October); that 'I washed and dressed Baby myself' (23 October); 'Baby christened. Enfield came to do it and it was v. nice indeed. All the colony of relations came to it' (17 November); 'Baby vaccinated' (3 December); and finally, on 21 December 'Went home [to Bollington] with Bertha, Baby and nurse'.

It all sounds rather impersonal. There are no terms of endearment or expressions of love. However, it was not Alice's style to include her own (usually strong) feelings in this non-private diary. It was quite another matter to report the feelings of others and here she doesn't hold back.

[Still in Bollington] Aunt Agnes gave a dance. Most jolly. Baby came down to be seen & charmed everybody. (6 January 1865) [Returning to Nottingham] Baby will be very much missed ... They are all *so* proud of him. (16 January)

Back in Nottingham, young William Enfield caught a cold and became quite ill; his parents had him to sleep with them and suffered the bad nights that parents everywhere in all generations know about. At last Alice allowed her own feelings to appear: 'Baby still very poorly ... He is very good & even merry at times, dear little thing' (22 February). Ben's account is noticeably warmer:

> The afternoon before his birth, Alice & I had taken a gentle walk along the Park Side, resting by the railings ... & thinking so much of the immediate future, & of our year of life together. Then came the first sight of Alice after Will was born & the happy days of her gradual recovery.

And fifty years later, on the morning of his Golden Wedding, he would remember 'how lovely she looked with her first dearly loved child in her arms'.

It is clear from the few things that Alice reported in her diary that Ben was extremely attentive to his young wife during this time: 'Ben spends his evenings with me always ... He carried me into the little nursery to see Baby washed for the first time. He reads Romola to me' (6 October).

The first year of marriage had been filled with pleasant activities. There was much obligatory calling but there were also many dinner parties and dances – in December alone, Alice noted five dinner parties, and her concern was whether she should wear 'the tarleton', the blue jacket or the white silk. In February, aunt Anne gave a grand party and for that Alice decided on the white silk.

At the time of their engagement, Alice had feared that aunt Anne might be 'difficult' after they were married. The implication was that Ben had become so much a son to this childless woman that she would be jealous of his wife. Whether she was or not, there is nothing in Alice's diary to suggest that her aunt made things uncomfortable for the young couple. Rather the contrary: she had been there to welcome them to their own house when they arrived from their honeymoon and frequent dinings and parties at Low Pavement (her aunt's house) were recorded in the first year of marriage, including dinner the night before her baby arrived; and members of their families (especially of course Alice's mother, who is aunt Anne's sister) are welcome guests at Low Pavement when there is no room for them at Alice and Ben's little house.

For general entertainment, there was skating in winter – 'Ben and I skated and had tremendous fun' (9 January) – and in the summer there were picnics, and there was watching cricket. These were activities they enjoyed together and it is obvious from the many entries that she really enjoyed watching cricket for its own sake. Thus: 'Notts v Yorks, most splendid playing' (30 June), and 'Notts v Surrey, the most exciting match that has ever been played ... I went down with Ben at 4 o'clock. Surrey won by 1 wicket. It was tremendously exciting' (29 July). There were almost continuous visits from members of her family and when they were not staying with her in Nottingham, she was often back at Bollington, Ben spending the inside of the week by himself in Nottingham.

At Bollington there seem to have been an almost constant round of parties and picnics:

A carriage of them went to Quarry Bank [for a party]. (8 July)
We went a tremendous party (a good many neighbours & Macclesfield people) for a picnic to R. ... very good fun. (9 July)

Alice's visits from and to her family in this first year of marriage seem indeed to have been so frequent as to be almost continuous ... And when the parents were away for minor illness or holiday – in this year they went for six weeks to Lucerne 'for their health' – Alice might go to London with Ben, or have a friend to stay. She could hardly have had time to feel lonely.

In the spring, she and Ben had gone for a week's visit to Esher to stay with his sister Fanny Martineau. In London they experienced a trip 'on the underground railway'; and on 11 April, there was the excitement of Garibaldi's arrival in London. It was estimated that the crowds on the streets to greet him numbered half a million. She wasn't in London to see him herself but she heard about it from her sister Amy and her uncle Richard who were. Garibaldi had been escorted from Southampton by the Liberal MP, Charles Seely, and she doesn't fail to mention that 'Papa would have seen him at Mrs Seely's if he had been well enough to go to London'. Of course this merits an entry in her diary: 'there was a great crowd to see him ... he stays with the Duke of Sutherland where he will see and visit all the grandees'.

When Ben had to be away for a few days on business, Alice felt very bereft: a cousin, Mary Enfield, would spend the night with her and they would share a bed and lie awake talking. Her former school friend Sarah Sharpe came to stay, and she too 'slept with me and how we did talk'. Sarah had just become engaged to Sydney Courtauld, and 'Sarah Sharpe's gentleman' (she calls him) came for a weekend during that time. They were married in London the following April and – typically – Alice is more concerned about her friend's last day at home than about the wedding day: 'Sarah Sharpe's last day at home. I wrote to her yesterday...' (3 April 1865).

This year, too, to Alice's great relief (as she confided to her diary), her former admirer, Albert Greg, was engaged and married: 'We heard the splendid news that Albert is at last engaged to Ellen Ronalds. Oh I *was* glad' (1 July) and '*Albert Greg married*' (13 September). The rare emphases are Alice's.

Behind and during all these activities and comings and goings, Alice was of course having to learn to run her little household, which meant engaging, organising and settling down with her staff of servants. She began with two servants: a cook, Ann Thraves (aged thirty-five) paid £13 a year and £1 'for tea'; and a housemaid,

Sarah Wilson (aged nineteen), at £6 and 10 shillings for tea. Sarah left in July and was replaced by Elizabeth Heys (aged 22).

As regards the tea allowance, Twinings have told me that tea in 1863-4 cost one shilling per pound and fell in 1865-9 to sixpence a pound. My grandmother abandoned the practice in 1867 and Twinings suggest that the fall in the price may have been her reason. Indeed it may – though she doesn't say so – since at sixpence a pound, each member of staff would have been able to buy twenty pounds, or eighty quarter pounds, the usual way of selling tea. Since there were at least two in the servants' hall, I would think there must have been tea over for the staff's families even at the 1863/1864 price.

When Alice abandoned the special payments for tea, she recorded in the diary that: 'from Nov. 3rd, they all have tea allowed them instead of the 10/–'. This seems to have meant that the servants would drink the tea left over from the dining room, since Alice's annual report on Elizabeth in 1869, includes this uncharacteristic little criticism:

> I found that the cold tea is not used up in the kitchen, which Elizabeth undertook to do, when I changed the payment for tea system some time ago. I had to talk to Elizabeth about it, & she has not been quite good not to speak to me before about it. She says with this cheap tea, they can't drink it cold it is so bad.

To me, it seems that the control of staff must have been one of the most alarming aspects of marriage for young Victorian brides but perhaps the situation was so much a matter of course, so much taken for granted, both by mistress and staff that, in practice, it was easier than it would be today. By Alice's time, however, Mrs Beeton had produced her *Book of Household Management* (1861) which contains a useful section on 'Domestic Servants and their Duties' and guidelines on the annual wage each type of servant should receive. (But Alice never mentions Mrs Beeton in her diaries.) However, it must have taken courage to face up to servants – Cook especially – who had more experience than the mistress and might have the advantage of age as well. It is noticeable that in listing the names, jobs and pay of her servants, Alice usually notes their ages. She had taken cooking lessons after she became engaged and she had some kitchen skills. She reports, for example, that in July she is 'very busy preserving raspberries and red currants' – but she could have been no match in knowledge for an experienced cook.

Young and callow as she was, however, Alice was not lacking in the kind of courage needed to run her household and assert her authority as its head and, as it happened, she had to call upon it in the first year of marriage: ' I had a great row with the servants or rather they had together and I had to give Sarah a great talking-to.'

Alice appears to have been ready to experiment and make changes in the duties and wages of her little staff, of a kind which seems certain (at least in today's eyes) to cause staff trouble. When Sarah had left after only a few months 'on account of health', her replacement Elizabeth (though three years older) was started at the considerably lower wage of £5 per annum 'and get her own tea'; and when the cook gave notice, Alice replaced her by promoting Elizabeth 'at £7 the first year [a rise of £2] to be raised another £1 if satisfactory'. In November that year, Alice added a nurse, Mary Brookes (aged twenty-one) at £10 and '10s.' for tea.

Before the year was out, Elizabeth was asking for more: 'Elizabeth complained about her wages, which seemed very ungrateful after all that has been done for her & distressed me very much' (31 October). A day or two later she had a talk with Elizabeth and agreed to give her £10 from November and 'no further rise to be expected for some time'.

Poor Alice! There was even more trouble about replacing Elizabeth as housemaid: first she engaged Anne Lee at the surprisingly high sum of '£11 in the first year' – well above what Elizabeth was getting as cook. Highly paid Anne gave nothing but trouble and left the following July 'having', Alice writes, 'behaved very badly indeed the last fortnight'. Next, she engaged Annie Selby (age not stated) at £9 10s. She 'was delicate when she came' and left after only three months, during at least one of which she was ill in bed and being constantly nursed. Alice saw her on to the train home at the end of October, to her great relief – 'I had feared she would never be well again', and indeed she died of consumption a month later. Alice replaces her with 'little Mary Bebbington' (a child of twelve) at £4 a year 'until we find a regular one. She is too small to stay.' During this time, Alice noted: 'We put out most of the washing with the understanding that it is to be done at home again when we get a housemaid.' So in this household, the housemaid performed as laundry maid as well.

Alice then had to borrow a housemaid on a temporary basis from one of her aunts, but there was not long to wait for the return to normality, for Martha Bennett (seventeen or eighteen) was in the post as housemaid at £9 10s. and 'get her own tea', by the end of the year. However, the following year was not without its domestic troubles: 'Martha gave me notice on account of some silly quarrel between her and Elizabeth; I had to have long talks with them & we were all 3 quite upset' (25 April).

A day or two later, the experienced Bar came for a few hours on her way home and 'set all right among the servants, to our very great relief'.

There seems neither rhyme nor reason in the wages paid – and Alice gives none. It looks as if the wages were very much a matter of bargain and supply and demand at the time of engagement.

One wonders how much her troubles with her staff were due to inexperience and how much to her frequent absences from home. During these two first years of her marriage, she continued to spend a great deal of her time during summer months or holiday weeks, away from Nottingham, staying at Bollington, and she was in fact there in July when the housemaid who had behaved so badly left. Though Ben regularly joined her at the weekend he was normally at work in Nottingham during the week. How, one wonders, was the little household in Nottingham expected to run satisfactorily in these circumstances? Alice does not raise this question or appear to worry seriously about any of the staff changes, except the felt ingratitude of Elizabeth.

The return of the young bride to her family home for long periods after marriage does not appear to have been unusual in those days – or at any rate not in Alice and Ben's circle. Ben appeared to take it very much as a matter of course in his Family Record. And he describes how (in the previous generation) his aunt Maria, being very homesick in the early years of her marriage, had spent not weeks but months back at her home. Other records show that this practice was also common among the Enfields and Needhams.

My grandparents' lives were not greatly changed socially by the arrival of young William Enfield. Whenever they were at home together in Nottingham, there seems to have been a fairly continuous social round – dances, teas, dinners, callings, watching cricket and, when there is nothing else happening, Ben and Alice played croquet together in the summer evenings or chess in winter.

Cares of a young baby notwithstanding, they started the year 1865 by giving two big parties themselves – each of about twenty guests: The first – 'Chiefly old. Talking & music. Went off pretty well but we were short of gents' (21 February); the second 'Chiefly young people. Music all evening and whist in the hall' (24 February). Alice added – 'of course I have been very busy preparing for these parties, cooking etc'. I suspect that it was unusual amongst young marrieds of the servant-employing classes for the mistress to help in the kitchen. Was this perhaps the kind of 'treatment' Alice was referring to when she accused Elizabeth of ingratitude in asking for more wages?

There is also in the diary for this year (as indeed for every year) what seems an almost continuous tale of illness – usually based upon colds but including headaches – and though rarely needing a doctor, often involving periods in bed both for Alice and her servants. And now of course the baby's ailments were added: during their August holiday at Southtown (Ben's family home) Baby seemed so ill – 'he does nothing but be sick and sleep' – that Ben's father walked to Yarmouth at six-thirty in the morning to fetch the doctor: '*Not* a homeopath of course,' Alice reported. From other references, I gather that she relied very much on homeopathy. 'He ordered grey powders and castor oil.' This sounds fairly drastic treatment for a sick baby less than a year old. However, in a day or two he was better and because there was a scarlet fever scare in the Yarmouth area, they returned to Nottingham at once. He was well enough to go on (with scarcely a pause) to finish their holiday at Bollington.

Alice writes often of her children and servants' toothache. She herself suffered a great deal from abscesses and a swollen face and from the discomfort of her false teeth. On 14 May 1867, for example, she reports that 'my teeth came entirely to grief and I had toothache very bad and can hardly eat', and a day or two later, that though 'my teeth don't ache so much ... they are very troublesome as to eating'. As the years progressed references to toothache became more frequent.

In 1883, she would have 'face ache all day, which got worse & worse and gave me hardly any sleep' and, next day, 'my face very bad all day. Mr White came and gave me some medicine & towards evening, it swelled v much and the pain went off', and a few months later, 'a horrid toothache grumbling all day ... kept me awake most of the night' and, next day, 'my toothache did punish me all day! I went to [the dentist] but he did me no good that lasted ... a laudanum poultice helped me to get a better night'. After which would come a more serious and permanent blow – 'At tea I broke my *last* front top tooth, such an indispensible one, it made me quite low!' (3 November 1883). She was not yet forty, and was ever more condemned to wear false teeth that were 'so uncomfortable and bulky'.

But now still at the age of twenty, Alice was full of worry about her parents' illnesses. Both were often ill with the usual colds, coughs and headaches and Alice felt that one, at least, of their

MRS GREG (NÉE NEEDHAM)
Alice's mother, with her eldest daughter, Alice's sister

daughters should always be in attendance. Her parents also had more serious troubles: her mother was so deaf that she went to the length of consulting a specialist in Leeds who found a hole in the drum of one ear and a tumour in the other, so that there was no hope of her hearing being restored. 'It was a disappointment to me,' Alice reported, 'but not much to her as she had not hoped anything.' (In the only known photograph of her, she is holding a large ear trumpet.) Alice's father too, now in his sixties, was frequently reported to be ill and called in at Nottingham to see his daughter on his way to consult London specialists, for what trouble is not stated.

Concern with baby, parents, household and social engagements was startlingly interrupted at the end of April 1865 with news which took up the whole of that day's diary:

> The dreadful news arrived about the middle of the day, that President Lincoln was assassinated at Washington on Good Friday. It was hardly believed at first, it was so horrible. (26 April)

Good Friday had been 14 April, so the news had taken twelve days to reach Nottingham. It was of enormous public interest. The main Nottingham paper describes at length a public meeting, convened by the Mayor, 'to enable the inhabitants of Nottingham to express their opinion on this dastardly and diabolical outrage', which – so the report goes – was 'crowded to excess, many being unable to procure even standing room'. The meeting passed the resolution that it 'regards with horror, indignation, and abhorrence the appalling crime which has put an end to the life of the great and good President Lincoln'.

Ben had been much concerned about the American Civil war in its early stages in 1862 when, as he saw it, England's attitude might possibly have affected events:

> The larger bulk of English people went with the North, but a strong section of thinking men & some leading statesmen sympathised with the South, notably Mr Gladstone. Lord Palmerston, in many ways inferior to Mr Gladstone, saw the right course ... Louis Napoleon made advances to England, with a view to joint action for stopping the war in the interest of the South but Lord Palmerston would not hear of it.

The cause of the South could have been seen as Britain's economic interest, because our cotton came from the South, and Ben reported that 'the suffering in the Manchester districts was intense, owing to the cotton famine'.

Given his undoubted interest at that time, it is surprising to find that Ben makes no mention at all in the Family Record either of the assassination of Lincoln or of the public meeting about it in Nottingham. Nor is there any mention of the Nottingham meeting in Alice's diary. Their uncle William Enfield was there officiating as Town Clerk but, on the day of the meeting, Alice records only that they 'went to Mrs Ransome's at 7.30. Very pleasant'. So they were not among those trying to get standing room. The assassination gets no further mention.

In August of this year, Alice had her twenty-first birthday: 'No longer an infant!' she writes, 'Ben was very busy so we could not go a drive or anything. It rained too.' However, the important matter in her thoughts now must increasingly have been the preparations for the arrival of her second baby: in early December, she wrote that she was 'tremendously busy preparing for number 2'. They bought a larger house (in Oxford Street, which is nearer into Nottingam) costing £540 (Ben reported) and were together planning the necessary alterations to it. Their permanent living-in staff was now three – cook, housemaid and nurse and an under-nurse would soon be added – so the new house had to accommodate at least six adults (excluding guests) and a growing number of children; they did not expect to stop at two children – nor did they. By the end of the decade they already had five and another on the way.

Ben's accounts for the first three years of marriage show their expenses to be £490 for the first year (1864), rising to around £600 at the end of the decade. The first big increase was in 1872, to £900, when an entry of £50 for education appears for the first time and expenses such as furniture and repairs, double. The wages bill increased by £10. The accounts in these years also show that they lived well within their income. A pencilled note for 1873 shows a total income of £1,977 (including Alice's settlement of £311 per annum and 'presents' amounting to £255). Expenditure for the whole year came to £880, leaving a balance of £1,097. (A modern-day equivalent can be worked out by multiplying by fifty.)

January 1866's diary is full of the dinners and dances attended by Ben – Alice not, of course – and plans for the alteration to the new house.

Their second baby, born on 25 January, was another boy whom they named Hubert. This time the birth was so easy and quick – from two a.m. to three a.m. – that Alice was quite taken by surprise. Once again, 'as soon as it was light' Ben went to take the news to all the relations, and, once again – on 10 April – his brother Enfield came to conduct the christening. Quite an occasion was made of it.

> We were so busy all day getting ready for the christening ... It was very nice but I could not listen to the first part because Baby was so restless. He didn't cry though. I sent him away afterwards.

Friends were invited as well as family and, says Alice, 'many stayed to tea and evening'.

The following year the third baby, Hester (my mother), was born on 11 July. 'We were so glad it was a girl,' Alice wrote. She was named after Alice's elder sister, who had died as a child, and whose birthday each year Alice never failed to remember and note in her diary. This time there was no christening party. Alice simply recorded on 18 August that 'Baby was christened at chapel after the service was over. She was asleep and so good.'

No christenings at all are mentioned after this one. There is no reason to think that Alice and Ben became less devout; they continued to support the Unitarian chapel and Ben indeed became chapel warden about this time. It is perhaps worth pointing out that nowhere in the diary is there any mention of godparents.

Though Alice recorded many things of her first baby – the day that

ALICE WITH HESTER, C. 1870

she washed and dressed him herself, the days when he was vaccinated, registered, christened – she said nothing about the all
important and trying matter of feeding. We have to wait to learn
about this from the next two babies: about Hubert at three and a
half months, she wrote (21 April 1866) that 'Bar left and I felt very
bereft, especially when Baby turned against his bottle'; and (10
March 1868) of Hester at eight months that 'I weaned Baby'. So it
looks as if Alice's babies were part breast-, part bottle-fed.

My grandmother told me once, in great confidence, that after
the pain of giving birth to her first baby, she did not want another.
Fortunately, after the first, the births of Alice's children were
increasingly quick and easy, in spite of the fact that they were big

babies – 9 lbs usually: with the fourth, she was taken ill about twelve o'clock and 'little Tom Greg' was born an hour later – 'quick work indeed,' she says and adds, 'I had a little chloroform the last 5 minutes'.

The chloroform would probably have been given by the monthly nurse whose arrival Alice records with the rather surprising comment that 'it felt dreadfully like the executioner'. However, though the births were easy, they were followed each time, after up to two weeks, by an unpleasant form of recurring fever, causing her mother to keep putting off her return to Bollington where (Alice kept reporting) she was needed and 'sadly missed'. Unfortunately, no sooner was Alice worse, than her mother (who slept with her) began to develop ailments of her own: (24/25 February 1866) 'Mother had *very* bad toothache' and 'her knee began to be bad again as it was last winter'.

A month after the birth of her third baby, Alice was still not well enough to have her well-loved brother-in-law sleeping in the house; and after the fourth, she gave the following graphic account of what happened thirteen days later:

After being perfectly well, I suddenly had a drawback – pains & tremendous shivering, headache, fever & tremendous perspiration. I had to be politiced & done. (11 December 1868)

Following this she was terrified of having another 'drawback', and, for the first time, stayed in Nottingham for Christmas. Her mother stayed too and Ben went to and fro to Bollington where the two little boys, Will and Hubert, had been sent with their nurse as soon as 'little Tom' was born. 'They went quite happily,' Alice wrote, 'tho' Will nearly cried when he came to say goodbye'.

This was not the first occasion on which little Will had spent time away from his mother. When Hubert was born, he had been sent with his nurse to stay locally with the Henry Enfields in Lenton Road, from where he had been brought to see his mother the next day – 'as he will every day' Alice wrote, and 'Ben goes round by Lenton Road on the way to and from here [to work]'. But this 'modern' treatment did not last under the pressure of events and indeed gave way that summer over two quite different problems.

The first had been the move to the new house. Alice was under extra stress in the week of preparation for the move, because Martha, her housemaid, was ill in bed and, at the same time, she had felt she must allow Eliza, the children's nurse, to go home overnight for a special family party. So she had agreed fairly easily to an offer from her mother to collect little Will and take him with her to Bollington –

> Accordingly the dear old thing appeared at 11.0'c with Walter [Alice's teenage brother]. Of course we were *very* sorry to lose him but yet thankful for him to go, in our *busy* conditions. (16 July 1866)

The next day, 'the house seems so quiet without him', but there had been 'very good news of dear little Will', and a week later came a letter from Mother to 'entreat that Will may stay a bit longer. He is getting into such good habits and is so good and happy'. Alice and Ben did not take much persuading this time either, for this was house-moving week:

> We began about 10.0'c & of course were at it all day. Harry and Mary E [cousins] came & helped with putting up bedsteads etc. We dined in the old house & Baby [Hubert] was washed at 6.0'c in the new house. (26 July)

The good relations between Alice and her staff stand out from the diary entry for this day and the next:

> The kitchen was one mass of things all over the floor, & it was a comical sight to see the 3 tired maids about 9.0'c sitting on 3 chairs in the midst of the chaos, sighing, with their heads on one side!

By the end of the following day there are still 'endless carpets & blinds & curtains to be done' but 'the kitchen & pantry apartments are beautiful and maids are delighted'.

71

One way and another, it was not until 10 August that little Will was brought home. He had been away from his mother for three and a half weeks. 'It was nice to see the dear bright little face again,' Alice wrote, 'and he quite remembered us'. The second special problem calling for the little boy's absence occurred only nine days later, in the form of a meeting of The British Association in Nottingham: 'We are all in such a ferment about the British Association next week. The whole town is. The H.E's are to have among others, 4 F.R.S's!!' (18 August). Ben and Alice had also engaged to put people up during the visit and had decided that 'it is better to have Will out of the way this Association time, though we were *very* loth to lose him again'.

There are glowing and full accounts in the diary of the sessions of the Association, and visits to local factories that Alice took part in every day for over a week, ending with an organised all-day excursion to Matlock:

> an *immense* party of excursionists, about 550 people!! We had a grand luncheon there and tea too! It was a very jolly day altogether & now I feel as if we had come to the end of our spirits for gaiety!

This second time, Will was away two and a half weeks. Given the way she conducted her family, Alice could not have had the interest and the fun that she had during the British Association visit, had little Will been at home.

Though she always had a nurse for the children (and an under-nurse when the third child arrived) she and Ben were not the kind of Victorian parents to see their children only in clean and tidy clothes after tea in the drawing room. The diary at this time is full of phrases like 'most dreadfully busy with the children' and it also makes clear that they normally had one of the babies sleeping with them, usually the youngest. This meant bad nights with sometimes only an hour or two's sleep.

Will began with croup at 11.0'c & was quite bad till 3.30 about. We did not have the doctor but we had him up twice & of course got very little sleep. (6 June 1868)
I always have to spend most of the afternoon sleeping, which takes up a sad quantity of time! (29 January 1869)

Scattered through both Alice's diary and Ben's Family Record are hints that Ben was an intimate father with his children. Theirs was an easy informal style of life: 'Ben bathed Will! He did not like it much' (1 July 1866). Will was then eighteen months old. And 'Katie, Mo and I had a cosy in bed before getting up, while Ben had Will' (11 August).

After the first four years of marriage, Alice was more at ease with her domestic staff too. She was very far from being the 'slave-driving', 'no followers' kind of employer that the Victorian lady is sometimes pictured to have been. The traditions of both her immediate and extended family were quite otherwise and she herself was instinctively liberal and humane.

As to family tradition, she mentions (2 July 1867) that – 'Jane, the servant at Lenton Road [home of aunt Ellen Enfield] was married from their house, which was quite a great event'. It is clear too that Alice's mother set her an example of friendly relations with the servants and she herself had been on intimate terms with the servants of her childhood.

Alice's staff were given twelve days' holiday a year to go home and she seems to have been ready to agree to reasonable requests for other short home visits for special reasons – a day to attend a chapel function arranged by the family or two days to help a sister to sort out problems with a drunken husband. She is also at pains to provide for her maids' enjoyment of life during their working weeks: they go to the seaside with the children (admittedly a convenience for Alice too) but they also go (without the children) to entertainments like the Nottingham Goose Fair, the Circus and the 'Panorama', or are despatched for an afternoon in the country on Ben's half day off.

Emily & Sarah [the two nurses] went today to Matlock by the Thursday special. It was a sweet day. We did nothing but read the newspapers etc. (21 July 1870)

Miss Wirz (formerly governess to the Richard Enfields) was staying for a night or two. Perhaps she helped with the children while the nurses were away; certainly both maids would have helped.

Christmas celebrations and presents for the maids were always a matter of excited day-long preparations:–

Mother has been very busy getting our Xmas presents, chiefly for maids. [Alice had just given birth to Tom.] We were busy doing them up & arranging some fun for the kitchen. (22 December 1868)
I put a lot of presents for our maids in a bath of sawdust that was discovered at the garden door & was a great surprise & delight. Mo had written some poetry for it … They had a very merry evening. (25 December)

On Shrove Tuesday 'two of the maids went to tea-parties' and 'they had a great kitchen party at home which was very successful' (9 February 1869).

The health of the maids is also always Alice's concern; they are cared for when ill, kept in bed and if necessary nursed and doctored, almost like members of the family – 'Elizabeth has such bad feet that I am going to make her rest them for a week and sit upstairs sewing' (8 August 1866).

Alice never hesitated to tell her staff what she thought of them and she seemed surprised when they showed resentment. However, she quite clearly regarded their jobs as worthwhile careers and this must, I think, have made it easier for her maids to accept her criticisms. She saw the job of living-in staff as a serious career progressing by experience from under-housemaid, to upper-housemaid and parlour maid, to cook at the top. Despite her being a remorseless critic, though, she was never short on the milk of human kindness and felt it keenly when she had to dismiss one of her maids – 'I was quite poorly all morning, for I had to give

Harriett notice to leave. After I'd got it over I got better!' (6 September 1869).

Once she started her family, Alice had little time for social or public activities between the births of her children. There were sixteen months between the first and second births, and eighteen months between the second and third. Nevertheless, she was always full of enthusiasm for anything intellectual that she could join in: for example, a course in English literature – 'It was very interesting indeed. There were about 50 ladies there' (20 November 1867), and another series of lectures in 1869. She enjoyed watching a partial eclipse of the sun (6 March 1867) and discussing temperance with an American general (her parents' guest) – 'such a *nice* man & so funnily free and easy' (22 August 1867). In October that year she records discussing a sermon by the Archbishop of York with her aunt and uncle Needham 'but of course we didn't agree about anything', and earlier, in February, cutting a formal engagement to tea with relatives in order to hear a speech by Neal Dow on temperance, 'a most delightful speech and *such* an enthusiastic audience. I did so wish for Papa and Ben' (14 February 1867), and attending a lecture on the Earl of Chatham (13 January 1869).

There had been a time, early in 1867, when Alice became depressed, and could admit to envying her younger sister Bertha, who had just become engaged: 'After my ecstatic delight for her, I have got a fit of reaction and envy!' Whatever her feelings (and I suspect they were short-lived) she didn't let them affect her behaviour. Bertha & Amy (her eldest sister) had come to stay for a few days for shopping – 'Ber is getting most of her trousseau here' – and Alice arranged no less than three parties for them in the ten days of their stay: a music party for a select twelve when her brother Herbert sang; a supper party for thirty 'mostly unitarians ... we had supper in the kitchen and made the dining room like another drawing room'; and a party of twenty, all

75

unmarried, which she clearly thought rather adventurous, 'but it did very well'.

And when it came to Bertha's wedding, Alice played her full part:

> Up at 6 to do flowers etc etc – helped Bertha to dress. Went to Chapel in carriage with mother *and Bertha* who was as cool as if it was someone else who was going to be married! (11 April 1867)

It is rare at this time for Alice to mention what is happening abroad and she only shows any personal concern where Italy and her hero Garibaldi are involved: 'Affairs at Rome and abroad are dreadfully interesting. Garibaldi and his people are trying to free Rome but the French Emperor is horrible and won't let them,' she wrote on 21 October 1867. She could mention the Austro-Prussian war as though it were of no interest to her – or to her country: 'The Prussians have beaten the Austrians terribly in the war that is going on, and they are advancing on Vienna' (6 July 1866). But her imagination and sympathy are engaged when 'There [was] a most fearful hurricane in the West Indies, which destroyed whole Towns and sank no end of ships' (23 November 1867).

On that same day she reported, apparently unmoved – 'Execution of the Fenians in Manchester'. Did disapproval of this beginning of a violent 'free Ireland' party perhaps cut out her natural sympathy for the humans involved? She made no comment.

Her sympathies were engaged, however, by a human saga closer to home:

> We heard a very sad story about the Dunningtons who live nearly opposite us; how he beats his wife so dreadfully & she has had to run away & leave her 7 little children. (22 January 1868)

Though she longs to help the Dunningtons, there is nothing she can do then. Three months later she hears that the Dunnington baby is very ill, and she is again shocked by Mr Dunnington, 'a most wicked drunken wretch'. This time there is something she can do:

> We sent across to ask Mrs Dunnington if she would like the youngest boy (the only one who does not go to school) to come & spend the day here. She was very grateful & glad for him to come, so he was here all day.

Ben, naturally, was much less constrained in his social and public life than his wife was and he is often reported as going to parties and dances without her. But marriage and children meant giving up a great deal for him too: 'Ben went to Beeston to play cricket & enjoyed it very much. He has hardly played for 3 years' (30 May 1867).

There are frequent references to Ben and his brothers going down to bathe in the Trent (usually before breakfast) but, cricket apart, there seem to have been few other summer outlets for the energies of the young men of Nottingham – though of course everyone *walked* much more often and further than people, even the young, normally do today: four- or five-mile walks from the railway station were quite common, and they walked from place to place in and around Nottingham where now people would usually take the not-yet-invented bus, car, or bicycle. And then as now (but perhaps more then) there was walking for pleasure – the diary mentions the children going for a walk in the meadows to get crocuses.

Large picnic parties were an established form of entertainment. For one of these 'the maids had been up till 11.30 making pies' and they were a family company of fourteen, which included uncle Sep, and a number of other relations, the two little boys, Ben and Alice.

> At 11 o'c we all started off in an enormous van. We went 1st to Hucknall where we saw Byron's tomb ... then on to Annesley Park

where we got out & walked & it was most lovely; then to a hill of gorse & ferns where we picnicked most successfully. A lovely most successful & delightful day. Will & Hubert very good except just coming home. Meadows [Martineau] paid for it all.

At Bollington – by now christened by Alice's friend, Sarah, 'B.B.' (short for 'Beautiful Bollington'), they were usually on holiday, and the house would be full of young people, so energetic activity was the order of the day: there was almost always some party in the evening, either at B.B. or Quarry Bank, when they rolled back the carpet and danced. But there were also formal balls; on 9 January 1868, they went to one given by the Macclesfield Fire Brigade, taking a party of twelve. During the planning, Alice had bemoaned the fact that 'everyone we asked has refused', so they must have had big ambitions. 'It was such fun. I was chaperone!' she boasted.

During the day at B.B. there were picnics or long walks, usually to some place of interest and on New Year's Day 1868, Alice reported a 'Paper Hunt' –

It was about 7 miles ... We girls went, cutting off the corners. It was v. good fun. Then dinner. Burbery & Norman Moore stayed till 8 o'c, Norman reading aloud and telling his funny stories.

Quite cleary, 'dined' here means a meal at an earlier time than today's middle-class dinner, but about the same time as the twentieth-century working-class evening meal, which [in my part of Suffolk at any rate] is called 'dinner'. However, on Christmas day 1868, Alice writes: 'Mother went to Lenton Rd for 3.30 dinner & got back at 8.30'. So there is as yet no unanimity.

There were still times when Alice was homesick for her mother and her childhood home – indeed, when she went back to Nottingham in January 1868, she wrote that she felt 'much lonelier than ever before on leaving home'. This was in spite of the fact that, on the day of her return, she and Ben had gone to 'a very pretty ball, about 140 there ... we stayed till 1.30'. It must be said that she recovered her spirits fairly quickly, writing in early February of an evening spent at home (Nottingham) 'laughing a great deal and being very silly'. However, her mood was not entirely a passing one; on 5 October of the same year (again coming away from Bollington) she wrote that 'it grows more hateful every time to leave Mother'.

Undoubtedly, in spite of her frequent pregnancies and her many home responsibilities, she managed to have a lot of fun in Nottingham. The entertainment there was croquet on summer evenings, dancing, music (which of course included singing), whist and chess.

Reading aloud was a staple evening occupation for the two of them when they had no visitors or outside entertainment. What were they reading? The titles she mentions are mainly of books that would become our twentieth-century classics: no Jane Austen or Brontës but George Eliot's *Romola* (first published in serial parts in 1862-3), Thackeray's *Vanity Fair* (1847), Trollope's *Small House at Allington* (1869), and *Last Chronicle of Barset* (1867). And of course Shakespeare. They go to the Henry Enfield's for joint Shakespeare readings. There is no mention of Dickens but as a child Ben had been brought up on Dickens, so it's unlikely that Dickens was not among their reading-aloud authors and they were certainly interested enough in him to go and hear him read: 'Very interesting it was to see and hear such a clever man but he does not look at all nice' (4 February 1869).

In short, the general picture is of a happy young wife devoted to her husband, missing him when he is away from home for however short a time, still tied by strong affection to her parents and childhood home, and taking pleasure and support in her extended family of uncles, aunts and cousins.

Cousin Mary Enfield (daughter of the Henrys) was a frequent companion but there were not many cousins of Alice's age. There was of course a special relationship with uncle William and aunt Anne at Low Pavement and to an extent also with uncle Richard and his family at Bramcote; there were young children there with whom Will and Hubert shared lessons but it is clear from the way she wrote of him, that Alice was a little in awe of uncle Richard, who was a senior partner in Ben's law office. It was with uncle Henry and aunt Ellen Enfield at Lenton Rd that she had the closest and easiest relationship seeing them more or less every day. Sadly, uncle Henry died suddenly on holiday in July 1869.

Quite a number of young Nottingham wives called and were called upon and invited to parties, but Sarah Courtauld was the only friend whom Alice wrote about in this period as being more than an acquaintance; she had been a 'best' friend at school and would remain of great importance to Alice throughout their lives. Their friendship at this time is well illustrated when Sarah paid a week's visit to Nottingham in 1868:

> Sarah came at 12.0'c. We talked away *all* day & could hardly get our scraps of letters written. It is 2 years last September since I had even a little sight of her & it was most delightful ... (30 May)
>
> Sally & I talked all the day long. She has brought the children a lovely scrap picture book & me a beautiful workbag! ... She is making me a bonnet. (2 June)
>
> We went a very nice drive. It was Ben's holiday afternoon but alack, he had to go to London at 5.0'c! I was very melancholy to lose him but Sally & I made ourselves happy. He sleeps at the Edward Enfields. Sally slept with me. (4 June)
>
> Sally had to go home to London & very sorry I was to lose her ... We seem to care about each other as much as ever. (6 June)

Alice celebrated her twenty-fifth birthday on 12 August 1869. It was a Thursday, so a half-holiday at Ben's office and they went by train to Derbyshire and revisited the little village of Baslow, where they had stayed on the first day of their honeymoon:

> Ben & I went by the weekly excursion train to Bakewell station where we had a *lovely* walk ... right across Chatsworth & the Park to the dear little Peacock Inn at Baslow where I have not been since 6 years ago. After tea there, we went to the churchyard & sat there a bit & then

drove to Hassop & home by train about 10.30. The day was *lovely* & we enjoyed ourselves most *immensely*. Meantime, the children & maids were very happy having a tea party in the dining room!

A fitting end to this chapter. There were now four children: the eldest (Will) was almost five; the youngest (Tom) six months old.

CHAPTER 6

Political Awakening

'What a year it has been, the fullest and most eventful of our lives.'

THREE IMPORTANT events occurred in Alice's family early in the year 1870: in March, Emily Drinkwater was engaged as nursemaid; in April, a second daughter, Maud, was born; and in May, Alice was introduced by her mother to the agitation for the repeal of the Contagious Diseases Acts.

Maud would grow up to be the support of all the family, and especially of her parents in their old age; and Emily would be the devoted nurse of the younger children and afterwards would become Alice's main assistant in running the family, remaining with them, part employee, part friend, until her death. However, as the new nursemaid, she was not immediately recognisable as a likely future paragon. Indeed Alice's first impressions were definitely unfavourable:

> She is not a bit like what I expected – *very* young looking & not what one would call 'superior' at 1st sight. We can't understand why Mother & aunt Agnes were so 'despritly' enchanted with her. (16 March 1870)

Emily came of a farming family in a village near Bollington and had been found for Alice by her mother. She was twenty-three and had never been in service before. As it turned out, her mother's judgement could not have been more right but, in the first few years, Alice and her new 'upper' nurse (as she became by the end of the year) certainly did not always get on quite smoothly together.

Emily was willing, friendly and responsible: from the first she could be trusted alone with the children and within a month of her arrival was sent by Alice to Bollington with the three youngest; she was happy to help Alice prepare for a grand ball in February the following year, doing for her what a lady's maid might have done;

and after her first annual holiday, she arrived back 'bringing such *loads* of things from her farm home – eggs, butter, cream (for me), apples, wheat and rhubarb, presents for the children etc., etc.' But she could be moody and, in particular, was not invariably willing to put her hand to anything needed in the household, as Alice tended to expect of her staff.

Alice's running of the house sometimes caused friction with independent Emily. Her second year with Alice began with 'all the children' having coughs and colds and 'poor Miss Rice' (the governess) too being very poorly – so no doubt a good deal had fallen on Emily.

And in mid-January, Alice had nevertheless given a 'regular dance' for some forty people, including two of her sisters who came to stay for some days beforehand 'to help with the preparations'. Alice herself got so 'knocked up' that she was only just well enough on the actual day 'to come down & receive the guests' – and 'Emily was v. poorly & gloomy too'.

Only a week or two later, Alice again had the house full of visitors: two of her sisters were as usual staying in the house and her married sister, Bertha, had come for a weekend with husband and baby (Basil) whose nurse had gone on holiday – 'leaving Basil on our hands. [He] is not very well so it is no joke', Alice wrote. 'Ber & Sib had a dreadful night with him.' The next night, Elizabeth (the cook) had Basil to sleep with her.

It seems pretty clear that at this point Emily was not prepared to add Basil to her normal and extra duties – she already had three in her nursery – and Alice's comment in Monday's diary, after the departure of Basil and his parents, was that – 'Elizabeth has been most good & helpful while they have been here (not so Emily)'.

After Maud was born, 'a dear little black-haired girl', there followed a happy, contented, easy period for the family: the new baby was 'the goodest, quietest & prettiest baby we have ever had'; and Alice now had, in Emily, a nurse of unusual quality. Diary entries mention evenings when 'Ben mowed the grass', and 'We play whist'. And, on 20 May, we have this happy timeless family picture:

I am very very busy of course, what with washing & nursing Baby, & Hubert's lessons & everything, but we are very happy and cosy. The maids & children, all but Emily and Baby, went to Wilford for the afternoon & had tea there & enjoyed themselves very much.

There is no sign here – or indeed anywhere in Alice's diaries – of a lady of leisure, waited on hand and foot by teams of servants.

It was while Mrs Greg was in Nottingham for Maud's birth, that she first told her daughter about the political issue which was to engage Alice's deep concern and very considerable effort for many years. This was the countrywide campaign for the repeal of the Contagious Diseases Acts.

Before Alice's marriage, there had been no hint of her having any interest in national politics, though we have seen that she had a romantic interest in Italian nationalism. Her traditional family liberalism was so much an unthinking inheritance that she found the opposing political views expressed by an acquaintance odd enough to make her smile: 'Percy Hervey was very amusing, talking his conservative politics' (August 1867).

But almost at once after her marriage, references to political processes began to appear though, of course, as a woman she had no vote. In April 1866 she wrote about the Reform Bill debate in the House of Commons and a few weeks later spent four hours in Nottingham market place listening to speeches, afterwards carefully recording the votes in the election. How far this interest was her own natural bent on growing up and how far her husband's adult interest can only be speculation. But she was still very much under her father's influence: staying at Bollington in November 1868, she had been shocked that

Albert & the naughty Tories [in Macclesfield] have been giving hot suppers to the working men as a bribe, which is most wicked & makes us v. indignant. The working men liberals are behaving most admirably & keeping clean hands, exciting Papa's enthusiasm.

A month later, she wrote with delight that 'the Liberals have won at Macclesfield with *clean* hands'.

Elections seem to have been a good deal more violent in Alice's day than they are now. Alice mentions riots both in Nottingham and in London at election time, including one, some years later in Ratcliffe, a small village outside Nottingham, where 'Ben presided at a meeting for Mr. Earp. He was almost mobbed and they would not hear a single word from either him or Mr. Earp' (22 October 1885).

In March 1869, she had become for the first time an active campaigner for a cause: in some papers sent to Ben, she had come across a proposed 'bill to protect the property of married women', a Bill which had been about since 1855; she had at once consulted with other ladies of her acquaintance, within a week was preparing a Petition to Parliament and a week after that was 'busy most of the day going about with my "petition"'. She seems already to have known a good deal about Parliamentary procedures for, next month (14 April), she noted that the Bill had been 'discussed in the House, passed 2nd Reading & referred to a Select Committee'.

This cause gave her a personal as well as a theoretical interest in the election two months later, when she and sister Katie dared 'to go down into the market place in evening to hear Seely [the Liberal candidate] or rather *see* him ... a most improper proceeding on our part'. And, on polling day,

> Sib & I went right into the polling booths & saw the people voting ... After dinner we were going down again [but] Ben looked in to say the Riot Act had been read ... & we mustn't go ... Seely got in but it was a close run thing. (11 June)

The first Married Women's Property Act was passed a year later.

Alice's reaction to this cause had shown how quickly and effectively she could act when her interest was engaged, but what seems to have awakened the political campaigner in her, never afterwards to sleep, was the agitation, seen as a *moral* cause, for the repeal of the Contagious Diseases Acts. These Acts (dated 1863 to 1869) provided that, in and around named ports and towns frequented by our armed forces, any woman could be forced by police to undergo a medical examination and, if found to have VD, be compelled to enter a special hospital to be cured and be subject to regulation by police thereafter. If she resisted, even to the extent of avoiding subsequent tests, she went to prison.

The Acts were opposed from the first. Then, in 1867, a propagandist association was formed, favouring the extension of the Acts to the whole civilian population.

These Acts have recently been described in a Fawcett Society Library publication, as 'an attempt to introduce into Britain a form of state-regulated prostitution on the Napoleonic or "Prussian" pattern'. It points out that little public attention was paid to the Acts while they applied only to garrison towns and ports and that it was when calls were made for the system to be extended to the whole country that the agitation for repeal really took off, and became a major campaign, second only to that for repeal of the Corn Laws.

All the House of Commons debates on the introduction of the Contagious Diseases Acts were held in secret session and public attention had first been drawn to them by leader articles written in 1863 for *The Daily News*. These articles were written by Harriet Martineau, but were, of course, anonymous at the time. She was then in her sixties and sported a large ear trumpet and, by all accounts, was a woman of formidable intellect and independence. Indeed, during her lifetime she would write almost fifty books, including novels that explained political economy to the laywoman, and over a thousand leader articles (all anonymous). The Contagious Diseases Acts were but the latest in a long line of causes she had supported, including divorce reform, education as a key to equality, and women's suffrage.

The repeal movement was led by Mrs Josephine Butler, another

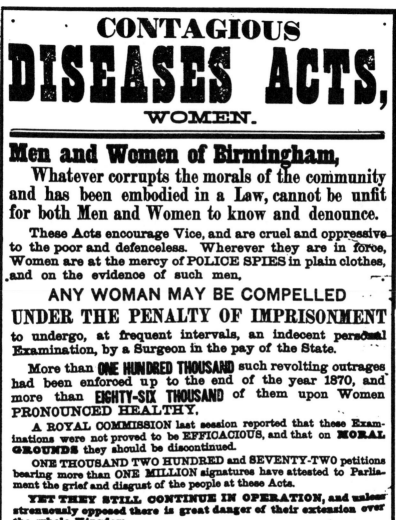

FLYSHEET OPPOSING THE CONTAGIOUS DISEASES ACTS
addressed to men and women of Birmingham

famous and formidable campaigner for women's rights, who became president of the Ladies section of the National Association for the Abolition of the State Regulation of Vice, when it was founded on 5 October 1869. She had spent many years working among destitute women and prostitutes in Liverpool, and made repeal of the Contagious Diseases Acts her 'Great Crusade'. She wanted prostitution brought to an end, as she felt it denied women their basic rights and made them slaves to 'male lust'. She also campaigned vigorously for higher education for women.

A 'Women's Manifesto', signed by 2,000 well-known women, was printed in *The Daily News* on 31 December of that year. It protested against the Acts on the grounds that: 1. they took away women's legal safeguards without full and proper discussion; 2. they removed women's sacred legal guarantee of security and put them absolutely in the power of the police; 3. the offence was not clearly defined; 4. the Acts punished the victims of vice and left the perpetrators unpunished; 5. they made the path to vice easier and declared it to be necessary and venial; 6. the measures were cruel and brutalising to women; 7. the disease had never been shown to be removed by such measures; 8. the conditions of the disease were moral not physical, and the cause of evil should have been dealt with before rushing into experiments legalising a revolting vice.

There followed 'a conspiracy of silence' in the local and national Press as a result of which the Abolitionists founded their own weekly paper, entitled *The Shield* and the manifesto was reproduced in that paper on 14 March 1870. Among the 250 signatures listed there, Josephine Butler, Harriet Martineau and Florence Nightingale were in the first eight. 'Mrs Majur Grieg' is also in the first eight; it is possible that this should read 'Mrs Mary Greg'. Apart from this possibility, no name appears in this short list from Alice's circle of families. Harriet Martineau, in a way, was 'family' since she was related both to Ben (she was an aunt of his brother-in-law Meadows Martineau) and to Alice's mother (she was a cousin of her sister Lucy's husband, Richard Martineau).

There was a good deal of disingenuous argument on the subject. The Acts had been based on the assumption that continence is impossible for men and that because of the diseases incident to prostitution, a sanitary cordon should be drawn round prostitutes. However, when it came to Government argument against the motion for repeal in 1870, you might almost have thought from the debate that the object of the Acts was to rescue 'fallen women' and return them to their families.

Feeling between the opposing views ran very high. On a campaign visit to Colchester, for example, Mrs Butler was obliged to leave her hotel at night, because the Proprietor was afraid of what the mob outside would do if she remained.

The first mention of the subject in Alice's diary is on 5 May 1870:

> Mother has been very busy since she came, collecting signatures for the repeal of the villainous Contagious Diseases Acts. She is very alive & indignant about the subject & indeed it is no wonder. Ben quite agrees with us about it, but strange to say, Papa doesn't, quite!

In 1870 alone, 817 petitions signed by over 460,000 people were presented to Parliament in favour of repeal of these Acts; two of these were from Nottingham in that year (in February and April), and one the following February, all three being presented by Colonel Sir Charles Seely, the Nottingham Liberal Unionist MP, about whose election, in 1869, Alice had been so concerned.

The petition of April 1870 was specifically from the Women of Nottingham. Signed by no less than 10,034 people, it called for the repeal of the acts on the grounds 'alike of religion and morality, of common justice, common decency, and common humanity'.

Alice was too late for this petition. She must have worked on the one presented in February 1871 which dealt solely with the Acts as they stood and not with the proposal to extend them. (This petition is given in Appendix 1.)

From the moment of being convinced of the cause, Alice watched eagerly to see what happened in Parliament and she was understandably angry when the first debate on the motion for repeal was held in secret:

> The debate on the C.D. Acts last night was carried on with closed doors & no reporters allowed!! Such a thing has not been done for 20 years! but it seems any member has a right to demand it! (29 May)
> Ben has read the report published in *The Shield* of the debate on the 24th which is dreadfully interesting and convincing. (6 June)

Alice was quite right. The ancient custom under which a single M.P. could have the Chamber cleared – i.e. the Press and Public Galleries – simply on stating, 'I spy strangers', was not changed until 1875. The effect of holding the debate in secret session was of course that no woman, in theory, could hear or report it since there were no women M.Ps. However, it is possible, as will be seen in Chapter 10, that when the Press and Public Galleries were cleared, the Ladies Gallery may not have been. If so, a woman could, conceivably, have been present. Could Harriet Martineau, deafness notwithstanding, have been such a one? And could that explain how she was able to write her articles? Alice might not have known that all the debates on the introduction of the Acts had also been held in secret session.

In spite of this, detailed accounts continued to appear in *Hansard* under the words – 'The following is believed to be an accurate representation of the several Members who addressed the House on the Motion'. Presumably, M.Ps gave their speeches to the Press if they wanted them publicised, and those arguing for repeal clearly did – the *Hansard* account of the debate on 24 May ran to forty pages, and on the adjourned debate, held on 25 July (also in secret) to thirty.

At the end of the debates in 1870, the Government announced the appointment of a Royal Commission. The main Government speech on the subject is not given in *Hansard* but the appointment was supported in debate as being 'the best means of probing the subject without giving needless offence to public decency', it being argued that if discussion on the floor of the House were held in public, the subject 'would be made painfully familiar to the young as well as to the old and brought next morning under the notice of ladies perhaps as well as men'.

Given the fact that thousands had signed the petitions, these excuses ring a little hollow. What is certain is that neither Alice nor her mother or husband felt the subject to be unsuitable for public discussion and that Alice became an active crusader for repeal from the first day that the cause was explained to her, arguing vigorously with relatives, friends and strangers alike, in public or private, at good times and bad.

She met some opposition within her family: 'I got a letter from uncle Richard about the C.D. question! & answered it at length. Luckily he did not seem to be at all angry with me in the letter' (30 January, 1871). His writing to her instead of speaking (he lived locally) as well as the tone of what Alice says, leave (I think) no room for doubt that he disapproved of her campaign. An argument with her father ended better:

> Papa & I (& mother a little) & afterwards Ben, got into a tremendous talk & argument about women's rights questions & C.D. acts etc ... which was very interesting & very good to have had. We ended very good friends & mother & I very thankful feeling. (5 June 1871)

However, her father continued to have doubts since next September, Alice again reports a long talk with him about the subject.

Just a year after the appointment of the Royal Commision, they heard that the government did 'not intend to do anything this year', and that 'the Royal Commission is not as we hoped in favour of repeal'. Alice writes that she, her mother and Ben have been '*immensely* busy over the last few days framing and sending off for signature memorials to different members of the Government about C.D. [Contagious Diseases] legislation' obviously in the hope of getting enough support in Parliament to obtain repeal in spite of the Royal Commission. Three days later, she was disappointed and angry enough to write personally to the responsible Government minister about it:

Mr Bruce said in the House last night that the Govt would not do anything about the C.D. acts this session – 'if there had been *any hardship or grievance*!!!!! they would have felt bound to but it is unnecessary and there is no time etc'! Oh, *weren't* we angry. I couldn't resist writing to Mr. B to tell him so! (18 July, 1871)

Alice's view appears to have been typical of the 'grass roots' attitude to Parliament at the time and indeed of Josephine Butler herself. Mr Bruce had apparently hoped to produce a government Bill which would satisfy everyone but it would have extended the Acts to the whole country and so would obviously have been objectionable to the repealers.

The next diary reference is to a meeting on 'C.D.' in Nottingham on 12 January 1872 to which Ben went: 'Very crowded and enthusiastic. All men,' she reported. And at an election meeting a day or two later, Ben went and questioned the candidate on the Acts and received 'a satisfactory answer'.

But after this, the general picture becomes gloomy. In June she reported that 'the news of CD is very disheartening indeed' and, the following January, that there has been a disappointing public meeting in Macclesfield. The report of this meeting given in the *Macclesfield Courier* makes the reason for the disappointment clear: most of the gentlemen, who had been announced to appear on the platform, did not turn up and though some eighty people attended, only fifteen or sixteen women went.

Alice was not discouraged; she kept up her proselytising to the extent even of enlisting the support of their landlady while they were on holiday in Filey and she also kept up her petitioning. She describes a pleasant evening in February 1873 'spent with aunt Ellen, cosily discussing how to manage the C.D. petitions'.

However, worse followed for the repealers, with heavy losses in the general election in February 1874. 'We have lost many of our supporters (C.D.) alas,' Alice laments. 'Mr Jacob Bright, Mr Fowler, Mr Rylands etc' but (she is able to add with glee) 'Sir J. Pakington is turned out, and other enemies!' Mr Fowler had been the mover of the motion for repeal in 1870 and also the chief speaker on the first day. Mr Bright was the chief speaker for the motion on the second day. Sir J. Pakington was amongst the 'enemies' who spoke in the debates.

No doubt these results reduced the activities of the repealers for some time but whatever might have been Alice's wish to continue campaigning, grave family concerns and problems now intervened which took up all her time and thought. It would not be until 1878 (with another election not far off), that she returned to active work for the cause – see Chapter Nine.

When Alice described 1870, as 'the fullest & most eventful of our lives', I don't believe that she was thinking in family terms. Maud's birth and Emily's arrival were, after all, very much part of the normal order of things to date. She must have had public events in mind: nationally, the C.D. campaign on which she had embarked with such conviction and ardour; and, internationally, the subject that occurs most frequently in her diary entries for the second half of the year, the defeat of France in the Franco-Prussian war.

Beginning with the report on 12 July of 'a great panic in London owing to the fear of war', and her disapproval of the declaration of war by France on 15 July – 'There is hardly a pretence of a pretext and it seems most wicked and unnecessary' – she recorded the course of this war on many days in July, August and September. She noted carefully the battles – always lost by the French – the guns lost, the numbers of soldiers killed and taken prisoner. But what she wrote of with most feeling was the suffering caused by the war:

> 2 great battles were fought at Worth ... they were most bloody & dreadful battles ... 10,000 killed & wounded ... (6 August).
> The Prussians are in such numbers that the French have no force adequate to oppose them and it really seems likely that they may go on to Paris! The *poor* Emperor! All the papers seem to think that this war

will be the end of *him* & one would be surprised at *nothing* which could happen now. (13 August)

The battle on Thursday was such a rout & the army so surrounded, that it had to capitulate & the Emperor gave himself up as a prisoner to the King! The Prince Imperial comes to England, they have proclaimed a Republic at Paris. (5 September)

The war gets no mention in her diary throughout October and November but reappears in early December with reports of sorties from Paris, now surrounded, and of battles round about Orleans where 'the French have been very completely beaten again. They have not bombarded Paris ... [They] seem to be going to starve it out'.

> The cold has been intense for 3 days – last night the thermometer went down to 6 degrees. It makes one shudder to think of the poor soldiers & French villagers (24 December).

Then, on 28 January was to come – 'Capitulation of Paris signed. The Germans are we think very hard in their terms,' and on 7 February 'Preliminaries of Peace signed. The terms are very hard indeed.'

Ben, writing thirty years later in his Family Record, remembered his relief at the time when the Germans won the first great battle of the campaign because then 'there was no likelihood of our being drawn in'. But his concern by then was with the historical and international aspects of the huge change that was taking place in the balance of power in Europe: 'The cry which resounded in the Paris boulevards, "à Berlin, à Berlin", did not seem unreasonable before the war began,' he wrote, but

> a week after war was declared, the strength of Prussia, supported by almost all the German States became apparent ... Within a few months the power of France had been completely overthrown; a marvellous result, considering the position France had held for so many years in Europe. The political outlook was completely changed; a new era had opened; whether for good or evil, time alone could show, few liked to prophecy.

CHAPTER 7

Difficult Times

'A dreadful fright I got into.'

NOTWITHSTANDING THE accepted practice in the Victorian middle classes, Alice and Ben did not employ a governess until there were six in the family. The first mention of education in the diaries comes when Alice was taking Will and Hubert to 'lessons' with their cousins, the Richard Enfields (who had a governess), at the surprisingly early age of three and two. Thereafter, however, it was a matter of course that she would teach the children herself.

There is no information as to whether, in taking on this early task of teaching, Alice was following a family pattern, but it is quite possible that she was. Young educated girls frequently taught in Sunday school, and teaching of a wider kind was a Greg tradition: we know that Alice's grandmother Hannah Greg had been a notable educationalist and the Greg aunts had taught at the school set up for children of the factory workers at Styal. Alice's and Ben's mothers (one a Needham, the other an Enfield) would have gone to Mrs Turner's enlightened girls' school in Nottingham where the pupils were taught all the normal academic subjects of the day except, probably, Latin and Greek. Neither Mrs Greg nor Mrs Dowson would have had any reason to doubt her ability to teach small children and Alice never questioned her own capability.

Teaching was one thing for Alice; discipline was another. She found her elder son Will increasingly difficult to manage, and 1869 had seen many tussles with him, especially after he and Hubert had come home from spending several weeks at Bollington at the time of the birth of their brother Tom, a stay which extended over Christmas 1868. 'It was a joy to have them back,' she writes, 'but I had quite forgotten what they were like! & Will is such a great boy that I was quite surprised to hear him talk so un-plainly'.

Trouble had begun with Will at once. Pathetically, she describes putting the little boy to bed with his hands tied 'as he keeps meddling with things'. Presumably Alice meant 'masturbating'. And 'naughtinesses' over his lessons with her had also increased over the months: she had tried stopping them for a whole fortnight, 'as a disgrace'; she had tried shutting him in his room 'for ever so long'. Finally, and 'after much talk', she had given up the idea of teaching him herself: 'it is very difficult to manage him properly and I fear I don't do it'. And so, a month or two before his fifth birthday, she had accepted defeat and sent him to a little school run by a Mrs Petty, 'but for the present only for 2 hours in the morning'. She had clearly felt this to be a very drastic – even harsh – step to have to take and there seems to have been no question in her mind of Hubert going too.

After this, a whole year passed without trouble with Will but all cannot have been quite well for on 19 April 1871: 'Katie gave me a good lecture (very well deserved, I fear) about my management of the children.'

Alice gave no reason for this outburst and appears to have accepted the rebuke from a younger sister with surprising humility. Her sister may, however, have been speaking professionally. The previous year Katie was starting a two-month training at Great Ormond Street Children's Hospital and she was staying with Alice while visiting hospitals in Nottingham at the time she made her comment.

Alas for Alice! The silence about Will's behaviour was well and truly broken that summer, first at Bollington and then at home, when his imaginative naughtinesses became so frequent, so inconvenient and even dangerous, that his parents decided to send him away to school:

Will was discovered in the cellar, breaking & stirring up eggs in lime with a stick!! I kept him indoors for that, in my room where I lay down & went to sleep & meantime he spilt a lot of ink on the blankets & sofa cover!! I was in despair & felt quite finished up. (11 August Bollington)

Next day was her birthday, and she seemed quite recovered in

96

spirits and able to enjoy the fact that 'Mother and aunt Agnes are going to give me a nice cool foulard silk dress'.

Back in Nottingham, Will began school again but there was trouble at once:

> Will was very naughty & troublesome too. I think there never was such a mischievous, troublesome 'trying' boy ... I get almost in despair about him sometimes – & yet he is such a darling too. (26 August, 1 September)

Things grow worse –

> We were waked at 3.0'c a.m. by hearing Will & Hubert downstairs. They had lighted a candle & been into every conceivable place & meddled with every conceivable thing. It was a mercy they had not set themselves on fire ... Ben had to have recourse at last to corporal punishment, & Will (who was at the bottom of it all) was kept in his own room all day in disgrace. It was a most miserable day, for I was very bad all day in body and spirits, & B had a bad cold. (13 September)

None of their punishments stopped Will. In a day or two, he was 'up again at 5.0 a.m. [with Hubert] at the sugar jars & [had] lighted a candle & almost burnt a bit of the kitchen door'.

Alice and Ben obviously looked upon corporal punishment as a last resort, for on another occasion, a reason for turning down a possible school was that 'they use the cane' (25 May 1872). The difficulty then (as, indeed, now at the end of the twentieth century) was to find another form of punishment that had any effect – and really they never did.

For some unexplained reason (but could it have been good nursery discipline under Emily?) these problems of behaviour never arose with the four younger boys.

Having known my uncle Will in a relationship nearer to that of daughter than niece, I can testify that he would grow up to be a man of great integrity, intellect and charm. But he always had a very adventurous spirit – the first man in all Nottingham to own a motor car and, with Arnold Lunn, one of the earliest skiers – and that adventurous spirit made him a natural intellectual rebel. At seven, his mind must have been full of questions and there is surely in his attention-seeking behaviour, a recognisable cry for his mother's notice. She would of course have been quite able to fill his intellectual need, but all her diary entries at this time show that she continued to think of him as a *baby*. He is always 'dear little Will', and 'poor little fellow'.

The arrival too of yet another baby could only have been seen by him as a tiresome interruption in his life, distracting attention from himself, making his mother ill for weeks and causing him to be sent away from his home. There is no evidence that Alice attempted to interest the children in the new arrivals. When Tom was born, for example, she wrote that Will and Hubert 'were very pretty with him' but she sent them off to Bollington without ceremony the next day. It could, perhaps, be significant that Will's behaviour reached a pitch of unexplained 'naughtiness' just before the birth of another child (his brother Robin) on 29 September.

Alice must have been pretty desperate at this point. Not only did she send all four children to Bollington before her next confinement, she sent Will away only three days before his seventh birthday.

The decision to send Will to boarding school was taken jointly with her husband. Alice, though, seems to have regarded the choice of schools as primarily *her* responsibility and the school she chose was very much a boarding version of Will's previous little school, being run by a woman (Miss Allen) and in premises so close at hand that Alice could – and did – take him out whenever she fancied.

Given the Greg tradition of sending boys away to school at seven years old, it is at first surprising that his parents were so loath to send Will away to school. But the Dowson tradition had been different: Ben's father had lived with an older brother while he went to school and Ben himself had not gone away to school until he was ten and had found the experience extremely unpleasant.

It would not be until 1876, when Will was twelve, that he was sent to 'a proper boys' school', as my grandfather called it.

Alice took Will straight to this chosen school on his return from Bollington with the others at the beginning of November; noting that 'he did not seem to mind going'. Two days later she got away to take him out and was greatly comforted to find him 'so happy playing that he was hardly willing to come,' and 'so shy apparently that he walked 20 yards behind me' (8 November 1871).

Alice's diary reports that there was a great deal of infectious illness in Nottingham at this time. During October 1871, there was an outbreak of measles which both Alice's babies (Tom and Maud) caught, and both children also caught ringworm. As well, one of their friends' children died of scarlet fever – 'after only 2 days' illness'. More serious still (13 December) 'the small pox is rife in Nottingham ... Ben & Baby were vaccinated' and (a week later) 'I and three maids were vaccinated from Baby' (a curious phrase perhaps, but arm-to-arm vaccination was not unusual in 1871, especially during an epidemic, when suppliess of vaccine were short. This method was finally prohibited in 1898.)

Alice had begun lessons with Hester at four years old but had found 'its difficult to make her attend or think they are anything but fun and rather grand' (21 August 1871). At last, she realised that she needed help with both Hubert (now six) and Hester. Hearing of 'a Miss Rice (nursery governess sort of a person)', she wrote to people she knew who lived in the same village, to enquire about her. Two days later, there is 'a most *charming* account of Miss Rice. Decided to write & engage her for a while, though B. did not much like it.'

Alice does not say what Ben's objection was. Did he perhaps dislike engaging their first governess without having even seen her? Alice, however, was clearly desperate for help – any help – at this moment: Tom, with measles, had to be kept away from the new baby and so had to be looked after solely by Alice or her mother; Alice herself had had one of her bad attacks the previous night and was not fit to get up at all on the day the letter about Miss Rice arrived; Ben was 'very very busy just now' – and was due to spend the next weekend at Bollington to be with the older children; they were short of one maid who had been sent away to avoid the measles; and 'Mother rushed about to find charwomen or helps but failed'. 'Alice was feeling the burden of our growing family very much,' Ben wrote in the Family Record.

Fortunately, the new help could not have come more quickly; the arrival of Miss Rice is reported 'only a week since we first heard of her'.

> In afternoon Miss Rice came – the new nursery governess & *helper to me* sort of person ... Mother was so busy all morning helping to get the breakfast room nice for her bed & sitting room all in one. (30 October)

And, in a very few days, Alice was commenting: 'Miss Rice is very nice I think & she does all Hubert's and Hester's lessons & is altogether a great help to me' (11 November).

Towards the end of that month, she was getting on so well with Miss Rice that they went to a 'female suffrage meeting' together, which Alice, at any rate, found 'very interesting & exciting'.

Tantalisingly, there is no information about the routine for the children at Bollington. Their grandfather was often ill, their grandmother's deafness, though rarely mentioned, must have been a disadvantage with the children and in any case she was mainly with Alice at these times, travelling to and fro between the two houses, according to where she was most needed: 'Mother went home, as they want her more there than we do here' (17 October).

It seems that, until a governess was employed, any schooling the children had while they were at Bollington was provided by Alice's sisters. She would not have thought this unsuitable and she took

100

it for granted that she and her sisters would 'stand in' when the governess was on holiday or ill.

Even as late as 1874, when Hubert was nine, she wrote that: 'Miss Rice went away for 9 days holiday, so Amy & I will have Hubert & Tom on our hands' (15 July 1874).

Miss Rice had, of course, to be fitted into the hierarchy of Alice's staff in wages as well as in accommodation. On her arrival, Alice had written that 'It is a little awkward at first of course finding what sort of position she will take etc.' Why she felt this we do not know: she herself had been brought up in a family with a governess. In any case, with her mother's help, Miss Rice had immediately been established with her own bed sitting room; and Alice's accounts (recorded at the end of the diary) show that Miss Rice was the highest paid of the staff, with £20.

One might have assumed that the Victorian governess was socially looked down upon – part way between the servants' hall and the drawing room – and Alice certainly made that assumption when she engaged her first governess. That being so, I can't help noticing with interest that her sister Bertha had married a Hugh *Ronalds* and her dear cousin Albert, an Ellen *Ronalds*. It does not seem unreasonable to suppose that they were related to Alice's own governess, *Miss Ronalds*. Alice might of course have made a social a distinction between the position of Miss Ronalds (her sister's governess) and the new Miss Rice whom she describes as 'a nursery governess' – Emily's position had also to be considered. But, in any case, her social attitude to her governesses was to change over the years as she developed quite close friendships with at least two of them, the most important being with Miss Badham.

That sister Bertha's daughter, Ethel, was also a governess could perhaps be argued to be further evidence of the Ronalds' relationship, though admittedly it was at an altogether different level, namely to children of the Russian aristocracy. I knew my cousin Ethel quite well and can't resist mentioning here, as a nice little footnote to history, that in her will she left everything to her charges who by then were driving taxis in Paris after the revolution.

By the end of 1871, Alice had a staff of four in addition to her governess: an 'upper' nurse (Emily) paid £14; an under nurse (Sarah) paid £9; a housemaid paid £10 and a cook (Elizabeth) who had now been with Alice for a long time and was raised from £15 to £16 because 'she has been so good & such a comfort to me this last year'. Ben and Alice never employed a butler or senior male indoor servant but about this time (May 1872) she did employ a boy at two shillings and sixpence a week as 'man Freddy' to 'break up our coals' and clean boots and knives.

To the obvious comment that Alice seems to have had a lot of help with the children, it is fair to point out that there were four children under six, including two babies. It might, in any case, have been felt, with reason, that an extra nurse was needed when some children regularly went to Bollington and some stayed at home.

Remembering that some of her family were usually staying with her, and that she did a good deal of entertaining, the demands there must have been on Alice's staff are pretty obvious. She had little more staff than she had had when she first married and she was beginning to get high standards; for some years now she had been requiring someone to be prepared to wait at table – the under nursemaid had recently been told that she might sometimes have to take this on; and Alice was, for example, greatly put out one day when:

> Uncle John & [aunt] Mary [Albert's parents] appeared suddenly just before dinner, when we were in a great mess generally & going to have a scrap dinner; altogether it was such a dreadful dilemma as I think I never shall forget. B. never came to dinner & there was no wine up. Oh it was so dreadful! (6 June)

In spite of the cares of family, Alice had two good holidays that year, in addition to the normal family removal to Bollington in August: the first, *without* the children, though 'with misgivings about leaving home', was for nearly three weeks with sister Katie, mainly in London, seeing friends, going to the theatre, shopping in Oxford Street and being shown over the Houses of Parliament; the second, *with* the children and Ben, to Filey, a party of twelve, '6 children, Miss Rice & 2 nurses, Sibbie & us'. Next day 'Ben bathed before breakfast & Sib & I at 12 o'clock. It was capital fun for I have never had a good bathe since I was married!'

There were also two important deaths about this time – of 'Bar' (her childhood nanny) and of their uncle William. 'Bar' (her real name was Faith Travis) seems to have been a kind of 'Emily' of that earlier generation, 'deeply loved by all the children, specially perhaps by Alice & Katie' as my grandfather recorded. Alice took the train the moment she heard of Bar's illness but missed her connection and failed to reach her before her death. Katie nursed her devotedly to the end.

The death of uncle William (her senior local relative and firm support at all times), no doubt felt quite keenly by Alice, must have been a special blow to Ben, who looked on his uncle as a second father; as he wrote:

> No man was more loved & respected than my uncle in the district. He had the spirit of the Good Samaritan, & always rejoiced to help the poor & needy ... As he came out of his house door after breakfast, he had frequently to run the gauntlet of quite a number of applicants for his charity, before he reached his office in the yard behind his house. Personally, I owe him much in every way. In the will he thought of everyone ... we had £1200 & a half share with Uncle Richard in furniture. The furniture was very convenient & helpful some months later when we were furnishing the new house.

The 'new house' had been planned and embarked on by Ben and Alice the previous year. This time they were daring to *build*. It was to be a house for an already large and still growing family and the wisdom of this was underlined when, in April 1873, twin boys were born, bringing the number of children to eight.

Ben had acquired a plot of land where it could be bought cheaply in a then remote area of The Park, and there they were building the house in which the whole family would grow up and in which, indeed, at least four of their grandchildren (including the author) would be born. It was called 'Felixstowe' and it would always be a happy house.

The roof of the new house was already on when the twins were born, though it did not become ready for occupation until the autumn. In the first months of 1873 Ben and Alice made many visits during building and decided on such things as importing 1,400 loads of soil for the garden because the ground was very stony and sandy. I cannot resist quoting these words from my Grandfather, about Hester (my mother) then five years old:

> One of our visits to the garden at this time I well remember. Hester had a little sycamore seedling; we got it up with some soil; she wheeled it with great care in her tiny barrow to the new house & then we planted it. It is now in 1899 getting quite a fine tree.

(The house burnt down in the 1960s and the land was sold so I have not been able to check whether the tree is still there.)

On the birth of the twins, there was a present of £50 from aunt Fanny Martineau which earned two exlamation marks from Alice, and the thought that this might make it possible for her to add a kitchen maid to her staff. 'The twins are angelic babies and give hardly any trouble,' she writes. 'When they went out for the first time in their lovely new white and blue cloaks they looked so lovely and sweet.' And there is this charmng description of a very early picnic with them:

> We drove in afternoon to the cowslip field taking both babies & 2 nurses & Hester & Maud. I sat in the carriage with both babies while the others got out to pick the cowslips & the driver took out the horse & went too! My hands were very full meantime keeping the babies warm enough & giving them bottle etc. (19 May 1873)

It was well that Alice had these short intervals of happiness, because, that summer, she and Ben were to suffer the most worrying and saddest time of their lives. Ben suddenly became ill with what the doctors described as 'congestion of the membrane of the brain'. For two whole months, Alice had to oversee the household without him, as well as the completion and furnishing of the new house and removal to it.

That spring, Ben had had many worries to add to his normal work. He was an executor both of Bar's and his uncle William's estate, and one of his brothers [George] had got into serious financial difficulties from which he had to be rescued by his family. These responsiblities along with 'increasing family ties at home combined to tell upon me,' Ben later wrote, '& towards the end of June, uneasy feelings began to creep in upon me'.

Ben's illness, when it came, was very terrible. Writing twenty-five years later at the end of the century, his memory of his symptoms was still exact and painfully acute: at first he hardly slept at all and was possessed by 'terrible thoughts'; he had an oppressive feeling in his head 'as though my skull were drawn in tightly at the back of my eyes'; for hours before he lost consciousness, he had the experience of hearing cathedral music; on coming round he had at first no hope of recovery; and, in convalescence, his hearing was so acute that the ordinary noises of normal life were very painful to him. The pain in his head, which he knew he had had, was the one symptom he had no remembrance of.

For Alice, the experience was quite as terrible. The acute period of the illness lasted two weeks and her anxieties were intensified by the pain she felt for him over the business worries that beset him and which she had no way of knowing the truth or falseness of:

> Ben was dreadfully bad all morning fancying he had made some dreadful mistake at the office & no one would ever trust him again. I didn't know but what it was all true. We had a dreadful morning of it which ended with a bad convulsive attack. Mr White thought his state very critical. (7/8 July)

During the acute period, two people had to sit with him at night and a male nurse was borrowed by uncle Richard from the local lunatic asylum. Alice was in general charge – she had to sack one unpleasant female nurse – and she took on herself much of the nursing during the day. She can have had little time or thought for her children, her household or the arrangements for the completion of the new house. 'I don't know what I should have done; she wrote, 'if the children had not been taken in somewhere'.

Fortunately, this was where their large extended family and some very good friends could and did help. Ben was to write that 'the kindness shown by our relations and friends in our terrible trouble was very great'. Aunt Ellen took in three children accompanied by the under nurse; Emily went to one of their friends with the twin babies; Hubert and Hester, the two eldest at home, went to the Richard Enfields.

Will was away at school but when he came home for the holidays at the end of July, he saw his mother only for one meal and his father for a few minutes, before being despatched at once to stay with the Richard Enfields, from where he was sent on for a month, to Fanny and Meadows Martineau. Once more, family pressures had resulted in the poor young boy (not yet ten years old) being sent away from home for months.

Everyone was concerned to help the family and Alice found time somehow (I can't think how) to record some examples: aunt Ellen 'writes letters to everybody every day' – (the families at Bollington and Southcott must of course have been in the greatest state of anxiety and need for news); 'Mrs Jacoby makes jellies and all sorts of things ad libitum for B'; aunt Ellen sent Alice out in her carriage every day; Ben's brother, Enfield, came to sit with him at night and Alice's eldest sister, Amy, shared some of the night-nursing; by no means least, Elizabeth (cook) came back early from holiday – 'she couldn't rest after hearing of our dilemmas and I *was* glad to see her. Our dear Elizabeth is like one of us.'

Ben could eat nothing solid, lived only on milk and became very frail. On 11 July – Alice doesn't forget to note that this was their daughter Hester's birthday (her sixth) – his mind was still 'sadly troubled with imagined sins or business mistakes or the idea of being ruined etc etc. It is most agonising.' A second opinion is asked for by Mr White (the doctor they have had ever since their marriage) and a family conclave assembled to hear the verdict that 'they think he is very bad but no danger of "an immediate sinking". He managed to sign his will'.

By the end of July Ben was out of danger and well enough a fortnight later to go with Alice into lodgings in Buxton for two weeks, taking Emily and the twin babies with them. From there to Bollington and Alice could leave him to take a short trip to Nottingham to see the other children who had been left with Elizabeth and the under nurse.

Ben was still by no means recovered and it was decided that he should go with sister-in-law Katie for a convalescent holiday in Scotland. Alice could not go with them because the children now needed her and the move to the new house was imminent. 'It will be quite a long time before I see Ben again,' she wrote; and indeed it was, for he was away four weeks.

Meantime, the move to the new house was made without him but (as during his illness) with ready help from their extended family and from good friends. One, Mrs Paget, gave invaluable help with all the details of moving books, pictures etc. that so need a second mind and pair of hands, as well as taking some of the children home with her for the night. Sadly, a week later Mrs Paget and her husband were drowned on the East Coast by a wave which swept them into the sea. Alice states this but makes no comment. I think she already had so much to bear that one more thing made little impact.

For, before this news, she had had one more serious blow to meet and to face Ben with when he returned home. Her uncle Richard, now (on the death of uncle William) sole partner in their law firm, told her that he wished to dissolve the partnership, but hoped she would not mention it to Ben at present. She waited a fortnight and then decided she must tell him. In his own account he describes this ghastly blow with a surprising absence of bitterness:

> I never knew the reasons which induced my uncle to desire a dissolution. I can only suppose that he was afraid my intellect had suffered and he might be compromised by something I might do.

He insisted that in every other way his uncle was generous, particularly in allowing him to take some clients with him.

Had he in fact (as he had feared in the delirium of illness) made some dreadful mistake at the office, which now decided his uncle to part company with him? There is no sign in what he writes that he thought he had, or doubted his continuing capacity as a lawyer – and it seems hardly likely that his uncle would have handed over clients to his nephew, if some really serious mistake had been made. But his uncle's decision, given his nephew's circumstances, is difficult to explain on any basis.

It is painful to imagine what Alice's thoughts must have been, with the responsibility of eight young children, a new large house in the building, and the breadwinner, recently on the point of death, faced with the removal of his means of livelihood. Added to the massive burden of these anxieties was the fact that her husband was undoubtedly very dear to her.

There is plenty of evidence in both their writings that they were a devoted couple. Their continuing pleasure in each other's company comes out very clearly in Alice's diaries. They shared the same pleasures, whether dancing or going to parties, walking or picnicking, watching cricket or, alone at home in the evenings, playing croquet or chess together or reading aloud – at the time of Ben's illness they were reading *Middlemarch*, which had been published 1871-2, and finding it 'very interesting'.

If, as becomes clear in his Family Record, Ben was more generally concerned with public affairs than Alice, he shared fully her interest in the repeal of the Contagious Diseases Acts and in the cause of women's suffrage; and they had the same intellectual interests, often going to lectures together on literary or philosophical subjects. Later, together they forrmed a society among their friends, called the 'Nomadic Society', which met in each other's houses to discuss such varied subjects as the moral influence of royalty, the treatment of criminals, the Eastern question and the principle of beauty.

It is rare for Alice to say anything about the content of Ben's work but there were examples during the years 1869/71, which involved him in travelling about the country:

> 'Ben had to go to Chapel-le-Frith to defend some boys belonging to Pleasley Co. who had stolen something at Buxton. He was away all day till 8.0'c. (26 August 1869)
> B. was away driving about the country all day, seeing about some new railway, which he rather enjoys. (25 October 1871)
>
> B. away again ...The railway business took him to Derby again & he didn't get home till nearly 10 pm. It is so dull without him. (22 November 1871)

His absence was always unwelcome. Again and again there are entries about the dullness without him and when he was away for the night she tried to get a friend or a cousin to come and sleep with her.

During the worst of Ben's illness, followed by the worry of the move and of the dissolution of the partnership, perhaps Alice was too physically and emotionally busy to contemplate the full horror of the possibility of her husband's death, leaving a penniless family. But at the end of the year, she recorded 'a very black Monday because of a dreadful fright I got into' and two days later 'my black fright gone now'. It needs no very active imagination to put down her black fright to delayed shock.

Happily, she was able to report that, on New Year's day, she and Ben joined the traditional staff party (enlarged to include the male nurse who had looked after him during the worst of his illness, 'the only gentleman', Alice wrote), that Ben made a little speech and that the occasion became a welcome home for him and a general blessing of the new house.

*　　　*　　　*

The immediate need was for Ben to establish his separate law firm. So successful was he that, almost at once, it was clear that he was going to need a partner and, surprisingly, when it came to choosing who that partner should be, Ben took advice: 'Alice's mother, knowing of my difficulties, set her mind to work,' he wrote, 'and came to the conclusion that John Kentish Wright was the very man I wanted. An interview was arranged and we easily came to terms.' By the end of the year, they were in premises that Ben had bought in Weekday Cross, where 'Dowson & Wright, Solicitors' flourished and were still in business at the same address (with, by then, two of his sons as partners) when my grandfather died in November 1918.

CHAPTER 8

Coping with a Large Family

'We put up a cowshed at the corner of the garden
and began with one cow...'

COMPARED TO the turbulence and unhappinesss of the first years of
the 1870s, the remainder could be described – at least in the main
– as calm and happy. Once Alice's major anxieties about Ben's
health and their means of livelihood were out of the way, she must
have enjoyed settling into the new house. Though it was not a
grand or showy house – Ben writes that their architect accused
them of building a 'quaker' house – it was at last large enough even
for their family.

I remember well the dark red brick, typically Victorian house –
in what I call 'St Pancras' style. When I knew it, there were five
good sized bedrooms and a billiard room upstairs, which in my
grandmother's time, must have been at least seven large bedrooms
and two or three smaller ones, with the servants' bedrooms in the
attic. Downstairs there was a drawing room, dining room, school
room and biggish entrance hall, a large airy kitchen and scullery.

Size of course had its disadvantages from the point of view of
heating. Alice wrote of one occasion in 1879 when the thermometer was down to 5 degrees below zero – 'We have 12 fires in the
house & all the pipes are frozen – *so* inconvenient!'

By this time she had stopped regularly putting her staff wages
and comments in her diaries and the latest indication of size of staff
to cope with the work involved with all these fires is in 1877. Then,
besides the cook, she had on her staff only a parlourmaid, a housemaid and a boy/man for 'about an hour a day' 'to clean boots and
knives etc and break up the coals'. On the other hand, it seems that
in 1876 she had three servants besides the cook and had borrowed
a fourth temporarily. In any case, it looks as if the servants must
have been hard-worked in the winter to keep the house habitably
warm. There is mention in the diaries of the use of charwomen, so

perhaps Alice obtained extra help that way – though she did not say so on this occasion.

It was natural in the circumstances that Alice should be very much aware of weather and she reported it regularly. According to her reports, the extremes of weather seem to have been, if anything, greater than they are now, and would recur in the 1890s too. In the previous year, 1878, there had been both extreme cold and extreme heat. In June, 'The heat was terrific; 95 in the shade! We dined in the cellar, the only cool place! Several of the children were more or less upset or sick.' In December, 'The snow in Scotland is dreadful, 6 or 7 trains hopelessly wedged in it ... such a long and severe frost has not been known since 1855 I believe'; and 'Thermometer on my dressing table in the morning (where we had had the gas all night) was 28 Degrees. The Trent was frozen over & about 200 people crossed ...'

It seems to have been the norm for the winters to be cold enough for skating and, in 1875, there was so much rain that the Trent overflowed:

> The water rose high over the railway in several places & came into the Midland passenger station ... several lives were lost ...row boats plied to the Trent Bridge Inn & the valley of the Trent above Nottingham was like a sea.

It would be interesting, if it were possible, to compare the incidence of the common cold in those days with our day of universal central heating. It would certainly be true to say that there were colds in my grandmother's family at least eighty per cent of the time. In her day, colds so often meant spending time in bed – if only to keep warm and avoid the frequent chest infections.

The garden of the new house was big for a town house: a good quarter acre of kitchen garden and as much for the flower garden, including a lawn big enough for the recently introduced 'lawn tennis'. Alice often refers to tennis parties held there and Ben – writing of the summer of 1876 – says that lawn tennis was 'a regular institution' in the family. He added that 'it had not then become the very serious game into which it has since developed', for it only evolved out of real Tennis in about 1870. So they were in the forefront in adopting the new game.

Because the new house was at that time in a little developed part of the Park, for a few years it was possible for the family to enjoy rural advantages normally available only in the country. They could keep and rear chickens – and even have a cow and their own fresh milk and butter. 'We decided to try our hands at cowkeeping,' Ben wrote: 'We put up a cowshed at the corner of the garden and began with one cow, a beautiful creature who went by the name of Paddy; we were all very fond of her ...'

The cow arrived and the first chickens (from eggs brought from Bollington) were hatched in the same week in April 1874. The cow had to be walked six to seven miles from its home farm in Ruddington to Nottingham and its arrival was a great family excitement:

> William the boy went for the cow early in the morning to Ruddington and did not get back with her till 12.30. He had had a hard job to drive her & she seemed rather distressed & excited. Of course we were all in the most frantic excitement about it & there was quite a levee to see her milked ... There are 7 chicks hatched out of 11 eggs ... (24 April) The cow is a great delight & interest. It gives about 14 quarts of milk a day. The chickens thrive beautifully ... (27 April)

The cost of the cow (later there were two) was shared with their friends Mr and Mrs Ellis (he was a Nottingham MP) and milk was delivered to them daily, sometimes by the children for a penny pocket money. At this time Alice's household numbered fifteen, two parents, eight children and five staff; assuming the Ellis household had a minimum of five (the Ellis children had not yet arrived) that would make a demand for milk from a minimum of twenty people a day. So Paddy's fourteen quarts (twenty-eight pints) would just about do. Later when they had two cows, Alice reported that:

113

Paddy gave three gallons in the morning & seven quarts & a pint in the evening & the other cow a gallon & a pint in the morning & three quarts & a pint in the evening.

That would be fifty-five pints in all. The economics of the arrangement, including the rent of the necessary land, were not stated. My grandfather simply said that 'the experiment did not last very long as the land was required for building'. Emily must have been a great help in these farm ventures but I cannot find any mention of the fact in the diaries.

The birth of Paddy's calf was anticipated with pleasure but produced anxieties and even fear because she became sick and quite violent and the 'Dr' had to be sent for:

Poor Paddy, our cow, very ill ... gave us a great fright, she got so violent when B & I were with her. The Doctor came 5 times. John sat up with her & B got up twice in the night ... (25 January 1875)

Alice always writes of the *doctor* dealing with the cow's sickness, never the *vet*.

Someone had to be engaged to look after the cow and this was Ben's responsibility. He seems to have had quite a number of troubles with the various boys or men he engaged; they were always getting homesick or bored, or were thought to have ill-treated the cow. 'He spends 3 whole days a week and comes the other days to milk etc', Alice reported.

Now that they had a living-in governess, the policy seems to have been that the children were to be taught at home as long as possible and only go to school when they were no longer really manageable by the governess. The result was that their first attendance at school happened at quite different ages: Hubert – the best behaved – went at ten and a half, Tom at nine; Robin – the most difficult after Will – at seven. The next stage was day school, not boarding, and the schooling chosen was the mildest possible: Hubert, though ten years old, went for mornings only at first and Tom and Robin were sent to a girls' day school.

Judged by what we know of Alice and Ben's family, day schools for boys – high schools – were only beginning to appear in the 1870s and 1880s. There were long established public schools like Rugby and Shrewsbury which were boarding schools and Alice's brothers went to these. And there were private boarding schools, including Unitarian schools, like those at Bristol and Nottingham, to which Alice's father and uncles and Ben and his brother went, or like Kitchener's to which Alice and Ben would send all their children except Felix.

But there appear to have been no equivalent boys' day schools – High Schools – until about the time that the four younger boys were of an age to go to them. There is evidence that there were private day schools for boys only, which might be run by women – Will boarded at two such in Nottingham (as seen above) – but the day school to which Alice sent her other boys was co-educational and she called it a 'girls' school. Two formal prize cards enclosed in the diary for 1881, confirm that the day school which the children attended in that year was co-educational, Hester (fourteen and the oldest of them), Maud, Robin, the twins and Gerard (the youngest, at seven). Had Nottingham High School been in existence at this time, it seems pretty certain that Robin, at least, would have been at it.

The fact that Kitchener's started as a 'family' school and blossomed into Newcastle High School while Alice's boys were there is further evidence of the emergence of High Schools at this time.

So, the choice for boys had been: a governess, a private day school (probably of the 'family' type and usually run by a woman) or a public or private boarding school, often far away from home.

In educating their sons in the way they did, Ben and Alice were departing from family tradition: as has been seen, Alice's father and her Greg uncles had been sent away to school at seven, and her brothers had gone to established public schools, one to Marlborough, the other to Rugby; Ben's first experience of school had been a boarding school far from home, where he had seen and suffered a good deal of bullying.

115

Neither Ben nor Alice gave any explanation of their policy –
though when rejecting one school they mentioned that 'they use
the cane'. It might have been a matter of money but I doubt it,
because Ben's accounts show that they were living well within their
income. More probably their policy was governed by Ben's determination to save his sons from bullying by keeping them at home
as long as possible and then choosing a 'girls' day school, leaving a
'proper boys [boarding] school' as late as possible.

Will, who had at first gone to a boarding school close at hand, in
Nottingham, now three years later was to go to one in in Southport.
He and Hubert had been great companions up to this time and it
was hard for them to part: 'In evening poor Will & Hubert were
crying dreadfully at the prospect of separation,' Alice wrote in
April 1874. (Will was then nine and Hubert eight.)

Their father must have sympathised with them for he and his
eldest brother had been just such close companions when they
were children but there seems to have been no question of altering
policy and sending Hubert to boarding school then too.

While they were still under a governess, Hubert and Tom were
old enough to cause a good deal of mayhem in the schoolroom and
they did. So much so indeed, 'that we are going to try Mother's
plan & shut [Tom] in the boxroom for 2 hours *instead* of doing his
lessons' (September 1874). Next month it was Hubert's turn to
spend two hours in the box room. The punishment seems to have
been successful with Hubert who was 'very penitent afterwards'
but five-year-old Tom endured 'box-room' treatment for six weeks
before he gave in.

The summer of 1874 was expecially trying for Alice because Ben,
still recovering from his illness, was away in Switzerland on a
doctor-ordered holiday. She missed sadly the help he usually gave
with the older children during holidays. The Swiss party included
Alice's two sisters, Katie and Isobel, and they went to a number of
places that Ben and his brother had visited on their walking

tour eighteen years earlier. He found many changes; in Zermatt, for example, 'the glaciers had retreated several miles up the hills, quite altering some of the views'.

'Alice would have dearly liked to come with us,' he wrote 'but our young family made that impossible'. In fact Alice was expecting another baby in a month or two. Her own unselfish comment was that she hoped they would be away for four whole weeks 'but what a long time it will seem'. Her frustrations this summer were certainly added to by the coming event. She was always far from well during the last weeks of waiting and it must have been the last straw for her that, in the two weeks before the birth, her governess happened to be on holiday, which meant that Alice had responsibility for the schoolroom. Never sparing of self-criticism, she told her diary that her 'patience & my courage are both exhausted. I am as cross & as wicked as I can possibly be.' Four days later, her ninth child was born, 'after 10! weary hours of it. He is a fine fat little boy – but 7 sons!!!' she exclaimed.

It is very noticeable that next year, when for once she was not pregnant, Alice could be young again – though she now had nine children, she was still only thirty-one!

By leaving some of the children at Bollington, one with sister Bertha in Edinburgh, and the rest at home with Emily and the governess, she and Ben got away for a two-week sight-seeing and energetic 'young' walking holiday in Scotland. And, in December, she could write of a ball in Nottingham that 'I danced every dance' – Alice's version, I like to think, of Eliza Dolittle's words, 'I could have danced all night'.

The following summer, when she was still not pregnant, they had no less than three holidays: their brother-in-law, Meadows Martineau, lent them a cottage at Esher where (for once) it seems that except for the three babies the whole family holidayed together; Alice and Ben had a few 'very successful' days at the Peacock Inn in Derbyshire, taking with them just Will and Hester;

117

and they managed a holiday by themselves in Cornwall which Ben thought 'if possible even better than our first wedding journey together'. Alice describes every day's activity with obvious pleasure – walking, sketching (Ben), reading *Lorna Doone* aloud (Alice).

Inevitably, there were also 'downs', even in these favoured years. One was the death of her father but she could only look on this as a merciful release because he had been ill and in much distress for many months. '*At rest, at last, at last,*' she wrote. Ben wrote of him that 'there was great charm about Mr Greg, gentleness accompanied by a nobility of mind that drew so many of all classes within his influence'. That he was widely looked up to is shown by the fact (reported by Alice) that for the funeral, 'in the village and Macclesfield all the blinds were down, shops shut and all the people so quiet and respectful'. A book containing some of his writings and a memoir about his life, written largely by his eldest daughter, Amy, was published in 1883 entitled *The Layman's Legacy* and went into two editions.

The other 'down' for Alice was the temporary loss of Emily and the permanent loss of faithful Elizabeth, both from ill health. Emily was the first to leave but she found it impossible to part from 'her twins', the favourites among her babies and was soon asking to come back. Alice had been very loath to lose her and was only too ready to agree to have her back: 'She is so lonely without them & so miserable. I am so sorry for her,' Alice wrote on an occasion when Emily had come on a visit specially to see the twins only to find them already in bed and asleep.

In fact Emily was back within a year and the close relationship between her and the twins lasted for life. (In my grandmother's house at Upper Broughton – when I lived there in the 1920s – there was a room called 'the nursery', the joint domain of Emily and my twin uncles.)

Between Elizabeth and Alice there was real affection and when after a five-week period away in the hope of getting her health back, Elizabeth came to say 'she really must leave us; she has not the strength to go on', Alice was devastated but accepted it as inevitable. 'What I *shall* do without her I don't know. It will be a *great* wrench to both her & us. But perhaps it is right' (11 September 1876).

It was not at all easy to find replacements. Alice described how she visited one agency after another and advertised widely but still no response – 'What am I to do?' she said in August and, in November, 'What is to become of us?' and 'We seem at the last gasp'. It was even more difficult to get a cook than a housemaid and at one point Emily took on the cooking. There was also a good deal of unpleasantness with it all because some of the servants were far from satisfactory – a cook who lasted only a few days was unpleasant in manner, doubtfully sober and couldn't even cook, while the under nurse, who had been with them for some time:

> was very ill behaved at last demanding board wages for the time that she was at home while we were at Esher! Which Elizabeth and Emily agreed with me was preposterous so we didn't give it to her and we parted uncomfortably.

It is an interesting comment I think on Alice's relations with her staff that she discussed what to do about the under nurse with her two trusties, Elizabeth and Emily. But it is also interesting that a request for board wages was then considered 'preposterous'.

Yet a third 'down' for Alice at this time came at the end of the year, with the discovery that a temporary servant had the 'itch' and had at once given it to one of the other servants – no doubt because beds were shared.

> Ellen (who is here for a fortnight to help) has got the itch!!! She has given it to poor Elizabeth [one of the housemaids]! ... I had to settle with both these maids to leave at once ... We *were* aghast! I sent Elizabeth to bed at once and fomented her side, poor thing. (15 December 1876)

Alice herself took the two maids to the station and 'saw them off comfortably' next day. The seriousness of the danger from the 'itch', as they saw it, is underlined by the fact that Alice felt it necessary to call the doctor and for the whole household to undress before him to be sure that they were safe: 'Mr White came when 10 of us undressed to show our spots and he pronounced us quite right, so we felt much happier' (19 December). The 'common itch' appears to have been another name for *scabies*; it became very prevalent in the Great War, and 'still persists in individuals whose ideas of cleanliness might bear revision', so an early medical book states.

Whether they were yet at school or not, her boys' behaviour and, as they got older, the need to find something harmless for them to do in the holidays continued to give Alice much worry and, in this, she relied very much on their father's help: he would take the older children away for a few days' sailing in Norfolk, or for a week to Jersey; and after the birth of their tenth and last child, when the governess went on three weeks' holiday, he took four to Yarmouth for a fortnight, releasing Alice to go to Bollington with only the new baby and Hester.

At this time, Hester was often mentioned as being helpful with the little ones, taking their lessons when the governess was away, or to relieve Alice in helping to look after the babies. 'Hester takes almost entire charge of Gerard. He sleeps with her & I with Mother these two nights while Amy is away,' Alice wrote on 16 October 1877. Hester was then ten and Gerard three.

Ben was also sometimes helpful with the few disputes among the older boys:

> Luckily B was at home all day, for I was almost knocked up. It is very very hard work for me when these big boys are at home, settling their disputes and their employment ... both are v. nice with the 3 little ones. (Bank holiday, 5 August 1878)

120

PRESSED FLOWERS
from the children's nosegays in the June section of the 1881 diary

That the disputes were few, I deduce from the fact that this is the only mention of disputes or quarrelling that has occurred in the diaries up to this date.

They were a loving family both of each other and of their mother and much was always made of her birthday: on one, 'the children stripped their gardens of flowers for me'; on another, they joined together in arranging a tea party for her in the garden. All the older ones, Will especially but by no means only, had a charming habit of giving their mother nosegays from which she pressed specimens on the blotting-paper between the pages of her diary. And there those flowers are still, even yet with a little colour remaining. Two examples, both from Will, are of a single sweet pea: one when he was ten, presented 'after he had been naughty over his lessons and had got the better of it'; the other, a year later, against which Alice has written – 'From Will, out of the *many* nosegays he used to give me about this time out of his garden'.

But, alas, Will who was clearly so devoted to his mother, caused her more anxiety than all the others put together – at any rate, he was the only one of her children about whom she *wrote* of her anxieties and mentions her disciplining: her 'very serious talk with my dear Will which we shall neither of us forget I hope' is recorded on 9 January 1875 when Will was ten.

By now, his parents had become far from satisfied with the Southport school for him and had decided that, at last, he must go to 'a proper boys' school', and the night before taking him to the new school, Alice had another of her serious talks with him – this time 'about some things' is all she says of its content. There is no suggestion that his father also gave him a talk.

In the choice of this school, Ben was as much concerned as Alice and together they inspected a number of possibilities, deciding on Mr Kitchener's in Newcastle-under-Lyme. They don't say that it was a Unitarian school but I think this can be assumed. Taking Will there for his first term, 'Oh how anxious I felt about Will,' Alice wrote, no doubt picturing horrid scenes of bullying. With the advantage of hindsight, Ben would write in his Family

Record that the choice of school 'proved a wise decision. Mr Kitchener's influence has been invaluable to Will.' And this was not just his parents' opinion. I have heard my uncle speak of Mr Kitchener with admiration. But Will's school reports were more often bad than good and Alice went on worrying – 'I had some serious talk with Will about his dangerous proclivities. He was touched & I hope impressed,' she noted on 18 April 1877, and four months later: 'Letter from Mr Kitchener with anything but a satisfactory account of Will; & very very anxious do I feel about him.'

Two years on, Will was joined at Kitchener's by Hubert, just twelve years old. Again Alice's concern to be involved herself at this important juncture in her boys' lives is very noticeable. She clearly felt that it was her place rather than Ben's to deliver Hubert to school on his first term, and she had to be dissuaded by Ben that it would be unwise for her to go – she was far from well and very pregnant.

> Ben went to B.B. [Bollington] to spend the Sunday with the boys [they had been there for some days to relieve Alice] & take them to school on Monday. I had to give up going though I was *very* sorry to do so. (26 January 1878)

Sadly, the result of her worries about Will was that when she felt overburdened, it tended to be Will whose absence was the greatest relief to her. Unfortunately, it also meant a much greater separation from his mother for him than for her other children, because he was also away in term time. I cannot avoid the conclusion that Will did not get a fair share of his mother's company in these childhood years – he was still only thirteen years old when Felix was born. That he was fond of his mother and his home and suffered from homesickness is undoubted. 'Will went off to school more heartbroken than usual, poor lad,' Alice wrote on September 1877, and she confesses that his departure caused her tears to flow, as well as his.

Even boys' boarding schools could be 'family' schools. Kitchener's was undoubtedly a family school to begin with and

Alice several times stayed *en famille* with the Kitcheners. Later it became Newcastle High School.

Ben was not concerned only with his children's education; he was also developing an interest in public education, a subject that was very much a concern of the time. 1870 marked a watershed in elementary education, and in 1876, the power to enforce compulsory attendance became general. In this year he was asked to be one of the eight Liberals to stand for election to the Nottingham School Board and was elected: 'It was my first experience of electioneering on my own account and I was heartily glad when it was over,' he wrote. 'I only got in by a narrow majority. We immediately set to work to get up a clear case for increased school accommodation.'

Thereafter, he found that his work on the School Board took up many of his evenings and Alice sometimes had to go alone or with their governess to lectures or debates at the many local discussion societies. They belonged to several public societies as well as joining their friends in starting two of their own and the subjects discussed were very varied: 'Recreation and duty', 'Home Rule', 'Revolution or Reason', 'The Gulf Stream', 'Is it reasonable to worship God?', and 'Curtailing the power of the aristocracy'. Alice doesn't usually state her own opinions but on 'the danger of being over-governed', on which Ben read a paper (31 January 1876), she did, and I find it interesting: 'No one there agreed with him!' she wrote. 'It made me feel rather depressed that people don't seem to see that danger.'

'All good things come to an end ...' In the summer of 1877, Alice was again pregnant. On 9 March 1878, we find her diary entry:

> I got all my wages paid & accounts done up & my talk to the various maids abt the arrangements for the next month etc – a very good job done.

Then on 19 March her eighth son was born. He was called Felix and (for his second name) Needham, the maiden name of Alice's mother. Alice mentions particularly that Hester and Tom were so delighted but adds that they 'were all rather disappointed at his not being a girl'.

As usual Alice's mother came for the birth and, as usual, some of the children had been sent to Bollington with their governess. As usual too, Alice had had a bad time in the weeks of waiting, There are many blank days in her diary for January and February, but the following entries tell the story:

> B away ¹/₂ evening – as so often now. It makes me lonely but perhaps is best so, for I am very poor company just now. (31 January)
> A very black dark Sunday for me. I am but sadly poorly nowadays. (3 February)
> Katie came to look after me a bit for I am in such a poor way that I never was worse, I think. (23 February)
> Awake nearly all night with about the worst headache I ever had. (2 March)

The headache was no doubt partly due to struggles with Robin the day before. At seven years old, he had become quite too much for the governess and it was decided to send him to school with his elder brother, Tom. On the first day, his father had to carry him to school, struggling and in tears. This would have upset Alice – 'poor little lad' she wrote – but worse was to come because the letter she sent with him to the headmistress 'about him and his lessons etc' was answered by 'such a letter as no lady could write, it was so grossly insulting!'

What can the letters have said? Alice gives no inkling but was so distressed that she went at once to talk it over with her friends, the Ellises. Since, on being consulted, Ben was 'not so indignant & counsels moderation' she contented herself with sending 'a v. short reply' and wishing that they could take both boys away from the school at once.

However, she now had something more pressing and immediate

to think of. Though the actual birth of Felix had been relatively easy, her recovery from it was not. She began to get ill at the beginning of April and remained so for many weeks. Ben wrote of this time that 'she had a very bad attack which lasted for many days & alarmed us all. She was dreadfully exhausted, could not speak above a whisper or move herself an inch.' They sent for her sister Kate (now a trained nurse) and she, Ben and Emily divided the nights, sitting up with her for some weeks. Alice herself describes the pain and exhaustion of that time but there are again many days when her diary is blank.

Many, many Victorian mothers must have died young from bearing too many children. There were at least four in Alice's own circle: her husband's mother at forty-five after her eleventh child; a Nottingham friend who died leaving seven little children; another friend, a widower with twelve children, and Alice's lifelong school friend, Fanny Bibby, whom Alice long ago had described as 'a little touched with gaiety & admiration'. Poor young woman, she died at the age of forty-one, with the birth of her fourteenth child –

> Heard of my dear Fanny Bibby's death after her confinement leaving 14 poor children to live without her! ... For them it is too sad but not for her, who was just worn out poor dear!' (27 February 1884)

That Alice did not die is, I think, due (demonstrably from the diaries) primarily to the immense amount of help she received from her extended family on both sides – from her husband's young sister (whose name Anna they even extended into 'Nanny') but especially and always and at all times from her own unmarried sisters whose home was a taken-for-granted extension of the maternal home and who were unquestioning, unstinting, unpaid, extra 'mothers' to all her children at all times.

Alice was fortunate in her husband, who was not at all the

remote Victorian father sometimes pictured – he would help bathe his first-born, take his full share of nursing his wife, and assist in very many ways with the older children. He must also have been more sexually considerate than was normal in those days – and she must have been sexually cleverer/wiser than normal.

What seems certain is that both Ben and Alice were thoroughly frightened by Alice's collapse after the birth of her tenth child. She had already had a difficult time with Gerard, her ninth, and it would seem likely that they had planned the three years free of pregnancies that followed, for even after their rare holiday alone together in the autumn of 1876, during this period, which Ben described as 'if possible even better than our first wedding journey'. There was nevertheless no pregnancy.

Ben had been very close to his own mother when she died, following the birth of her eleventh child. Now his wife had had this frightening collapse after her tenth; and that Alice herself was very much aware of the problems of the young mothers of her generation, hardly needs saying. It certainly looks as though Ben and Alice agreed that somehow or another their tenth had to be their last. Alice would not have used her diary to spell this out, but that she greatly feared another pregnancy is surely clear from the following entry in August 1879: 'I was in very low spirits these few days with a fear which I found was groundless.' What else could that have been but the fear that she was pregnant again?

Alice was now only thirty-four, but there would be no more children.

CHAPTER 9

Middle Age

*'He and I got into a furious discussion about the laws of the sexes
and I got so fierce the children were quite astonished.'*

FOR FIVE years after Ben's illness, Alice had been largely inactive
politically – inactive but not unconcerned. She had always shown
interest in elections and she mentions, for example, attending a
three-hour sewing meeting for 'the poor Bulgarians'. A Bulgarian
revolt in 1876 had been brutally suppressed by the Turks, thus
sparking off a war between Russia and the Ottoman Empire that
would last until 1878. There are plenty of examples in the diaries
showing that it was Alice's (and no doubt also Ben's) policy to
involve the children in public matters of concern to them. 'Hester
(& Tom partly) are making some flannel petticoats for them'.
Hester would then have been ten & Tom nine. She also took
Hubert with her to a women's suffrage meeting when he was only
eight. 'We went with Mr & Mrs Ellis and it was so cold & slippery
that the horse fell down on the way home' (10 March 1874). When
Tom was nine and Maud seven, she took them over the Blind
Asylum (9 May 1877); 'a depressing sight' being her only comment.
Nevertheless, she thought it a suitable education for such young
children.

On 31 May 1877, she and Ben went to a great meeting in
Birmingham at which Gladstone was the main speaker, so she had
something really exciting to write about. Ben described the occasion as 'historical', and Alice gave it the very rare title in her diary
of 'Red letter day. An era.'

> I actually went with Ben & Enfield to Birmingham to hear Gladstone
> ... It was *splendid* to see & hear *the man* ... the hall in the evening
> had nearly 30,000 people in it ... I was nearly made ill with the
> excitement, heat, noise & crowding ... One of the greatest treats I have
> ever had.

ALICE IN MIDDLE AGE

Ben was by now a prominent Nottingham Liberal, and their friend Mr Ellis, another Liberal, also went.

The meeting was historic, for it was the inaugural meeting of the National Liberal Federation, arranged by Joseph Chamberlain (father of Neville and Austin) and then called 'Radical Jo'. The hall in which it was held was called Bingley Hall – described in Roy Jenkins' biography of Gladstone as 'a big hangar-like exhibition hall with no seats for the multitude but an elastic standing capacity'. Roy Jenkins tells us that there was speculation about whether so many had ever before assembled under one roof, Gladstone putting it at 30,000 and Chamberlain at 25,000.

Alice's enthusiasm did not blind her to everyone except '*the* man', for she adds to her account of the meeting that 'Mr Chamberlain spoke well – very'. There is no suggestion that she was aware of the oddness of Gladstone and Chamberlain being on the same platform, but others certainly were. Roy Jenkins says of it that 'There was an undercurrent of tenseness to the whole Birmingham visit. Gladstone was gracious but reserved. Chamberlain had been welcoming but undazzled.'

Ben describes a comic print circulated at the meeting, which 'hit off the political situation very cleverly', representing John Bright (member for Birmingham) as Polly Peacham, Chamberlain as Lucy Lockitt, and Gladstone as Captain Macheath, made to say 'How happy could I be with either were t'other dear charmer away'.

Later in the year, when Gladstone came to Nottingham to lay the foundation stone for the new College buildings, Alice took '3 children to outskirts of crowd that they might set eyes on Mr Gladstone, which they did *well*' (27 September 1877). That evening Gladstone made a speech at a big political meeting which Ben described as 'A tremendous indictment of the Sultan and all his doings; probably the climax of his Bulgarian atrocities campaign'.

Alice could not go to this meeting but she wrote that Miss Ida (the governess) went with Ben and 'they said it was splendid'. It is doubtful if this described Ben's feelings since he seems to have been out of step with Gladstone's anti-Turk stance.

My grandfather had always had a special interest in international matters and sometimes (as on the American Civil War and the Franco-Prussian War), his comments have seemed to me worth repeating where they can be regarded as giving a contemporary view of historical events. In the case of public feeling at the time of the Bulgarian atrocities, he held the view that Russia 'was taking advantage of the strong feeling against Turkey to push her own interests'.

Earlier in the year he had read a paper on the Eastern Question to their Nomadic Society but found 'little agreement among our members; they were too pro Russian'. He describes Turkey as being entirely at Russia's mercy in the war and says that their 'terms of peace' were 'a great shock to Europe'. Clearly he welcomed the fleet being sent to the Dardenelles but says that, though Lord Beaconsfield was welcomed from the Berlin conference as bringing back 'Peace with honour' – 'The country, when the whole story was told, including the Cyprus convention, was not altogether satisfied and it told against Lord Beaconsfield at the next general election.' The convention, entered into with Turkey on 4 June 1878, ended 300 years of Turkish rule; henceforward Cyprus was to be administered by Britain.

My grandfather also commented on public feeling about another foreign issue, the second Afghan war, which occurred later in the same year: 'There was much division of opinion, not only about the policy of the war but whether there was moral justification for it.'

Alice, on the other hand, had her very individual way of putting things: when Gladstone replaced Disraeli as prime minister in 1880, her comment was – 'What a wax the Queen must be in!'

Alice resumed her activities against the Contagious Diseases Acts with, this time, structured meetings of women's committees to organise public protests. They met in each other's houses and there were sometimes speakers – male and female – from another town. Alice mentions two meeting at her house in the second half of 1878 and in both cases she and Ben put up the speaker (a man) for the night. Mrs Emily Medley seems to have been very much the leader of the Nottingham ladies and this began an important friendship for Alice.

A very successful public repeal meeting was organised in Nottingham at the beginning of 1879:

We went to the *women's* C.D. meeting in the big Albert Hall. About 7 or 800 there. Mrs Medley (poor thing) in the chair but she did it so nicely ... Miss Tod of Belfast, Mrs Goulder & Mrs Wilson of Sheffield, were the speakers. (13 January)

This was followed next day by an afternoon and evening conference at which the main speaker was Mr Hopwood Q.C. who stayed with Alice and Ben. Alice wrote of the conference that it was 'well & influentially attended & most interesting'. Mrs Goulder who also spoke had stayed with Alice for some days beforehand to prepare. 'She is working very hard,' Alice wrote '& so indeed are Mrs Medley & I, so far as we have time'.

In February 1880, the ladies of Derby were not so well organised. Alice calculated that there were 300–400 at the women's meeting there, but when the Nottingham contingent arrived (Alice and Mrs Medley with six other ladies), they found that 'they were entirely depending on us'. Mrs Medley had to take the chair, one of the Nottingham ladies spoke for over an hour and 'I actually made a wee speech to eke it out'.

The women's meeting in Derby was followed by a conference for both men and women on the Nottingham pattern but so dependent was Derby on Nottingham that Mrs Medley took the chair at this meeting too. Mrs Josephine Butler was a speaker and Alice wrote (10 February 1880) that she had 'never heard her before & was very interested to do so'.

There was another big women's meeting in Nottingham's Albert Hall in 1881 and, this time, Mrs Butler came to Nottingham to speak and Alice herself was also one of the speakers: 'I got through it fairly well but felt very anxious,' is all she said of it in her diary for 15 February. No mention of either of these important Midland meetings appeared in the Press, no doubt due to the general policy of silence already mentioned.

Two years later, in April 1883, a Resolution was passed in the House of Commons 'disapproving of the compulsory examination of women under the Contagious Diseases Acts' and, although the

Acts were not then repealed, it was admitted in answer to questions in both Houses, that from that time onwards, the compulsory examination of women ceased. History has made much of this – as resulting in the acts no longer being enforced – and less of the actual repeal in 1886. But this was not how Alice and the C.D. protesters saw it at the time. The debate in April 1883 is mentioned in Alice's diaries, but not the resolution, and it is clear that vigorous campaigning continued right up to the repeal in 1886. In February 1884, Alice reported 'the great prayer meeting in London today about repeal', and in July 1885, she was distributing repeal leaflets 'all afternoon in the heat. Horrid work.' While as late in the campaign as October, she is 'very busy writing here & there to get a question asked about repeal at the candidates meeting' (22 October 1895).

At last, on 2 April 1886, came the longed-for news – 'telegram from Mr Ellis to say the Repeal bill had just been read a third time & passed the Commons! Hurrah!!!'

Rather surprisingly, considering the immense effort that went into the cause, there appears to have been no special local or national celebration. The campaign does not appear at any time to have been strictly a political matter: certainly, in Alice's circle, the main activists were Liberals and the main opponents tended to be Tories, but the Acts were first introduced under Palmerston's Liberal government. The wide campaign and its success seems to have been a real Victorian example of 'People Power'.

The Nottingham Repeal Committee met in June 'to consider what work [they could] now take up in its place' but only a day or two later, they met to wind up the association. This was merely organisational and certainly not for lack of other public work. For some time Alice and Mrs Medley and Mrs Ellis had been members of a committee campaigning for the appointment of Women (Poor Law) Guardians and, in 1880, there had been a big meeting on women's suffrage in which Alice was involved. She had mentioned going to women's suffrage meetings on several occasions in the 1870s, and in 1880 –

In the evening went to the great women's suffrage meeting at the Albert Hall [Nottingham], which was *crammed* and Mrs Cowan presided at an overflow meeting. The speaking was good but not special. I seconded the vote of thanks. Ben could not get in at all. (30 November)

Ben would of course have got a full report from those who did get in and wrote in his Family Record that 'she did it very nicely, her clear voice being heard distinctly in all parts of the Albert Hall'.

The following day a meeting was held to establish a women's suffrage committee for Nottingham. Perhaps not surprisingly, considering all her other commitments at the time, Alice wrote firmly that 'I shall take *no* part in it'. But it would be a cause she supported with enthusiasm for the rest of her life.

Alice had always been a general supporter of the Liberal party, increasingly so, I think, since the Birmingham meeting. Most of the individual causes she worked for concerned the wrongs done to women and, when she felt strongly, she always spoke with fire; she recorded one discussion with a cousin when she had surprised her family: 'He and I got into a furious discussion about the laws for the sexes and I got so fierce the children were quite astonished' (21 March 1879).

In the year before the repeal of the Contagious Diseases Acts, she and Ben had both been shocked by what Alice described as 'the frightful disclosures made lately in the Pall Mall gazette', and were supporters of the resulting campaign in favour of raising the age of protection for girls. W.T. Stead, editor of the *Pall Mall Gazette*, had published a series of articles under the title 'The Maiden Tribute of Modern Babylon', in which he claimed that it was easy to buy a thirteen-year old 'virgin' in the East End and that he had in fact done so to demonstrate the fact.

The campaign, which was supported by Josephine Butler among many others, resulted in the age of consent being raised to sixteen in the Criminal Law Amendment Act of the same year. It does not seem that Alice herself took any active part in this short campaign, what time she could spare being spent on the Contagious Diseases repeal, but she reports that Ben had a good deal to do with organising the big meeting on the subject that was held in Nottingham. 'Ben came bringing v good accounts of the meeting last night. They are being held all over the country, yet the London press is persistently silent! Shame!' she wrote on 29 July 1885. Her feelings are understandable, but this is an outstanding and highly quotable example of the difference between the Press of those days and of today. Alice would have been even more shocked at today's Press voyeurism.

Later in the year, Mr Stead was charged with abduction and sent to prison, much to Alice's indignation –

> Mr Stead was sentenced to 3 months (without hard labour). What an abominable sentence for such a man ... We were all very indignant to see in the papers how he is treated like any common felon, with every indignity! (11/12 November)

Mr Stead's sentence was in the first division. The women who helped him, a midwife and a reformed prostitute, got penal servitude. Though the 1885 agitation was short-lived, it contributed, in the short term, to the setting up of the National Vigilance Association and brought the issue of child prostitution into the open in such a way that in 1912, when W. T. Stead went down in the *Titanic*, an anti-white slave traffic paper could call itself 'W. T. Stead's Memorial'. Relating this story more than a hundred years later when we are asking ourselves why we are failing to prevent the appalling abuse of children, it is interesting to come upon this account of child abuse in the 1880s. We can't claim that we have not known or had time.

As well as their political activities, Ben had his demanding social work on the Nottingham School Board and, since his election, Alice had taken on school visiting of some sort. It was sometimes quite demanding of her time but I cannot find that she describes anywhere the precise nature of her responsibilities, though they appear to have been largely routine. In August 1879 for example, she wrote that she 'was at the schools all morning, Maud with me, calling over registers etc' and in 1880, 1881 and 1884 she mentioned spending a whole morning 'at the schools' and/or giving prizes at two local schools. She seems to have had – or taken on herself – some kind of additional inspecting role as well, because one afternoon, she received a call from a Mrs E. E. Smith, who was –

> very much hurt at something having come round to them (with additions) which I had said about their school! Poor things it is too bad & of course *most* uncomfortable, tho' I don't think I said more than I ought under the circumstances.

Alice's diaries for the early 1880s are so packed with family details, that it is surprising that she and Ben had any time at all for political activity or other public work: they had their ten children to bring up, varying in age (in 1880) from sixteen to two, and consequently, in the treatment of all kinds they needed – not least in education. They had bought a second house in Broughton, in a village outside Nottingham, which they used as a kind of weekend cottage; relatives and friends stayed with them for days at a time, and they often put up speakers who came for political meetings. With their growing family, they had naturally to entertain more and more, giving tennis parties and dances for the young. There were thirty-eight at their dance in 1882, forty-five the following year. Alice gives this satisfying complete description of an early family dance in 1881 – 'when we mustered 2 sets of lancers. They danced from 7.45 till 10.15. Our children thought there never was anything so splendid' (2 May).

They continued to find as much time and interest as ever – usually at least once a week – for evening lectures and discussions on all sorts of literary, social and scientific topics. Little wonder that Alice wrote (in December 1879) that Ben 'has had 10 things he wished to be at in the last 5 evenings!'

Taken-for-granted additions to Alice's responsibilities were letter-writing – a prominent 'must' every day – and 'calling' usually a whole afternoon at least once a week. She seems usually to have done her own shopping as well, and this would have taken up whole mornings or afternoons.

At least, however, Alice was no longer attempting to be her children's teacher – they were either at school, in the nursery under Emily, or in the schoolroom under the governess – but she did teach some of them some French and music and she still didn't find discipline easy.

The duties of Alice's governesses included overseeing lessons during holidays for the children who were at school – even sometimes for the older boys at boarding school. But Alice's governesses seem to take pretty much as long holidays as they like; four weeks are mentioned more than once and on one occasion 'nearly 7 weeks'. The holiday duties of the governess fell on Alice, and her sisters when Alice was ill or away but, so far as I can gather, it was not something that Ben ever undertook.

Of course Alice had a staff to help her but they had to be paid, fed, their work organised, their not infrequent disputes dealt with and their needs for relaxation and entertainment provided for. And time had to be spent on finding and engaging them.

Alice was beginning to become increasingly dependent on Emily to take charge not only of the nursery and younger half of the family but of the household, while she was with the older children or ill or on holiday. And the tussles between these two strong characters had by no means ceased with Emily's return after her nine months' absence in 1875. The arrival of baby Felix had been a high point of happiness for Emily: for the first time, Alice did not employ a monthly nurse and Emily 'washed baby all herself & slept in my room ... & was in great delight and pride' over him. But there were many ups and downs in the next few years. 'Oh how naughty she is,' Alice complains. 'I do so wish I knew how to bring her to a better frame of mind' (August 1879). And – 'Jane [servant] still quite ill in bed & Emily not very pleasant about doing her work which worried me much'. (27 September 1882) Alice herself that day had gone with a friend on a day-long excursion to Belvoir Castle.

One more example (17 October 1863) gives, as well, a good picture of two of Alice's crowded days: she went (vainly) in search of two possible cooks; spent an afternoon shopping; was worried by her two daughters being in trouble over their lessons and the governess, consequently, 'put out etc'; attended a Contagious Diseases meeting; despatched half the household to Broughton and joined them there herself and 'had to give Emily a lecture or sermon'.

Reading between the lines of what Alice says here and elsewhere in the diaries, I think that Emily was more aware than Alice was of what was due to her in the special position she was beginning to take up as, in effect, Alice's deputy. I am sure, in any case, that she was determined not to be 'put upon' and had never subscribed wholly to the view Alice took that everyone should be prepared to do whatever job was needed.

Of course, illness, always coped with at home, was another regular addition to Alice's responsibilities. In the 1880s, as in the 1870s, hardly a day passed without mention in the diary of one or more member of the family or staff being ill with colds which often involved a day or two in bed.

Fortunately there were no fatal illnesses in her family. Ben's meningitis was the nearest they had ever come to a death. The children had measles and whooping cough and Hubert had scarlet fever which was killing more children than measles and diptheria put together in the 1870s and 1880s. In the 1870s one child of their acquaintance had died of scarlet fever after only two days' illness and an outbreak in the Yarmouth area when the family were there on holiday, has caused them to flee back to Nottingham at once. Now, in 1881, an outbreak of scarlet fever at Bro'ton resulted in two deaths, and was so feared that village relatives were afraid to go there.

In these circumstances, though Hubert's scarlet fever was stated to be slight, it was treated with the greatest seriousness. Alice was away at Bollington when he developed it and returned next day –

glad to be back at my post, feeling I was needed. B & I went up to Hubert in evening in other clothes. All sorts of precautions are being taken with disinfectants etc, Emily nursing him & top landing given entirely up to them. (23 October 1877)

In the early 1880s, there was continuing anxiety about Hester's health, leading them to consult Dr Garrett Anderson in London. Hester seems to have had no definite illness but, at fourteen, 'is very weak and eats nothing'. The diary entry about this is worth quoting because it is so typical of the amount of illness amongst children and servants –

Jane and Mary Ann [servants] both in bed all day, they are so poorly. Annie too [servant] is poorly but up. Miss Rice [governess] too, & Gerard & Hester ... What should we have done without Amy & Miss Ida! We fixed to take Hester to London but it has been *so* difficult to arrange everything. (8 March 1881)

Mrs Garrett Anderson made a most thorough examination of Hester & says it is her stomach, poor blood and weak heart, *not* hysteria, hurrah! Very careful dieting is needed. (12 March)

Next year another doctor pronounced Hester 'completely out of health. She is to take an iron and aloe medicine, and liver oil and 2 quarts of milk and 8 to 12 eggs a day!!! (9 August 1882) Perhaps the doctor had been reading Mrs Beeton's advice that 'children's food should be nourishing rather than stimulating', and that, for invalids, milk is 'the best and most natural food' and eggs 'a very valuable food, containing all that is necessary for life in a most concentrated form ...' However, it does seem an extraordinary diet.

Hester's state of health continues to be worrying off and on and in April 1886 (when she was eighteen she became suddenly so ill with what they called 'croup' that the whole household were awake most of two nights –

> Towards 8 or 9 Hester's croup got much worse & was really dreadful. Good useful Tom went in p. carriage with John Poole for the Long Clauson Doctor. [They are at Broughton] Maud & Rob could not rest in bed; the maids stayed up too & Ben & I were up with her all night. So anxious. B. stood by her nearly all night supporting her while I made poultices, heated water and endless things. (28 April 1886)

Alice wrote that they kept steaming water by her bedside and mentioned their 'luckily having some remedies' and going to buy others but tantalisingly, she omitted to say what they were.

Alice did not carry the whole responsibility for family illnesses. Ben's help with Hester shows the contrary and there were also occasions when the boys were ill at school, and it was he not Alice who took action. In 1883 and 1884, for example, when Tom was ill, it was his father both times who travelled to Newcastle to see him: he was nursed at Bollington one year but the other, Ben brought him home when, as it happened, Alice was on a week's holiday in London taking Hubert with her; it had included a five hour visit to the House of Commons, which had interested her *very much* and when Ben suggested she should come home early on account of Tom's illness, she decided against because much else was planned. Once home she wrote that – 'It has been rather awkward my being away'. She does not say whether the awkwardness was in the management of the house or in her husband's reaction. She and young Hubert were of course separated when listening to the debate in the House of Commons because Hubert could go into the Speaker's Gallery, whereas Alice had to go to the Ladies Gallery.

Alice's task as a household organiser seems to me to have been indeed immense. The places left by her older children as they left home – the twins and Maud never did leave – were, as it were, filled by an increasing number of visitors staying in the house. Alice listed them at the end of each annual diary – fifty-eight in 1892, seventy-one in 1893. The two months of October and November 1884 are a good example. A friend 'came to stay a few days, with her maid' (1 October), cousin Annie Martineau came for a week and Ben's sister was a house guest (18 October), two cousins from Tasmania came to stay a week (6-13 November), and on 10 November, twenty-one people slept in the 'cram-full' house. On that day, the whole family were probably in Nottingham but usually there was the added complication for the planner that some of the family and some of the servants would be at their house at Broughton, however much also a relief from having so many of the children together in one place. No wonder my grandmother wrote (14 October 1884) that – 'There is so much to do, & my strength is not unlimited'.

The following is a good example of the to-ing and fro-ing between Nottingham and Broughton, twelve miles from Nottingham.

> Hubert & Rob went to Bro'ton by bicycle & Maud & I & the two new maids by train. Hubert rode back to Nottingham next day. Ben came next day. After 5.0'c tea Emily and 'the 3 twins' [the twins and Gerard] went back to Nottingham, leavng Felix with us. (12/13 April 1883)

Will, Hester and Tom are not mentioned in the above arrangements. Probably they were at Bollington which, in spite of their second house, was still very much taken for granted as 'in use' for Alice's family. From 1875 onwards, the family were always divided between Bollington and home for Christmas and also for part of the summer months and it is also used for family emergencies: when (for example) Tom was taken ill with measles at school, he went to Bollington to be cared for and the younger children sometimes went to Bollington while dances for the older ones were held in Nottingham. In the summer of 1884, an unspecified number of the children were at Bollington – for no stated reason and very much at Alice's decision apparently – in spite of there being several other visitors there – 'They have got such a party at B.B. of Lode Hills & Mary Ogilvy & Bertha's Ethel & governess etc besides ours. I had meant ours to return today but they begged off till Monday' (29 August 1884) and 'Hester & the little ones beg to stay longer at B.B. (1 September).

Clearly the little ones enjoyed being at Bollington where there was a lovely garden to play in and Hester, now seventeen, enjoyed the company of her aunts and the luxuries she could expect only at Bollington, of a room to herself with a fire in it. Whether it was so attractive to the older boys may be doubtful. In Nottingham, there must have been many more things for them to do and there was Broughton too where they were free of the discipline (and sometimes disapproval) of their aunts.

Will was probably a special case, as usual. Since early childhood he had tended to spend more time than the others at Bollington, sometimes leaving home near to tears. Whether in later years he went more willingly, is not stated. He may well have been his grandmother's favourite since the early days when she took him home with her as a baby, but Alice writes of bad reports of him from his aunts, and bemoans the fact that he doesn't try to make himself agreeable to them.

At last, in 1879, Alice had had something good to report about his work at school – 'he got a chemistry prize, Hurrah!' (2 June 1879). He had always been interested in flowers – 'the only thing he cares about' (10 August 1877) and perhaps that led, through botany, to science. (His passion for flowers was lifelong. I have a vivid memory of his excitement as he took me with him, sometime in 1920, in search of a rare specimen of 'grass of Parnassus' in some hills somewhere in, perhaps, Derbyshire.)

On leaving school, Will had gone to Owen's College in Manchester and two years later, he was sent to Düsseldorf for some weeks to learn German – two lessons a day. Now, aged twenty, he was preparing to embark on his first job.

Their friend, Ernest Hollins, had come to see Ben that October 'to offer to have one of our boys in their business' and within weeks

FAMILY GROUP IN THE GARDEN OF FELIXSTOWE, C. 1885
Standing (*left to right*): Will, Felix, Tom, Alex, Hubert;
sitting: Rob, Alice, Hester, Gerard, Ben, Bernard, Maud.

had proposed to take the eldest at their factory at Pleasley. Ben and Alice had been invited to stay with the Hollinses at Pleasley to go over the factory and discuss matters, and had been delighted to find not only that Will was to get '£100 a year!' but also that arrangements had been made for living space to be made available for him in premises occupied by one of the Hollins family.

Although £100 a year, then, was equivalent to only £5,000 at today's values, it delighted both Will and his parents, at a time when many apprentices and young men starting their careers (e.g. as lawyers) were expected to pay while learning their job, instead of being paid.

Alice at once took charge of arrangements for equipping what she called Will's 'Den', interviewed a servant for him and, on the last day of the year, went with him in an obvious state of happy excitement, to see her first-born established in his first separate home for his first job:

> Will & I went off to Mansfield with a lot of luggage & drove to Pleasley to start in his new home & most interesting of course it was. We had afternoon tea at the Hollinses. Then we unpacked crockery & linen & made the little Den look lovely & cosy & Will seemed at the height of bliss, as well he might & I felt as if we were very full of blessings – as well I might. (31 December 1884)

What of Alice herself? On 12 August 1884 she was forty. So, at last, by Victorian counting, the young girl, young bride, young mother, has reached middle age.

Usually there had been some celebration of her birthday but this day there was none, though she remarked that she received a lot of birthday cards. She spent the day at 'dear Broton', clearing up to leave it ready for friends who were to rent it for a fortnight. She was very much aware of the cost of the second house and had reported earlier 'that the R.E.'s [Richard Enfields] are to take it for 4 months which will lessen expenses'. (14 March 1883)

Alice still had a lot of minor ill health herself. She had headaches and colds for what I calculate to be most of the year and was often what she called 'but poorly' and she was finding the mere size of the family and the roughness of the older boys exhausting –

> They are keeping Tom & Rob for a few days longer at B.B. so I shall have a little quiet resting time which I need very much. They are so rough & noisy & they seem so many. (January 1884)

It was a long time before she recovered completely from the breakdown which followed the birth of her last child. Even two years later, her mother was saying that 'I ought to get away for 6 months' and she took the opportunity to consult Mrs Garrett Anderson about her own health when she took Hester to see her –

'She gave me medicine and bade me lie in bed for breakfast for some months as I am but weak!! (1 April 1881)

Alice's only comment was the two exclamation marks but that year she did manage, in spite of her domestic responsibilities, to take an eight week holiday in Switzerland with Ben and her sister Bertha. The arrangements for her holidays that were somehow made (with the help of her husband and sister) to do without her at home, the fact that they could be afforded and that she had such a capacity to enjoy them, must I think have played a major part in her survival into old age. After the long holiday in 1881 she was so well that she could write (27 August) 'I felt so well & happy all day' and, though (this year, 1884) on leaving for a three week holiday in Cornwall, she wrote that 'the poor children sadly doleful, so that I felt quite guilty going away for pleasure' (16 May), she could say on her return home that she had 'the most delightful welcome home that ever was' and that the welcome from her friends 'added another drop to my full cup' (6 June).

The help that Alice had from her extended family was not wholly a one-way matter. When it was the other way about and members of the family needed her help or hospitality she gave it in full: it has been seen that her mother's needs took precedence over almost anyone and her house was always open to relatives. Her sisters, her married sister and brother and their children came to stay and when uncle Richard's wife died suddenly and her children needed mothering, Alice packed her bags and went and spent nights with them.

Alice's so frequent minor illnesses must have been difficult to meet with invariable good humour both for her and her family but she must have managed a reasonably cheerful stance or she would not have inspired and kept so much love in her husband and children, so much cooperation from her staff and so much affection and help from her wider family and her women friends.

Of course she must have given love to be able to inspire it, though how much time or energy she had left to *express* it at the end of each overful day, must be doubtful. She rarely wrote in her diary about her love for family but she had always been outspoken about her school friends (Sarah Courtauld and Fanny Bibby) and she did write about her new friend, Mrs Medley – 'I admire & love her more the more I see her. She is so lovely.' Mrs Ellis was another new friend made through a mutual interest in women's causes. In the convention of the time, it was not until after she had worked with these ladies for some years, that she came to Christian names – Emily [Medley] and Maria [Ellis]. The Christian name, unless used from childhood or at school, seems to have meant an almost family intimacy.

Alice's love for her husband and her dependence on his company are not in doubt. Again and again she says how she misses him and how dull it is without him but she does seem sometimes to count his needs lower among her responsibilities than those of the rest of her family, especially her mother. In this year 1884, he had had much to bear with the deaths both of his aunt Maria (his surrogate mother) in February, and of his father, in July. Aunt Maria's death involved him in a great deal of extra work as her residuary legatee and at this time, sister Bertha remarked that Ben was very quiet and seemed unwell: but – by no means for the first time – Alice nevertheless left him because she thought her mother was 'but poorly'.

Given their so busy lives and the fact that (for holidays or daily leisure) more often than not, one had to be with the older children, the other with the younger, one wonders what time or opportunity they really had to enjoy each other's company, except on the quite rare occasions when they went on holiday alone together.

CHAPTER 10

Her Daughters' Education

'My own dears, you must try to make yourselves very busy,
that is the best cure of low spirits.'

IN JANUARY 1885, Alice and Ben sent their two daughters to school
in Germany. Hester was seventeen, Maud fourteen.

Up to this time, the girls had been educated very much on the
same lines as their brothers – under a governess in the first years
out of the nursery, then day school – they had gone to school for
the first time in January 1880, the same school to which their brothers went, in spite of the fact that there were three years between
Hester (aged thirteen) and Maud (aged ten). Why Hester waited
for Maud or Maud was hurried to accompany Hester is not
explained. It may have been simply that they had always been
educated together to the same standard; certainly this is what was
to happen with Hester's own two elder daughters.

Why then were they sent abroad? Alice had always attached
great importance to the children learning French. There is, for
example, a bill tucked into the 1874 diary, for payment for French
lessons (three hours a week) for Hubert only, at five shillings a
week, and Hubert and Hester together (Hester then seven years
old) at six shillings a week. Even after the girls went to school, a
French lady still came to give them extra French lessons. Tom
began special French lessons at thirteen; Alice herself was teaching
Rob French when he was eleven.

So why Germany? It is quite possible that Germany was the
fashionable place to go for education abroad at this time. Family
knowledge and the family contacts were with Germany. We hear of
Alice's sisters going for health or holiday to the German spas;
Ben's brother had been at Heidelberg University and now, in 1884,
their cousin, Harry Enfield, had a glass factory in Düsseldorf and
lived there. And Will had also stayed in Düsseldorf.

There were two families in Alice and Ben's own circle who sent, or had sent, their daughters abroad for a part of their education, and both to Germany: two Courtauld girls were at school in Germany at this very time, and the daughters of James Wilson, a relation by marriage of Alice's uncle William Rathbone Greg, so Alice might well have known about this.

Alice does not seem to have considered Belgium, or France which, after all, was our most recent historical enemy and was Catholic. And Britain had strong royal links with Germany.

The possibility of the two girls going to school in Germany had first been raised when Alice had accompanied Will there on his first trip. She used the occasion to visit two schools at Godesberg (near Bonn) 'in case the girls should ever go there'. This is what Alice wrote of her first meeting with Frau Bredau –

> Madame Bredau, a lady from Bonn, (of whom I had heard as having a sort of girls' school) came for a few hours & we all liked her extremely & I think we shall send the girls there. (1 September 1884)

No sooner said than done, and no later than the following January, the girls left for Bonn.

Preparations for this very considerable undertaking included providing all the clothes they would need, and all had to be made at home. This was not yet a time when there were shops where one could just go out and buy what one needed: there is mention in the diaries of Emily making summer clothes for the twins at this time, they were ten years old, of the tailor coming to the house 'about the boys clothes' and of Alice herself having someone come in to make her dresses, though very occasionally, she did *buy* a coat in a shop. The girls needed outfits for a year but by mid-November they are almost ready – '10 of them each! They are nearly done now, thank goodness'.

They left Nottingham on 14 January with '3 enormous boxes', their father travelling with them to Bonn. In those days, they could not travel without escort. Even on their third journey back from Bonn, their father put himself out very considerably to meet them and see them across London. (The need for three boxes became clear in letters: one box contained all their summer clothes and would not be unpacked until needed; besides the ten dresses each, they took with them such necessities as towels and wax matches, packed carefully in a tin box.)

Their father stayed a day or two with the Bredaus before leaving so as to have Edie Blount (a relative of friends), who was at school in Godesberg, over for the day – the third English girl mentioned as being at school in Germany at this time. No doubt Ben also wanted to see something of the Bredaus and their school while he could. Adding a few words to the girls' first letter home he wrote that 'the girls at Frau Bredau's are not very aristocratic. Our girls will be cock-of-the-walk I expect as soon as they know a little German.'

A veritable flood of letters followed between Bonn and Nottingham, of which upwards of 200 survive, a mass of letters which, covering such a short period of life in Victorian England and Germany must, I think, be unique. They make it possible to see a small intimate picture of the way of life in the two countries during the two and a half years of the girls' stay. Both spent a year there in 1885 and 1886, in two stretches divided by five months' holiday, and Maud went back for a further six months in 1887.

Alice wrote some eighty-three letters to her daughters, each of at least three pages (usually a good many more), beautifully but closely written, on both sides of thin foreign paper bought especially for the purpose to save on weight and so the cost of stamps. Though Alice's letters are always legible, they are often difficult to read, especially now that, after more than a hundred years, the ink is sometimes faded. Her daughters' letters are also on this special thin paper and often on maddeningly tiny sheets.

Alice's letters add an important dimension to her story because, in them, she expressed her feelings, stated her beliefs and opinions and, quite often, explained her reasons for holding them – all of which are almost always lacking in her diaries. For the first time since Alice Greg's private diary written before her marriage, we gain a private view of Alice Dowson, now mother of ten and organiser of a large growing-up family.

Alice wrote that she felt 'very flat and forlorn' after seeing the girls off to Bonn. It was no wonder: within the space of two weeks, her eldest son had left home and she had parted with both her daughters for (as she then thought) a whole year. The decision to send the girls to school abroad was not without criticism from other family members. In one of her first letters, Alice reported that aunt Fanny Martineau 'seems to pity you dreadfully for going off among strangers so far from home and seems to think you will be so awfully miserable. She can't think how I could send you!'

Homesick Hester and Maud certainly were. And no wonder – they thought they faced the prospect of a whole year away from their home and country. There appears to have been no criticism from their mother's side of the family. In her first letter, grandmother Greg says nothing of possible homesickness, only how nice it is that everyone there seems so kind. Moreover, neither Alice nor Ben seems to have doubted the rightness of their decision.

'How comfortable it is to think of you both amongst such kind & nice people. We were fortunate to hear of the Bredaus,' Ben wrote. His letters are rare – I have found only twelve – but they are always those of a loving father and the letter he wrote the day after leaving them in Bonn shows that he did understand about homesickness. No doubt remembering his own solitary first days at boarding school, he wrote how lucky they were to be together, and ended with these words: 'When you look at the moon and the stars you can think that the same moon and stars are shining on us at Nottingham and the same God is over all.'

Alice was just as worried about their possible homesickness but her reaction was to suggest thoughts and occupation which she hoped would make it easier to bear –

I am afraid you may be feeling rather forlorn, so little accustomed as you are to *bearing* things. My own dears, you must try to make your-selves very *busy*, that is the best cure of low spirits ... It is better to try to put oneself *on one side* and work away at something. (17 January 1885)

Homesickness, she argued, could even be a matter for a kind of congratulation, 'the shady side of love' she called it.

Writing a few days after the girls arrived in Bonn, their aunt Amy said that she hoped they were getting on with their German, 'as that is the main object of your being there'. And Alice herself emphasised again and again how important it was that they should not only learn German (and French too) but learn to speak it with the right 'enunciation'. The girls wrote to her (11 February 1885) that there were three days when only French was spoken and four days German, and that 'the lessons we do the most of are French and German. We have to work very hard here; all the time is taken up.' They must have worked hard, for by June they were taking parts in (and enjoying) reading a German play and, by October, they were translating French literature into German.

Then, as now however, they were faced with the problem that all the girls spoke English as well as their own language and Hester expressed the perennial English feeling that – 'foreigners must be much cleverer at learning languages than us. Everybody here can talk 3 languages and the Dutch girls can talk 4.'

Of course her early letters are full of the anxious enquiries and comments that a mother would make in these circumstances. Are their dresses suitable compared with those the other girls wear? Their answer is that if anything their dresses are more 'swell'. Are they making a point of going to bed early? Are their bowels work-ing all right? How fortunate that there is no one in the school whom they dislike. They must be thankful that a school as good as the Bredaus' can be afforded for them. She thought it right that English books were banned except on Sundays – and she was happy for them to read them then, provided they had first done their religious duty-reading.

Interspersed with her words of sympathy and comfort were pieces of her own philosophy of life: advice on how to get on and make themselves acceptable among strangers, for example, find something, however small, to praise. And –

> Remember that you will get twice the good if you will *pull with* those who are over you. This is the whole secret of doing well at school. I do hope & pray, my darlings, that you will not be like I was in that respect. (20 January 1885)

> You are learning things besides German which will be useful to you all your lives & help you, I hope, to make better mothers & mistresses than ever I have been ... & acquire habits of tidiness & discipline & such sort of things in which I feel my failure very painfully. (27 January 1885)

And during the *Faschings*, when everyone out on the streets was in fancy dress:

> I daresay the carnival may seem rather silly but I think it is very nice of people to be pleased with such simple things, so don't you look contemptuous! (2 February 1885)

She also wrote often about her tiredness, her sense of inadequacy and how she missed her two daughters –

> I was in bed for breakfast & had a little weep. I think I am getting very old or something. I seem to be losing my wits & not to know how to think about what is best. (January and February)

Both girls were full of sympathy especially about her tiredness and frequent ill-health and wrote that, much as they relied on her two letters a week (the same number as the boys got) they *could* just manage with one. Bearing in mind that letters were the only means of communication, this was no small offer.

Alice tried to make her longed-for letters amusing to her daughters as well as informative and instructive. In a letter dated 6

November 1885, for example, she describes being much surprised to be invited to tea with her four youngest children, by a Mr Thompson, clearly a little known acquaintance,

> We went, they first, I following about 5. It was the comicalist tea party I every was at ... there were two young ladies helplessly trying to entertain the children with a picture book in a tiny room where there was hardly room to turn around & no Mr. Thompson! He turned up in course of time & proceeded to make the tea ... there was no table cloth, a huge tin kettle on the wee fire, a few miscellaneous cups & saucers & plates of food & about 5 teapots, for his fads of tea making ... To crown all, Felix whispered to me that he *must* go somewhere! Of course I did not know from Adam the geography of the house; I could hardly ask Mr. Thompson or the young ladies! However, one of them kindly came to my rescue ...

Her letters were often revealing not only of contemporary conventions but also of Alice's attitude to life. In another letter, for example, dated 27 February 1885 she writes that –

> Ethel Perry is engaged! To Mr. Forman, one of the editors of the Nottingham Guardian!!! I feel quite vexed with her – he may be nice, but he is a man of no position much, even in Nottingham; & you would think she ought to be a Duchess! At any rate there are a lot of nice young men that we know something of that I would rather she would have had.

Wise and confident as Alice's words of advice usually were, there is one matter on which she showed indecision: Maud told her that when she was saying goodnight one evening, Herr Bredau had asked if she would give him a kiss too, and she had said 'No' – 'I think it was great cheek. I wouldn't have done it for a sov,' she wrote. Alice's comment would probably not have been today's –

> I am almost sorry you declined to kiss Herr Bredau. It might hurt his feeling for I am sure he is a nice kind man – still I wish he had not asked you! I can't think how you dared to say no!

She didn't hesitate to include criticism where she thought it due, even in these early letters of sympathy and high thought: Hester was not to use the slangy word 'awfully'. Alice had counted it used twelve times in one letter! And she *must* improve her handwriting. She and grandmother Greg had both, for example, read her word 'carnival' as 'general' and 'your 4s are indistinguishable from your 7s'. If she didn't improve soon, bad handwriting might be a problem all her life. To Maud, she had this to say:

> I'm afraid you are not much in awe of Fraulein Theresa if you shook your fist in her face, Miss. I am horrified.

Almost sixty letters home from the girls in Bonn remain. It quickly becomes clear from their early ones that the Bredaus' was a very small, though fast expanding school of the 'family school' type. By the time Hester and Maud left, there were twenty-two girls there, but when they arrived, there were only four besides themselves: two Dutch and two German, apart from two grown-up English ladies. No mention was made of basic school subjects like maths and science and Maud wrote that she was the youngest there. There was a Mademoiselle to teach French – 'and she can't speak any English at all so we must learn' – an Irish lady to teach English, and music and drawing masters who came in, but all the other teaching was done by Theresa, the daughter of the house, except for a few German lessons given to the older girls by Frau Bredau.

They both like Theresa and are sorry for her for having such a heavy load of work when she is only twenty-three. 'We have to call her Fraulein because she is a teacher'. 'Lessons are nice on the whole,' they write, 'but Theresa is very strict. She expects us to sit up straight all the time.'

They take trouble to describe the routine of the household: breakfast (coffee and rolls) was at 8.30; roll and butter at 10.30; 'dinner' (soup, meat and pudding) at midday; coffee and rolls at

4.15; supper (meat, tea) 7.15 to 8.15; bed at 8.30. There was only one servant and Frau Bredau herself (assisted by a lady who had meals with the family) did the cooking. After dinner there was a compulsory walk, especially appreciated by Hester who describes her enjoyment of the beauties of the Drachenfeld hills and of walks by the Rhine – 'watching the great river flowing on so quietly'.

They shared a bedroom with two other girls, had a bath every other Friday, hot water at night for washing in winter (if asked for) but only cold in summer, and they were left with a candle at night. Theresa washed their hair every week but in eau-de-cologne instead of soap. As sisters, they were expected to share a bed (and their father wrote that this should make it feel like home), but quite a row developed when Hester got into bed with one of their friends to comfort her when she was unhappy. As has been seen in earlier chapters, this was a wholly acceptable way to give comfort in Alice's family.

It seems indeed that the differences between the two households were chiefly in the kind of behaviour expected, Germany being more formal. In one of their first letters, they wrote (28 January) that 'M. Bredau is fearfully shocked at our unladylike movements & untidy ways. Everybody here seems awfully tidy.'

Hester had reported (17 February 1885) that Maud 'romps about with the other girls an awful lot' and she was not innocent of wild behaviour herself: perhaps not surprisingly with eight brothers, they seem to have been what, in my day, would have been called 'tomboys', and Frau Bredau might perhaps have been excused for being upset by Hester's behaviour and, if she heard it, her (surprisingly twentieth-century) way of talking, twelve months later –

> Last night I was dancing about in our bedroom & made the others laugh. The English governess is an old stick & stupe. Frau Bredau was so waxy she said she wouldn't say goodnight to us ... (29 December 1885)

There were things that they definitely must *not* do – they must not read letters at meals but wait patiently while there was general talk over coffee following the meal; they must not go out without gloves or hats; they must not skip in the street; they must not put their hands in their coat pockets though they might put them in their muffs – Hester said that her hands were covered with chilblains because she hated muffs.

On the other hand, they were surprised that the other girls didn't change their dresses during the day, that the Bredaus' grown-up son kissed his father and that, in the hot weather, the ladies took fans to church.

Religious observance at the Bredaus' took the form of formal 'readings' both after breakfast and after supper. What can only be assumed from the diaries, becomes clear from the girls' letters, namely that a 'reading' means a religious observance in the home – a reading of the Bible; the girls were allowed to follow with an English Bible at first.

In this, practice seems to have been the same as in England but the German Church was more formal about, for example, confirmation. Two of the German girls, who were their friends, were confirmed in April 1886 and Maud wrote that, in preparation for the ordeal of answering questions in church before the whole congregation, they had had two lessons a week for two years, and two a day for the last few weeks – 'If they don't know their questions, it will be out of fear, not out of ignorance.' For the ceremony, the church was packed from early morning with relatives wanting to be sure of getting in – Frau Bredau having to pay to have seats kept for 'her' parents – and afterwards the confirmants were given presents by friends as well as relatives.

By chance, the girls' letters also tell us more about what was expected in the way of religious observance at home than has appeared in the diaries. Maud wrote, for example, that she had learnt by heart certain psalms, as asked to by her mother and she mentioned that, at home, they were not allowed to read non-secular books on Sunday and that there would not be dancing during Lent. Finally, in the matter of doctrine, there was the following request for guidance – 'We had better not go to the

English church had we, as they read the Athenasian creed?' – the Athanasian creed with its worship of 'one God in Trinity' being anathema to Unitarians.

Enclosed with the parents' letters went quite a shower of letters from the brothers, some forty of which survive. There would have been more had not the parents imposed a limit for stamp economy. Both the number of the boys' letters and their obvious spontaneity confirm what can only be guessed from their mother's diaries, namely, that they were a very loving and close family. The four or five letters each from the two eldest, Will and Hubert, are interesting as showing both intimacy and trust between them (now really grown-up young men) and their sisters – both write of the dances they have been to, give the names of the girls they danced with and how many dances with each.

The girls' letters always include thanks for their brothers' letters and for the letters they have had from their aunts, of whom they are clearly fond. In one, Hester presses for her aunt Katie to be there when they come home; in another she wishes that her aunt Isobel could come to Germany (obviously to take some action) because 'the cab horses are really sometimes a dreadful sight ... no more than skin & bone, their knees all trembly ... a pitiful sight'.

Politics, especially foreign affairs, bulk so large in Ben's rare letters to his daughters as to seem almost obsessive. He starts a letter to Maud, when she is just seventeen, with the words – 'My dear little Maud, so you would like another letter from me. I must see what I can find to say that you will care about', and he follows this solely with comments on political matters which would have interested Hester but probably not Maud.

Alice too is a political animal but, up to now, most of her interest in individual subjects has appeared to be in those affecting women. In these letters she shows a wider interest – she writes about the death of General Gordon in the siege of Khartoum, the possibility of war with Russia, the tension between England and

Germany, socialism, poverty, the Trade Unions and Irish Home Rule. To what extent she learnt and wrote about these subjects more because they were Hester's undoubted interests than they were her own, it is difficult to judge. But she certainly held widely liberal views. She wrote of one of their friends who might be coming to stay and was 'a home ruler and radical and a dissenter', that 'it is nice that we think the same sort of ways'.

From the first, the girls' letters show Hester's passionate interest in politics. She is for ever asking for newspapers to be sent out to her and Maud wrote (29 March 1885) that: 'Hester has got all the papers and spread them out all over the floor to cut out the pieces she wants.'

It seems likely, from one of Hester's letters, that the tragedy of General Gordon's death occurring within a month of the girls' arrival in Bonn led to some early tension which became person-alised into a sort of popularity competition between Gladstone and Bismarck –

> The Germans I have met don't seem to think much of Mr Gladstone ... It makes me very waxy the way they talk about *poor* Gordon & blame Gladstone for it all.

Fortunately for social peace, Theresa seems to have been accepted by the sisters as an exception, Maud writing that 'Fraulein Theresa likes Mr Gladstone and she and Hester have long discussions that are very interesting'.

The first news of the Gordon tragedy came in Alice's diary –

> The *sad* news came from Egypt that Khartoum fell to the Mahdi only 2 days before the English Vanguard got there, which force was wrecked on its way back & is now in a very perilous position. They fear Gordon is killed. (5 February 1885)

By 10 February, when Ben wrote, there was still no reliable news –

> There never was a time when the newspapers were more exciting ... they are going to send out a quantity more troops & have engaged a

great many large steamers ... If he is dead, they won't feel bound to push on so quickly ...

Two days later, when the news was pretty certain, a letter from their aunt Katie described how *all the papers* were hailing Gordon a hero and Alice wrote with what, in the circumstances, seems to me to be a surprisingly objective view:

> Its very sad but I think it will make things easier for the Government. If he had been alive Wolesley must have pushed on at all hazards to rescue him. He could not have done this till he got some reinforcements & by that time the Nile would have fallen still further & the hot season would have been coming on & it would have caused immense loss of life. As it is I do hope the country won't push the Government on at present.' (12 February 1885)

It is a matter for note too that, stalwart admirer of Gladstone that she is, Alice is prepared to criticise him when she writes about the vote of censure in the House at the end of the month:

> I should think Mr. Gladstone won't be very sorry if it goes against him & he has to resign; *poor man*, it is a sad ending to all his attempts to do the right. I can't help thinking that he has been *so very* anxious about passing the Reform Bill, that he has been led into doing & allowing things in Egypt that his judgement does not approve, in order to get on with his favourite Bill. (27 February 1885)

The Reform Bill she refers to would no doubt have been the Franchise bill of 1885. Gordon was of course employed at the time by the government of the Sudan, not by Britain. In his *Life of Gladstone*, Roy Jenkins shows Gladstone to have been among those in his Cabinet who were least enthusiastic about the despatch of troops to Egypt. He recounts the tragic telegraphic error in which Gordon's appointment was mistakenly thought to be approved by the British government – the phrase '*declines* to sanction' being transmitted as '*decides*'. He mentions that Gordon repeatedly declined to be rescued and he reproduces Gladstone's letter to Queen Victoria (who took the public's view about Gordon the hero) stating that Wolesley might have got to Kharoum in time 'had not a large portion of [his forces] been delayed by a circuitous route along the river, upon the express application of General Gordon'.

There is no sign that Alice was much concerned with what might or might not be done in Egypt after Gordon's death but the apparently imminent war with Russia at this time is mentioned in no less than five of her letters. On 13 March she sends the girls a copy of the Nottingham paper – 'from which you will see that a war with Russia is really imminent! The Russians are behaving abominably,' contrary (she explains) to agreed arrangements to settle the boundary in a Conference.

Ben's confirmation that war with Russia was probable is in a letter dated 29 March in which he sets out the position at length. The following are extracts –

> England is in a great state of turmoil about this last Russian advance in Asia & the country is pretty well making up its mind that it is better to resist at once even at the risk of war ... We are very confident that the advantages will be on the side of England if war takes place ... Some say it will be a nice excuse for stopping the Soudan campaign ... There will be no considering cost if the war is once begun because on the result will turn the command of Asia ... Work being short at present, the calling out of the reserves will be welcome. A war would tend to improve trade ... The gun makers of Birmingham are working day and night...
>
> They say Mr Gladstone has taken the negotiations with Russia into his own hands & is determined not to be played with – isn't he wonderful? He has been a friend of Russia ... & has treated them as gentlemen. Now they in return have attempted to take advantage of England's difficulties in Egypt & the desire that good men have in England that peace should be maintained.

On 10 April, Alice writes that –

> the Russians have begun hostilities & have had a fight with the

Afghans on their frontier, killing a great many ... It is most disgraceful behaviour.

And on the 24th comes the surprisingly ignorant statement that – 'the Afghans don't seem at all to want us in their territory ... so I suppose it would have to be war in Europe!' (The exclaimer, as usual, is Alice's) – a statement that could not have have shown more clearly the huge gap between the nineteenth century and the century that knew the First World War. There is no further reference in the letters to the possibility of war with Russia but, as history tells us, Afghanistan has continued to be a source of contention ever since.

There is criticism of her own country in Alice's letter of the 13 March:

> It is dreadful to think of the number of messes of one sort or another we have got into, with so many different places. I hope the dispute with Bismark is about ended as Lord Granville has 'explained' or apologised. I think for many years we have not been in such an anxious condition all over the Empire almost as we are now.

The reference to the reply to Lord Granville is explained in a letter from Hester, in which she says that 'here they seem to think Lord Granville was wrong to publish private dispatches without Bismark's leave. He should admit being wrong.'

In February 1887 when Maud was alone in Bonn, both Alice and Ben wrote of talk of war at this time between France and Germany. Ben wrote assuring her that of course he would come at once to fetch her if there were war and, on 22 May, that

> I suppose Frau Bredau or Theresa has told you of the demonstrations there have been in Paris. How, at great expense, a Monsieur Lamoureux brought *Lohengrin* out in Paris and how the so called patriotic mob wouldn't allow it to be performed because of its being a German work & how after one or two nights the Minister asked Mr Lamoureux to give up the performances & how he had to do it. Then again perhaps they have told you about General Boulanger the French

War Minister & for the moment the popular idol in France. A great deal of his popularity seems to be caused by the idea that Bismark is against him ... Because I feel sure that Bismark will not stand any nonsense or allow Germany to be insulted. I don't think for a moment there will be any war this year now; so feel quite safe ...

The care that Ben took to state the British viewpoint on this and other occasions was no doubt partly to inform his daughters but it could also suggest that he was expecting what he said to be passed on to the Bredaus. Indeed Herr Bredau's views are specifically asked for about the possibility of war between France and Germany in a letter dated 28 January 1887.

However, when it came to the conquest of Burma in 1885 he clearly felt that no explanation was needed and described it to his daughters with a complete lack of criticism. I feel a duty to quote what he wrote as presumably reflecting, as he says, contemporary feeling:

The country is pleased at the efficient way in which the Burmese campaign has been managed ... It seems absurd that less than 3000 English should have steamed up the river & quietly seized the king & possessed the government of a great State with so little ado ... Its almost a pity that there are none of our boys of the right age & acquirements to seize upon the chances that will be there. There will be quite a rush there I expect; & before long railways right up to the Chinese frontier. (13 December 1885)

The Irish question occurs and recurs in both the letters and the diaries at this time. In April 1885 Ben wrote:

Do you see that the Prince and Princess of Wales & Albert Victor have been paying a visit to Ireland? They must have been v. nervous. They have been quite into the worst parts of Dublin looking into the dwellings & even shaking hands ... & only one or two attendants with them. I think it is very brave.

On 12 June 1885, Alice wrote that 'the Irish Members as usual joined the Tories to try & upset the coach' on a vote on the spirit duties in which the government was defeated. Then on 19 March 1886 Alice commented that

> it has leaked out that Mr G is going to ask the English to lend the Irish 100 million to buy the land from the English landlords ... Either the English must find the money or the landlords must be abandoned ... to be ruled by the Irish Parliament & dealt with as it pleases ... Papa is doubtful if he [would vote for this] I hope [Parliament] will support it with a rousing majority.

On 13 April 1886, Hester wrote from Bonn:

> I hope Gladstone won't pass his Bill though I suppose I ought to hope the opposite. The other English girls are awfully conservative which makes us stick up for him much more than we otherwise should ... I wonder what the poor landlords will do if his Bill passes, or is he going to make some amends to them. It seems rather unjust if he does not do something.

And then, on 7 June 1886, Alice's diary is full of the Home Rule debate for which both she and Maud were in London.

> the great day of the division on [Gladstone's] Home Rule Bill for which we had actually got places in the House!!! Mr. Ellis showed us over the House & took us up to the Ladies Gallery ... Mary & Amy took our place at 6 ... At 9.30, I left Maud in bed & went with Mrs Ellis to the House & heard the debate & Gladstone's fine speech & saw the Division. Government beaten by 30! Got home at 2.30. Waked the others & had a chat & our supper. Oh what a wonderful day for us!

Maud also wrote an account to Hester but her letter was mainly about being shown round the House before the debate, and about the unsuccessful struggle they had to get seats in the front row of the Gallery. She describes the proceedings as beginning with prayers. The Ladies Gallery at that time was screened off from the House by a metal grill through which the ladies could see the

THE LADIES' GALLERY
at the House of Commons in the Nineteenth Century.

House but the MPs could not see the ladies – and no doubt it made the front row the only one from which there could be a really good view. The result of the grill appears to have been that the existence of the Ladies Gallery tended to be forgotten and that this is why it was not cleared for prayers as the Press and Public Galleries were. Later, in the 1900s, one of the suffragettes would chain herself to this grill and could only be released by taking out the grill with the woman still attached to it. The grills were removed in 1918.

On 26 December 1886 Ben wrote that:

the excitement now is Home Rule. It is said Mr Gladstone has made up his mind that home rule must be conceded. I am against home rule & hope there is some mistake about what Mr Gladstone intends.

But on 14 April 1887, he said:

the feeling now is strongly toward home rule for Ireland ... One of the most hopeful signs is the desire of the Irish leaders & the greater part of the population to keep order & do nothing that shall give an excuse for violent measures. The Irish have seemed to realise that only a little more patience is wanted of them & the battle is won. If Mr Gladstone went to Ireland now, he would be almost worshipped.

At the end of this year, 1887, the annual meeting of the National Liberal Party was held in Nottingham and Gladstone was received with great enthusiasm. The occasion was widely reported in the local press which seems to have quoted Gladstone's long speech, all about Ireland, verbatim; it runs to six uninterrupted columns and the description of his triumphal arrival takes another column. There is an excited entry in Alice's diary. She was in the crowd which waited for an hour outside the station to greet the Gladstones' arrival and was in the Albert Hall for the speech for which she had platform tickets ... 'Ben & [some others],' she writes, 'could not get in at all with their delegates' tickets'. To the modern reader the speech seems to have been more words than matter but this is Alice's account –

Oh! never to be forgotten day! ... I never saw such a sight for crowd-ing, packing, and enthusiasm; it was splendid; & Gladstone's speech was up to the occasion & to all expectation. Wonderful! We *were* all in a state of excitement!

Up to this point, Alice's enthusiastic commitment to Irish Home Rule has been referred to again and again in her diaries and letters. Then, came the Parnell scandal – 'Mother & all of us are very unhappy about Parnell & that the Irish leaders mean to stick to him,' she wrote on 20 November. 'Dillon has not spoken though'.

She was greatly shocked and her strongly expressed reaction is worth recording as that of an interested, liberal-minded, thinking, Victorian matron. She has enclosed a newspaper cutting of Gladstone's letter to John Morley of 24 November. Her comment is 'how *thankful* I was to see in the paper that dear old Gladstone rings true'. On 28 November, she writes that – 'Parnell has thrown off the mask & is showing himself a thorough scoundrel!' Her last entry on the subject is on 13 December – 'The Irish affairs are almost worse & worse, if that is possible! Parnell seems *mad*'.

It seems that, in her eyes (as in Gladstone's), Parnell's behaviour affected the whole Irish cause. I think it would, at the least, have reduced Alice's enthusiasm for that cause.

According to Alice's private diary, the monarchy, in the 1860s, was held in what I can only describe as a species of 'loyal awe'. Her change of feeling by the time of the Jubilee in June 1887 may well have been typical of middle-class, middle-England Liberals. Her 'democratic' attitude to the monarchy when the Queen had to make Gladstone prime minister, expressed in her remark, 'what a wax the Queen must be in', was of course influenced by her admiration for Gladstone. It seems, however, to have been an attitude shared by Ben, who wrote to Maud that money was being collected by the ladies of England for a present for the Queen on her Jubilee, but that – 'the silly old thing is going to have £10,000 spent on an equestrian statue to Prince Albert who already has statues & memorials without number'.

Alice came round to Ben's way of thinking but, as usual, she was for seeing the best in everything. She wrote that she thought it 'a nice idea' to collect for a present to the Queen after fifty years on the throne and that – 'It has given a number of ladies something to do & has brought them in contact with their poorer neighbours' (15 March 1887).

*   *   *

From letters and from the diary accounts of the celebrations when the girls returned from Bonn, a convincing picture emerges of a loving united family, enjoying games of all sorts – almost to the point of obsession when it came to cricket. Though, obviously, age differences called generally for different holidays, schooling and leisure activities, they enjoyed being all together as a family and the affectionate protective attitude of the elder two-thirds towards the four younger boys, is very marked. The letters and the diaries of this period also support what hitherto can only be inferred from what is *not said* in the diaries, namely the absence of quarrelling. The first welcome home for the girls was at Broughton in August 1885 and it produced an usually emotional diary entry –

> Red letter day! ... Will and Hubert arrived on bicycles, then all started to the station, Felix Allie & Gerard concealing themselves to 'bo' out at them on their way home ... Oh what a joyful meeting!! & what a happy party we were! I think I never felt so proud and thankful & rich ... They set to cricket almost directly, all eleven of them!

Their father isn't actually mentioned; he has to be inferred from the fact that eleven play!

Now that the twins were no longer babies, their father had begun to take them on holiday as he had the older boys in the past. This was particularly the case at Broughton where he felt as much on holiday as his children. Walking tours had been among his holiday pleasures ever since his young tour in Switzerland with his brother and they were a matter of course to entertain his children. At the end of this August, 1885, for example, Alice wrote that: 'B & twins started for a two day walking tour in Wansford & Stamford' and (1 September) that 'Ben & twins got home at 6.30 having had a delightful two day walk. About 23 miles each day.' The twins were then only twelve years old but Alice makes no comment – not even one of her frequent exclaimers.

In June the following year Ben had bought a yacht which Alice thought 'very rash but I hope it may answer', and there followed a particularly happy family holiday in Norfolk. She had to admit (9 August) that 'B does so enjoy his yachting and so do the boys' – 'We started from Bro'ton, a party of 11 ... Ben, Tom, Rob & Gerard to the yacht, the girls, twins, Felix & I to Geldeston where good Susanna [Ben's youngest sister] took us all in ...' (7 August 1886).

There was bathing and toing and froing with the yacht and the small boat they called *The Jolly* and Alice describes seeing them off one evening on the river:

> We all went down near sunset to watch them row off again, such a *pretty* sight, in evening light, with reflections of boat, girl's dresses etc & such happy faces. I wished I could always remember it!

A long account in letters to Maud about the Easter weekend 1887 completes the picture with the family enjoying themselves at Broughton. Five of the boys had walked all the way (twelve miles) from Nottingham and they are described:

> having fine fun of it, especially over their lunch at the Plumtree Inn where they laughed so much they could not give any orders ... Will was very uproarious; I sent him & Rob to put the beds down to the barrack room fire to air; next thing, I saw beds & pillows tumbling out of the window, where they arranged them on the gravel & were very indignant when I would not let them jump out of the window on to them in their boots! When at last I made them take them in, Will made a tobagganing place down the stairs & the boys slid down on their fronts head foremost, amidst shouts & fits of laughter!

Was there perhaps something in the size of the family that kept the older ones young? Certainly they were what I can only describe as boisterous for their age: Will was twenty-two.

In previous chapters, the large amount of intellectual activity that Alice and Ben managed to fit into their packed lives has been very noticeable. So it has been with a shock of surprise that I have come upon the following words in a letter dated 25 February 1885 –

> I shall be so very glad too if you get a real liking for knowledge, a thirst for learning which I had hardly begun to get before I was married & my busy life put a stop to my self-improvement, as far as learning went!

I find this statement immensely moving, emphasising as it does how much my grandmother missed – how much the women of her generation missed – from being born in the wrong century; not only were they without the vote and without the opportunities for the enlargement of life that can come from responsible mind-stretching employment, they were without the wonderful advantage of being able to spend time in pursuit of learning at a university.

With the right education, Hester and Maud might have gone to university; Girton was opened as 'The College for Women' in October 1869 and from information in the letters added to scraps in the diaries, it emerges that Miss Badham, the children's governess, went to Cambridge as an undergraduate after she left Alice's employ. She took some of her exams while still with Alice and they remained friends after she left, Miss Badham writing weekly letters to Alice and coming to stay with her. In a letter from Hester to Maud, in Bonn, about a visit that she and Alice made to Cambridge, there is an interesting description of the first university-type college for women.

Did Alice at any time argue to herself that what Miss Badham, their governess, could do, her daughters could do? She might have wanted it, but she (and Miss B) must surely have realised that the girls' education up to now would not have fitted them for university.

The two types of school then available to women were 'family' schools and 'collegiate' schools but the latter were very recent and few in number – Cheltenham Ladies College was founded in 1854, Roedean not until 1885. The Bredaus' was of course a family school. This did not necessarily mean non-academic – Alice tells the girls in one of her letters, that Kitchener's (to which the boys all went and which was a 'family' school) had a number of Cambridge wranglers to its credit – but the girls' letters had made it plain at once that the Bredaus' was very definitely non-academic; was indeed, strictly, hardly a 'school' at all.

So their ordinary school education had virtually ceased when they went to the Bredaus', Maud's at only fourteen. Alice did consider sending Maud to Cheltenham instead of back to Bonn but the routine she arranged for the girls on their return from Bonn in April 1886 (just after Maud's sixteenth birthday) shows that she had no idea what would fit her daughters for Cheltenham; it was at least half domestic –

> I find myself making plans for how you will parcel out your time ... I tho't between 9 & 10 one of you would practice alternately & the other dust the drawing room & your bedroom; then the other would practice & the one read history for $^1/_2$ an hour and then write a recollection of it in German. Then would come perhaps the school of art 3 days a week, another day cooking, another shopping in the town for me. Then in the afternoon there would be Felix's lessons & superintending the schoolboys' lessons & perhaps Maud giving them music lessons. And in the evenings, there will be 2 college lectures we shall want to go to [together] ... (12 March 1886)

She concluded with the words – 'Now what do you think of that programme I wonder?' I cannot find that they answered this question in their letters but they went home the following month so may have felt that any comment could wait.

They would not have been surprised because it had always been Alice's expectation that Hester, at any rate, would take on teaching the younger boys when she got back from Bonn. In a letter of 6 November, 1885 referring to her social work, she had written –

> How nice it would be if you were at home to help me with such things. But then I reflected that Maud, at any rate, would be too busy with her school work at the present & Hester, perhaps with her college classes & teaching of Felix & the boys.

In fact, the first weeks of their return were taken up with Alice going to London, leaving Hester in charge of the household, the girls going to Bollington, and family boating holidays on the East coast. And in June, nudged to a decision by Frau Bredau, they decided against Cheltenham and for Bonn, for two terms the following year for Maud. That of course meant no Cambridge for her, if indeed it had ever been thought of.

Starting only in October, Hester was encouraged to pursue studies of a more obviously academic kind at Nottingham College; her letters to Maud in 1887 tell of having 'to stew up a bit for the Cambridge history exam' which included Stubbs' *Constitutional History*; of doing very well in that; but, of a Latin exam, that 'I expect I shall do very badly as I have missed so many classes but I don't much mind. It is always fun going in for exams.'

It doesn't sound as if Hester herself was much concerned about Cambridge (if, again, that had been her aim) and certainly Alice expected her to take on social 'good works' as well as her studies, as well also as taking charge of the household in her mother's absence; she writes of Hester being 'a good little mother' while she herself is on holiday in London.

It is easy to blame Alice for what appear today as the gaping holes in her daughters' education. But, given that university education for women was such a new thing, she could not have foreseen it for them when they were little, or perhaps be expected later, to realise all that the steps leading to it involved, much as in her 'thirst for learning', she may have glimpsed its distant promise.

CHAPTER 11

Her Family Almost Flown

'My days are fuller than full.'

IT IS an interesting fact that, though the girls' education at school had been on the whole lacking compared with their brothers', their later education was better, because the need to take a job, when it offered, interrupted the boys' higher education. Ben's own time at London University had been abruptly terminated to allow him to accept his uncles' offer of a place in their law office. Will had gone to Manchester College and come away after two years to accept the Hollins offer of a job in their business. That Hubert would join his father as a lawyer was taken for granted and nowhere discussed in either diary or letters; Alice simply noted his going to London to take his exams, his passing them and his acceptance as a full solicitor. Though the number of 'honourable mention' cards from Kitchener's that are stuck in the diaries are quite as many as for the older boys, showing that the younger four had plenty of intelligence, only the youngest, Felix, would go to university.

For the older boys, worries about education were being replaced by worries about employment and both parents' letters to Bonn had included discussion of their plans for Tom and Rob. Tom wanted to be a doctor, was good at exams so might have succeeded, but was 'a good lad' ready to do what his parents thought best and, at the age of seventeen, accepted the offer of a job in industry with Alice's brother Herbert. Rob was interested only in how things were made: he would have liked to combine engineering with a life at sea and, at fifteen, had taken an exam in naval engineering but, in the end, at the age of eighteen, was apprenticed at the railway works in Derby – 'The dear boy went off to his lodgings at Derby, where he will be for the next 2 or 3 years, I suppose' (9 April 1890).

Later, Will left the Hollins business and set up his own lace manufacturing enteprise in Nottingham and Tom would become a stockbroker; later still, Rob would establish his own engineering business in South Africa. In 1891 however, with the youngest, Felix, aged thirteen, a new worry set in:

> I am nearly distracted with our complicated plans for the holidays, for the 4 younger boys after that and about their futures, about which we are feeling v anxious now. (28 July 1891)

Language tuition was continued for the boys as well as the girls – Rob learned Spanish and the younger boys went to the Bredaus for holidays.

The girls' education could be, and was, continued at Nottingham College in Latin, modern languages, art and music. There were also evening lectures and, several times a week, readings in German, French, or Italian in which Alice herself joined.

Alice had been without a governess ever since the girls went to the Bredaus. She had tried a German governess (found for her by Frau Bredau) for the '3 twins' but this had failed within a month because the boys could not understand what she said. Alice made no secret of her relief when Miss Grosse left, there being the added embarrassment that Alice couldn't understand Miss Grosse either. After her departure, the twins had started at the Nottingham High School, an outcome that was welcomed by Alice's sisters, among whom Amy thought the boys inclined to be too "babyish" and better at school in any case.

What happened, when the girls returned, was, as Alice had always expected, that they took the place of a governess, helping Alice with after-school and holiday responsibilities for the school-boys. In March 1888, for example, Maud was 'teaching the children their music these holidays'. It was decided in June 1888 that 'The girls are going to try and do Fee's [Felix's] lessons for the rest of this term' and, 26 July, 'Felix is doing his exams for Hester and Maud'.

Contrariwise, I come upon the surprising statement for Sunday, 5 Jan 1890, when Maud was ill in bed, that – 'Felix taught Maud's

173

Sunday School class by his own desire! and managed very well!'
He was eleven years old. Who did his lessons after the
governess left in 1885? Presumably Alice. He only started
Nottingham High School in 1888.

When the Kitcheners retired and closed their school after a big
formal 'do', attended by Alice and most of the boys, Sedbergh was
chosen for Felix, and when he went there as a boarder at the age of
fourteen, both Alice and Emily were desolated; again and again
during that and the next year, she wrote 'I did miss my little
Felix', and she was so sorry for Emily that she sent her for a week's
recovery holiday with Tom and the '3 twins'.

Thereafter with no nursery, Emily appears much less often in
the diaries. Her former position as Alice's deputy in the house
must have been affected by the presence of the two grown-up
daughters. But she remained an amalgamation of family friend and
upper servant or housekeeper, in charge of the younger boys on
holiday, taking the younger servants on pleasure outings which
Alice arranged for them to Goose Fair or the theatre, or on a day
excursion to Derbyshire and, in one case, on 'a few days jaunt to
Skegness'. She also took charge of such important annual under-
takings as spring cleaning, both at Nottingham and Broughton
which, surprisingly, included 'whitewashing' (2 June 1892).

Pleasant relations with her servants continued to mean a lot to
Alice. 'I continue to like our new cook so much. It is such a comfort to me,' she wrote on the departure of Mary Ann who left to get
married – after nineteen years in service with them. She was marrying George Poole, a Broughton farmer and the wedding took
place from Alice's home in Nottingham:

> Mary Ann's wedding day. Emily was in great force, managing all the
> affairs for the guests – ie M A's sister, old Mr and Mrs Poole, Jenny [a
> former servant] & her husband & our old Lizzie. They all except the
> bride & groom, came & had dinner here after the ceremony, to which
> Maud, Felix and I went. (5 January 1895)

I remember Mary Ann quite well. In the 1910s, she lived in the house opposite Broughton church. Her daughter was called Maud and was a member of my aunt Maud's patrol of girl guides, to which my eldest sister and I also belonged.

While her daughters were away in Germany and her sons were either in employment or at school, Alice had found herself for the first time alone in the house. She had her friends to call upon and the poor to visit but, one senses her loneliness in diary entries such as 'Ben at a meeting in evening. Hubert was out too, so I read aloud to the maids' (22 October 1885).

Once or twice in the past, she had tried to involve the servants in her 'good works' but without success, except in the case of Elizabeth – now her 'dear old Lizzie' – with whom she had developed a real friendship starting in the first years of her marriage. But Lizzie was no longer with her when she had tried again in this lonely time:

> I read to the maids and talked to them about helping our less fortunate sisters & the poor but I don't think it was any use, for they were quite unresponsive & it was v hard work! (23 November 1885)

With the girls away and without a governess, Alice had become depressed as well as tired – as the Bonn letters have shown – and this may have been a reason why, once both daughters were at home, she and Ben indulged themselves in a month's cruise to the Canaries, in May 1888. The holiday may, however, have been needed as much for Ben as for Alice: he too had missed the two girls, especially when they were both away at Christmas, though it was quite usual for some of the boys to go away to Bollington then.

Alice sometimes used her diary to sum up her feelings on New Year's Eve and she had done this in 1886, with the unwelcome prospect of Maud's return to Bonn for the first six months of 1887 very much on her mind – 'How I shall miss her':

> I sat up over my fire, thinking about my children, my family, & my dear friends, about Tom's future & the parting with Maud etc etc.

Then woke the girls to hear the bells, & so to bed.

No mention of Ben. Was he possibly at Bollington? He might have been if any of the children were there. It seems that he was feeling no more cheerful than Alice was, for a few months later, she made the quite unusual decision to break off a visit to Bollington, though feeling very torn because her mother was having one of the frequent bouts of illness that always had Alice hurrying to her bedside – 'It was time I came home,' she wrote. 'B is not capital just now, so grave & silent & anxious' (26 May 1887).

Earlier he had been worried about money, even thinking that perhaps they ought to sell the yacht and they did take the drastic step about that time, of letting the Broughton house for a whole year. Or was he really worried about the possibility of war in Europe with Maud away in Germany, or perhaps about local politics? (He was one of the Liberal members of Nottingham Town Council.) Or was he feeling that, in all that was happening in the busy lives of his wife and his children, there was too little time left for him? To any reader of the diaries, it would not have been surprising.

He can never have been in doubt about his wife's devotion. Again and again she tells her diary (which he certainly felt free to read) how she misses him when he is away, and how dull it is without him, e.g., 'Ben went off at 11 to Norwich to return by London in a few days. It does feel dreary without him always' (17 February 1890).

But it does not follow that he had much of her *time*. They were no longer so much divided by the needs of their large family but other calls on Alice's time were taking their place. In the first week of the year 1887, Alice had written that 'the innumerable invitations or engagements of sometimes some & sometimes others is quite confusing' and in the first months she had been very busy with Hester. She and Hester seem to have gone everywhere and done everything together, including the evenings – except when one or other had one of their frequent headaches or colds. There had been too their visit to Cambridge. Alice was probably concerned to see that Hester did not miss Maud too much and, now, her mother's bouts of illness were increasing. Still, she managed to find time to read 'a charming book called *Little Lord Fauntleroy* by Mrs Burnett – such a *pretty* book, about a sweet boy of 7' (8 March, 1887).

Within days of her return home in May 1887, she had arranged to have breakfast at 7.30. She explained to her diary that this was done partly so that the boys could go to the baths on their way to school and partly to get the maids up – 'for they *will not* get up in the morning & it does so worry me'. But it was also 'to lengthen the mornings'. Unusually, she cried off a musical party that she and Hester had been asked to, because – 'I thought I would not leave Ben alone', and a week or two later, she and Ben escape together to Broughton, taking only Felix with them:

> B & I got up at 6 ...They were milking the cows outside. We got a glass of the new milk and went a little walk before the dew was off. It was so nice and romantic! tho' rather exhausting! (30 June)

Given the dim lighting before electricity, it seems likely that people normally went to bed earlier than we do now. That might explain the fact that they got up earlier. It is noticeable throughout Alice's diaries, that she regards it as no hardship to get up with the dawn on holiday and the diaries of the Gurney sisters show them getting up regularly at 6 a.m. to do a period of study before breakfast.

At the local elections in November, Ben lost his seat on Nottingham Council. It isn't clear how much he minded; Alice said that it was rather a relief to him. However, her main comment distanced them both very strikingly from anything that could be said or done – or not done – today:

> He is beaten alas (by 71 votes) by a most inferior man too. In some wards publicans & low sporting people have been elected & the tone

of the town seems v. low! I am so glad B would not canvass or stoop in any way. (1 November)

She was much happier that New Year's Eve, writing that, apart from a worry about Felix's deafness (which turned out not to be serious) 'We have everything to be thankful for in every way'. And the next year, she was quite back to her normal brave attitude to life – 'What a wonderful year it has been' she wrote. 'I think there will never be another like it for us' (31 December 1888). It had been a year when both girls had been at home; she and Ben had been on their holiday cruise; it was the year of their Silver Wedding, celebrated by a happy expedition to Bakewell with all their children except one – and their family had been all together at Christmas. She had also felt especially settled and fulfilled in her public work, much of which was for charity, though she continued to work on many political causes, both old and new.

A comment in a letter from Hester in Bonn had produced a very full statement of Alice's views on economic policy, trades unions, free trade, unemployment and poverty –

Yes dear Hester, it *is* sad about the poor. Of course there are heaps of institutions & agencies at work in England for them &, when they are in work, they get really *much* higher wages than in Germany ...The Trades Unions have done very good things in some ways by raising the wages of the working classes & shortening their hours of labour but sometimes they overreach themselves & are foolish & tyrannical. A man in Nottingham got a big order for lace & offered a lot of people work, at reduced wages – still v.g. wages – but the silly things refused at the bidding of their Trades Unions. So ... the master sent the work to Germany. If only people would learn to be thrifty & lay by, they would be comfortably off in bad times. (18 February 1886)

Whatever Alice thought she thought about economic policy, she didn't mean quite what she said in that last sentence. She had always been full of sympathy for 'the poor' and she told Hester in this same letter that, in London, £40,000 had been collected and in Nottingham, £1,000, of which £600 had been spent on soup and bread for the unemployed. (She didn't, by the way, think unemployement was due to 'free trade' and did think it would be better if all countries adopted it.)

Taking part in 'good works' was quite definitely regarded by Alice (and her contemporaries) as a lady's duty. It was in the air she breathed. When she was still a child in Bollington, her mother had brought down orphan children from London to be brought up in the country and, as has been seen, she and her sisters were expected – as they grew up – to conduct sewing classes, make clothes for the poor, arrange and assist at charity sales and generally to take part in any social work in the village. After she was married and visited her brother-in-law, Meadows Martineau, in London, it was a taken-for-granted interest that she should be shown, with him, the work for the poor in London in which he was involved:

> In an open carriage down the Embankment & through the City, most interesting, to Meadows' office. He came with us & showed the Whittington Club for 150 poor boys – *so* nice – and to Toynbee Hall which I had often wished to see. Such a treat. (8 June 1886)

So Alice made it her business to get Hester involved, as soon as she came back from Bonn, in a recently established charity which she had been concerned with setting up.

> To the Girls' Evening Home at St Mathews Schools ... with a view to Hester helping there. There were 30 or 40 girls there & it is a capital thing. There are 7 homes over the town. (26 October 1886)

There was also the annual Christmas Tree party for poor children, held every year in the first fortnight of January, a practice also observed by the Bredaus and so taken very much as a matter of course by Hester and Maud during the one Christmas they spent in Germany. The main work for these parties always fell to the women of the household, but Alice involved her sons where she could. She describes going round 'with Gerard & Felix to call on the various poor people to ask them for the Christmas tree'; in 1885, twenty-five children and two mothers – 'v poor' – came; in 1889, thirty-five children and five mothers who 'got as much to eat as they wanted & games & the tree & they all had some clothes, a toy & some sweets. They *did* enjoy it poor things!'

I have a still vivid memory of two such parties in the drawing room at Broughton before the First World War, when my aunt was the moving spirit and my twin uncles had the job of arranging the games for the boys. Each child was expected to be grateful for an essential garment such as shoes or socks or an apron, plus a toy or sweets.

It is noticeable that the charity Christmas parties were always held well after the day itself and that the family Christmas was less of a function in Alice's day than it is nowadays: it was always an occasion for present giving, both amongst themselves and to the servants, but this was in the evening; the day was treated much less formally – Alice might stay in bed much of it if she happened to be tired and the children scattered to go skating. Conversely, more was made of New Year's Day, except for present giving. The servants had a well-established kitchen party on New Year's Day and it was usual for Alice and family to go to a big gathering at the Richard Enfields.

'Penny dinners' get mentioned often, particularly in December. As usual, there is no explanation, but from one of Alice's letters to Bonn, it is clear that this was a locally run charity for poor children – 'I went to a Penny Dinner committee on Monday, when we decided to begin them again. I undertook to go down on the Wednesdays' (6 Nov 1886). And two weeks later she described a Penny Dinner at Radford as having 'Abt 200 children in different relays'.

Always too, of course, there was regular 'poor visiting' in the Lenton area of Nottingham near The Park where she lived. And when Ben was buying property there, she got him to set aside some houses for her to establish and run as 'my almshouses'. At

Broughton too, where after all she went mainly for relaxation, she was visiting no less than sixteen houses (18 April 1887).

Contemplating the much larger amount of private charity in grandmother's day than today, I remind myself that circumstances were very different. There were, for example, no state pensions in the nineteenth century.

The fact that there was so much poor-visiting seems to me to highlight another wide difference between charity then and now. There were already some big charitable organisations like the SPCC (of which my grandmother was the local and very active secretary) but more often charity was individual and personal; you might go (as Alice did) to see people in their homes and you might invite them to your home. There was, of course, a degree of patronising in this – and there was also a certain amount of looking-up by the recipients in the 'humble' acceptance of charity by the poor, but it is arguable that there was also more real humanity.

Alice's new social and political causes in the last fifteen years of the century included arguments (unsuccessful) with shopkeepers that seats should be provided for shop girls; the women's committee of a Social Guild (objects unspecified); a Charity Organisation Society (C.O.S.); a new Saturday (talking) Society; a new sewing and reading society; and a society which appeared only as 'L.V.R.S.' which held monthly meetings, but the object of which was not explained. The atrocities committed against the Armenians in Turkey bulked large and the question of Contagious Diseases was reopened in connection with India. My impression is that whenever some matter of public conscience or need arose, the first thought was to apply to Alice – she took on the secretaryship of both the local Women's Suffrage Committee and the ladies' committee of the S.P.C.C. – 'just to start it' – in the same year, 1894.

District nursing appears for the first time, but it was not a new cause; Alice wrote of her sister Katie being involved in it back in 1878 –

Katie went to Liverpool to begin her nursing work ie overlooking of district nursing. She is to live (in lodging) with a Miss D'Arcy who is in the same position. (6 November 1878)

The initials 'L.V.R.S.' occur for the first time in February and March 1895 – 'The Mayor has given us £5 for L.V.R.S. from his relief fund' and 'I was at Mrs Handford's the whole morning at L.V.R.S. monthly meeting'. From then on these initials occur often and with great regularity. Alice not only attends monthly meetings of this society but takes a very active part – on 30 October 1895, for example, she records 'a long conference with Mrs Crewdson who mangled my L.V.R.S. report horribly, which depressed me'.

This cause was obviously pretty important to her. What could the letters stand for? 'L' could be Liberal or Ladies or Local and 'V' could stand for Vigilance or Vice or Visiting, 'R' for Regulation or Relief. Amalgamations of any of these could make a cause that would have interested Alice. Then I came across a clue: 'First annual meeting of the Lenton Visiting Society at Mrs Crewdson's. Mrs Handford in the chair.' (16 October 1895)

Only the meaning of 'R' remained to be established and looking back with this guide, I found that, in December 1894, Alice and Maud organised a big meeting to discuss setting up a society for visiting the poor of Lenton –

> Maud and the others got the drawing room ready for 60 people. Only 25 turned up ... Our Visiting & Relief Society was started. I hope, well & on a good footing.

So – that established 'R' for Relief and L.V.R.S. became, quite definitely, the Lenton Visiting and Relief Society.

Alice's new causes were in addition to her old-established ones, of which the most important were the Women's Liberal Association and Women's Suffrage.

It was in the last decade of the century that a serious split occurred amongst the Liberals and the Women's Suffrage movement, following a debate on Women's Suffrage in the House of Commons on 27 April 1892:

> The Women's Suffrage paper I was to have read to the WLA next Monday is put off. The Division in the House last night was v. good, only lost by 23 but Mr. Gladstone and 'the party' have behaved very ill in opposing it.

This was followed the next day with a report that she had heard at a W.L.A. meeting 'that the majority (Anti-Suffrage) on the W.L.A. Federation have resigned!!! What will be done now!'

This is the first mention of the Women's Anti-Suffrage Society which is covered in Chapter 15.

Alice was extremely busy with all her public work and private charities. Somewhere in the diaries she writes that 'My days are fuller than full'. It may well have been at this time. On 1 April 1896, for example, she remarks that there are '4 things in one day'. At the same time her intellectual activity was as great as ever. February 1894 was crammed with events:

3 Feb	Health lecture at college
6 Feb	'Visiting & Relief meeting' in afternoon. Lecture on Old Testament history in evening
7 Feb	SPC meeting at Exchange in evening
8 Feb	Lecture on political convicts in Siberia in evening
10 Feb	Lecture on health at Nottingham College
13 Feb	Lecture on Wordsworth's *Prelude*
14 Feb	Women's Liberal Association meeting in afternoon
20 Feb	WLA tea party and lecture
21 Feb	Women's Suffrage Council meeting
27 Feb	Lecture on Wordsworth's *Intimations*

By this time, Alice was becoming very dependent on Maud's help in her public work: 'she is so efficient & methodical & does the greater part of the [S.P.C.C.] work for me' (1 February 1895) is a typical comment.

Unfortunately she did not expand on the objects or organisation of her causes or say what she herself did about them. She said no more about seats for shopgirls than that she argued with some shopkeepers; nothing about their reaction. We know from the diary that her district nursing committee produced awkward argument in Nottingham, since she wrote (1 December 1893) that discussions on it 'disturb me v much – being so peppery!' But she doesn't say why or what the duties of her committee were.

What is pretty clear is that of all her new causes, the plight of the Armenians in Turkey was the one that most touched her heart and that she tended to see everything else in the light of its affect on that cause – 'All England is dreadfully excited about Jameson's raid into the Transvaal & the attitude of Germany re. It is very serious & poor Armenia will sink into the background' (4 January 1995), and 'Electioneering in full swing ... In the heat of "party" I fear all will forget the poor Armenians & the weightier matters' (10 July 1895).

Again, she doesn't say whether she got any organisation going on the subject. Certainly she would have argued to everyone who would listen but the only indication she gave of any action came from an entry in February 1896, in which she said that she had written a letter to the *Nottingham Daily Guardian* in support of the fund for the Armenians, which 'the Mayor has at last opened' and 'I have been corresponding re'.

I understand from the Fawcett Society Library that the re-emergence of the Contagious Disease question in 1896 was due to the India Act 1895 which amended the statutory position about the control of venereal disease in India. When the Contagious Diseases acts were repealed in India, they had been replaced there

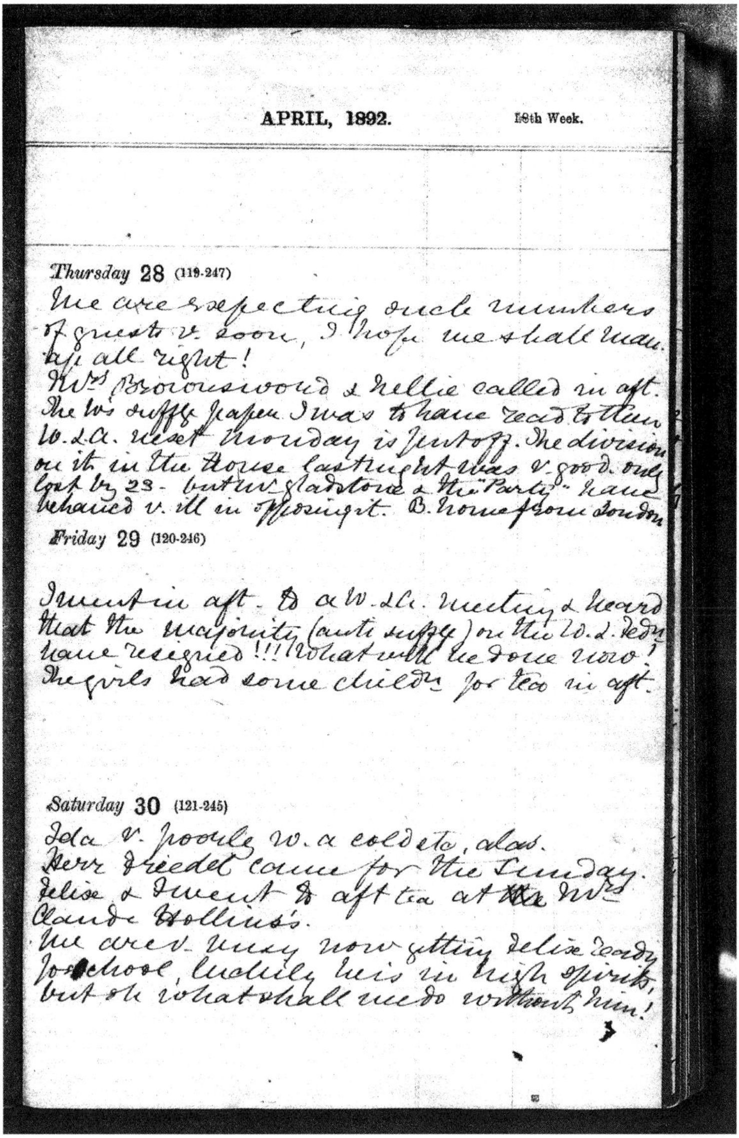

APRIL, 1892. 18th Week.

Thursday 28 (119-247)
We are expecting such numbers of guests v. soon, I hope we shall manage all right!
Mrs Brownswood & Nellie called in aft. The W's suffge paper I was to have read to the W.L.A. next Monday is put off. The division on it in the House last night was v. good, only lost by 23 - but Mr Gladstone & the "Party" have behaved v. ill in opposing it. B. home from London.

Friday 29 (120-246)
I went in aft. to a W.L.A. meeting & heard that the majority (anti suffge) on the W.L. Comm have resigned!!! What will be done now? The girls had some childn for tea in aft.

Saturday 30 (121-245)
Ida v. poorly w. a cold etc, alas.
Herr Friedel came for the Sunday.
Felise & I went to aft tea at Mrs Claude Hollins's.
We are v. busy now getting Felise ready for school, luckily he is in high spirits, but oh what shall we do without him!

PAGE FROM ALICE'S DIARY
in which she records the split in the W.L.A. over women's suffrage

(and nowhere else) by a new Cantonment Act, under which the local Indian governments could continue to control prostitution but in military areas only. The 1895 act applied to disease generally, making no mention of V.D. This was thought, by implication, to have done away with the control of prostitution, and caused an agitation for the complete reintroduction of the acts in India – which, in turn, set alarm bells ringing in England.

Alice was among those who were alarmed: she went to a Conference in Birmingham in November 1896 'about the threatened re-opening of the C.D. Acts question' and to a Women's Suffrage meeting on 30 March 1897, which met 'partly to pass a resolution against the threatened C.D. acts in India'. Not content with that, Alice set about organising her own meeting, inviting Lady Ridding to come to Nottingham to address it. Lady Ridding came and the meeting 'formed ourselves into a society, as a nucleus for the future', but it was a very small meeting since of the fifty whom Alice had invited, 'only about 7 came'. Well – it was 6 August, holiday time ...

She seems to have been surprisingly calm about the small gathering – perhaps because she went straight to Broughton to plunge into the organisation of 'our' party for her birthday the following week, which was a very large and grand affair:

> In the morning an enormous tent came & was put up on the lawn ... guests began to arrive at 7.30 or so. About 85 came, & mostly on cycles; it was a lovely evening for it ... the whole village turned out to see ... they cycled home by moonlight. (12 August 1897)

During these years, two important letters were written by Ben to the main local paper, the *Nottingham Daily Guardian*. One, headed 'Expulsion of the Jews' was dated 28 September 1891. In it, he describes their sufferings as 'piteous' and their expulsion from Russia where 'they have lived for generations' as 'reflecting the greatest disgrace on the Russian Government'. He suggested that people in England 'would gladly subscribe their mite or make some garments for the exiles if agencies were started in our large cities'. Alice made no comment in her diary and there are no further references to the subject, so if any action was taken, it must be assumed that she was not involved.

Ben's other letter was about vivisection. It raised a social storm at the time and produced an agitation in Nottingham, lasting some years and greatly involving Alice.

All through the family story, there have been examples of concern about the treatment or fate of animals: my grandfather wrote of his remembered concern about the cruelty to a dog and a horse that he had witnessed in his childhood; his brother, Enfield, risked his life to rescue his pet dog from the sea; and my grandmother's sister, Isobel, was known for her concern for animals. Hester's letter to her from Bonn about the treatment of cab horses there has already been mentioned and Alice told a charming tale in a letter to Maud about her sisters' rescue of three baby crows that had fallen out of their nest: they were hand fed and their feathers were preened with two old toothbrushes and on the approach of their human 'parents' – 'they began to caw as hard as they could with their 3 great wide beaks'.

On 30 May 1892, Alice had reported that she had written to the local paper 're the vivisection question which is coming up in Nottingham just now' and, two days later, that – 'Hurrah, the anti-vivisectors have won as regards Nottingham College! It is given up again.'

No doubt relying upon this as an indication of local feeling, Ben wrote to the *Nottingham Daily Guardian* on 11 July of that year, referring to the fact that the British Association was to meet in Nottingham the following summer. Stating that public opinion in Nottingham was against vivisection, that it was known that one member of the Association has a licence to practise vivivection anywhere without anaesthetic and that experiments 'of a highly painful character were carried out at Norwich at an earlier meeting', he asked for the assurance of the president-elect 'our respected townsman, Mr Joseph White' that vivisection would not be practised at the forthcoming meeting.

The following day, the paper carried a letter from Mr Joseph White giving that assurance, but this was called into question immediately by a letter the next day from Dr W.R. Ransom also a citizen of Nottingham saying that he 'had no doubt that it was far from the President's intention even to seem to imply [that] the rights of the members of the Association could be restricted' or that he supported 'those who seek to limit the freedom of the search for knowledge'. This in turn produced an immediate answer from Ben, who wrote on 14 July, that Mr Joseph White's reply would be accepted 'until he withdraws it' and concluded with the following statement:

> Dr Ransom's astounding contention that no-one should even wish to limit the operation of a law they deemed to be bad, will not be accepted by many. There are not a few in Nottingham who ... are determined to do what they can to confine the practice of vivisection to the narrowest limits possible. They consider that licences are far too carelessly given; that the present restrictions are insufficient; and that further legislation is necessary.

This public exchange of letters between prominent citizens of Nottingham caused very considerable social excitement and embarrassment, particularly in Alice's circle, many of whom would be offering hospitality to the members of the Association for the meetings. Here is the entry in Alice's diary for 13 July 1892.

> *Such* a ferment! A letter of B's appeared in Mondays paper, asking a question re vivisection & the coming conference, & the doctors were in such a rage & fuss! B was going to publish their very insulting letter ... & Dr Marshall & Dr White called to beg him not to & to smooth things over, & promised to withdraw it etc. It was v. upsetting & exciting, but B was splendid, so decided & firm, yet quite composed, tho' angry.

Worse social trouble followed but my impression is that Alice found it more exciting than embarrassing:

Mrs Whitelegge came in great distress because her brother, Mr Victor Horsley, the great vivisector, who is staying with the Ransoms, was v angry with her for staying with us, the Ransoms having poisoned him against us. These things are very upsetting. (27 July)

Alice was certainly not put off by these social difficulties and continued to support the cause vigorously:

A very busy day for me, for I had to give an address on viv in aft to a few women at Mr Simpson's – wh went off very well. (12 September 1893)

Meeting of British Association in Nottingham. B & I are taking no part in it as 2 vivisectors are taking the principal lectures. Maud Hubert & Will take tickets & some of them went in evening to the opening lecture, v dull. (13 September 1893)

Hester and Maud went to various sections of the meeting over the next few days but clearly nothing very unpleasant occurred and Alice continued to support the cause: 'With our lady guests to the anit-viv conference'. [There was a public meeting this evening] 'which however was not very good and how tired we all were after it' (28 November).

In February 1894, there was a meeting of their new Saturday Society, at which Dr W. Ransom was to read a paper on vivisection. Alice wrote that:

I was too nervous to go, as Will meant to speak, & of course we were in a complete minority! Ben spoke very nicely, Maud said & Will also ... and it all passed off amicably. Rob & I were alone at home.

A particularly revealing picture here, I think, of Alice's character – feeling so strongly about the subject, but sitting at home, too anxious about how her eldest would acquit himself, to bear to be present.

She continued to attend anti-vivisection meetings through the years but Ben was not a natural committee man. She reported going to a well-attended meeting 30 September 1897 when – 'I could not get Ben to go. He hates meetings.'

The Anti-Vivisection Society was founded in 1876. Alice and Ben may have been members – or their society may have been affiliated – but Alice does not mention it.

The situation of having two grown-up daughters and a still very active mother all living at home could not last happily for long, however much charitable and public work there was to do, especially as one of three was Hester who was bursting with energy and high spirits. She could not have been happy simply to stay at home, supporting her mother, going to dances and helping with 'good works' and political causes, however well intentioned.

In January of 1888, Alice had arranged for Hester to go to stay with her aunt 'Nannie' Taylor at Starston. This was Ben's sister, Anna, who had been such a help to Alice when the children were young. Now Anna needed help with the births of her own children. Hester liked nothing better than to look after babies but it didn't last because, as Alice reports and letters from Hester confirm, she found it 'rather trying at Starston as to politics'. The letters make clear that they differed over Home Rule for Ireland on which Hester went so far as to describe her aunt's views as 'rabid'.

So, by March 1888, Hester was back at home and she must soon have begun to think about a career. The choice at that time was really only between teaching or nursing: she was good at teaching but (as I have already suggested) she would not have had the education for the new type of collegiate school. Her letters from Bonn show that she was very fond of her aunt Katie, who had taken up nursing as a profession, and she must have discussed the pros and cons of this career with her.

I cannot find any mention in the diary of discussions about what she should do. The first mention of nursing is on 17 September 1889, when the decision had already been made:

To London to see the Gt Ormand St Hospital (v. nice sister) the Evelina (horrid matron), & the Shadwell (v. nice) with a view to Hester's training.

As usual, Hester was suffering from one of the headaches (she never called them migraines) often lasting two or three days, with which she would be a martyr all her life.

The next mention of nursing in the diary is on 3 October, when Alice and Hester joined sister Katie in Manchester to look at a hospital there, But next day, 'Hester & I decided that she should take the January vacancy at Shadwell hospital'.

That New Year's Eve Alice wrote that

some of the family went to the midnight service at the chapel ... the twins saw the year out with Hubert in the kitchen & Hester was upstairs with *us* over *our* fire.

The italics are mine – so often she is sitting over *her* fire. Hester's being alone with her parents is of course explained by the fact that she was about to set off for her career in London.

The first years of Hester's career as a nurse were full of stress, anxiety and sadness for her family, especially Alice. She had typhoid at the end of her first year and a year or two later scarlet fever for which she was sent to an isolation hospital where Alice, who had come up from Nottingham, was not allowed to see her. Both illnesses were life-threatening in those days.

She was so ill with typhoid that Alice was sent for and stayed eight weeks in hospital, sharing the nursing. When at last Hester was declared fit to go home, two doctors carried her down to the carriage and two nurses went with them to St Pancras. Alice found both Ben and Maud in a poor state of health: Ben had worried terribly about Hester's illness and 'looked aged & anxious'; and Maud was 'thin & white but she has kept house so nicely in my absence'.

191

No sooner were the two girls thoroughly recovered than Maud was hit by an epidemic of influenza, an illness apparently new to Alice and mentioned here for the first time in the diaries. She had a sudden shivering fit and 'was very bad' one day, had a temperature of 103 degrees and 'was v poorly', and the next was 'much better'. 'It is undoubtedly this influenza which is so mysterious,' Alice writes. 'Several people in Nottingham have died. 70 M.P's are down with it. They roll over like ninepins' (13 May 1991). In the first half of 1890 almost 600 deaths from influenza were recorded in London alone.

Hester went back to Shadwell that month but troubles for her and Alice were by no means over. It was in February 1893 that Hester developed scarlet fever.

Alice's spirit was not overwhelmed. She describes giving two dances that very month, congratulating herself that 'I didn't feel at all shy' and reporting that 'we danced away like anything, which really did me a lot of good' and that the next day she went to the Notts v. Derby football match where Rob was playing. Twenty slept in the house one night, nineteen the next.

In June 1925, my grandmother wrote me a letter telling me about my mother's life as a nurse in London and what I know of those years comes more from that letter than from her diaries. She wrote that, in 1896, Hester had formed 'a violent attachment' to a nurse who died suddenly of scarlet fever, turning Roman Catholic at the last, and that Hester wrote to say that she wished to become a Catholic too.

> This *was* a blow to me & off I went in a hurry to try to get her to put it off, to think it over – not to put herself in *chains* as it seemed to me! ... but she would not wait & insisted on being received into the Church without delay.

'I thankfully confess', she adds, 'that it has never interfered with our love'. Certainly the diary entries show that she made every effort to see with Hester's eyes, going with her to services at the Oratory whenever she was in London.

There were two important family happenings in the last decade of the century. One was the marriage of Will to Helena (Nellie) Brownsword in July 1894. The other was the death of Alice's mother in April 1895. The marriage was at the Baptist chapel and Alice comments that 'Hubert was v. useful as best man' and that 'it was a beautiful marriage service'. Will followed his parents' example in going to Cromer for the honeymoon.

Alice's descriptions of the family's behaviour on the death at last of her mother on 18 April 1895 after so many alarms over the years, are interesting: it was intimate, familiar, accepted, unfearful in a way not known today, so far as I, at any rate am aware. Whether it was special to her family, I have no means of knowing.

It happened that Alice was not there on the day her mother died though she knew she was very ill. She went to Bollington at once where her three sisters and her brother, Walter, were:

> We had afternoon tea & supper in mother's room as of old, she lying asleep as it were. Katie & Sibbie slept there. (19 April)
> We wrote & sat in M's room, beside her dear form & it felt like the house of God & the Gates of Heaven ... We do not leave the room, someone stays there all along. (20 April)
> still we sit & live mostly in mother's room, the fire burning & window open, rooks cawing & sun shining – all as usual but for the great change. (22 April)

On the day of the funeral, 'Katie helped to put her into the coffin'.

The following year brought more family trouble, again for Hester, who was dismissed from University College Hospital for writing to the *News Chronicle* about the howling of the dogs being used for vivisection in the laboratory next door. This caused a serious interruption in her nursing career but led to the great adventure of her life – her joining the small group of trained nurses who volunteered to go out to India to nurse the victims of the plague in Bombay.

CHAPTER 12

A Daughter in India

*'We seem to be living on a mine as regards Hester
and everything else seems trivial.'*

As IT happened, Hester's letter about vivisection was published on
her twenty-ninth birthday: 11 July 1896. Under the heading 'A
terrible story', it described

> the distressing howling and moaning of dogs coming from buildings
> opposite the hospital where licensed vivisection is carried on ...
> sounds which disturb the patients and are terribly distressing and
> appalling to the feelings of the nurses, increasing tenfold the already
> trying and weary hours of night duty in hospital ...

The *Daily Chronicle* did not name the hospital and the letter
was signed only 'A hospital nurse' but the anonymity of both
hospital and writer was seen through at once. Maybe University
College Hospital was the only London hospital with a research
laboratory where vivisection was practised. Hester was by now a
senior nurse and had been in charge of a big children's ward, on
night duty, so would have been easily identified.

Today many will feel, as I do, an appalled sympathy with my
mother in those night watches, unable to get away from the sounds
of suffering or to relieve them. Alice, however, describes in her
diary how Hester, on holiday at Broughton, was flooded with cor-
respondence 'saying how wild the authorities are about her letter'.
Alice was, of course, in sympathy with her daughter but neither
she nor Hester seems to have expected that it would cause her to
be dismissed. She reported (16 July) 'a very severe letter from the
Sister Superior to which [Hester] wrote a long & good answer' but
on the 4 August came 'a formal dismissal from hospital from the
Sister Superior which upset her (and me) v much' (4 August).

Although Hester had this responsible job, she was still working,
as she had in other hospitals, as a 'paying probationer, paying her

guinea a week', as Alice reported. So, in sacking her, the hospital were making a considerable sacrifice – which may explain why dismissal came as a surprise!

Hester knew, however, that she had general family approval in writing her letter, especially from her aunt Katie. This must have made the outcome easier to bear. But finding another hospital job would not have been easy – indeed there is no evidence that she tried. Now, she decided to look for paid work and the following month set out to find a post as a district nurse in London.

By this time she was well trained. She had worked at Guy's for a year and, before joining London University Hospital, she had spent six months at the General Lying-in Hospital (where she obtained a 'monthly nursing certificate') and another six months at the Great Northern Central Hospital. She had also had a period of maternity training when (Alice wrote) 'she used to go about in the slums with a trained midwife helping the babies into the world'.

Later, Hester told her children about her midwifery training and gave them a romantic picture of the beautiful little babies being taken out of the mother's body in conditions of great poverty and dirt. In consequence, we never needed to indulge in speculation about where babies came from.

For her period of district nursing, Hester lived with her young brother, Bernard, who was studying in London for his solicitor's exam and there were early reports of her being happy and finding time to go to the British Museum Reading Room. However, for whatever reason, her stint of district nursing did not last long. Within a year, she was nursing privately (including sick members of her own family) and was making enquiries about Government employment: there was a possibility of going to India where the plague was raging, and she was also considering a post in Malaya, to which Alice was much opposed.

Then, on 26 October 1897, a letter came from the India Office, 'asking if Hester was prepared to go to India, at a week's notice, to which she immediately said yes'. A cutting from the *Evening Post* for that date is enclosed in Alice's diary, describing the situation there. It mentions that thirteen doctors and thirteen nurses had been sent out from England six weeks earlier and that this number had been found quite inadequate –

> the mortality is exceedingly high. The Indian Government has determined to call for further aid from England ... & now 25 doctors & 12 carefully selected nurses are being sent.

On 17 November, Hester was summoned by the India Office 'for a medical on Friday and be ready to start on Thursday next week for Bombay for plague duty!!! All evening taken up in considering how to proceed & making a list of her requirements.'

Alice went to London with Hester to help her with getting her uniform and arranging about the journey, but mainly, I feel sure, just to be with her. And Hester was greatly in need of her mother's support: she spent much time at the Oratory, slept badly and entirely lost her appetite. Clearly, even her bold spirit was frightened by what she had undertaken. They went back home together for the last days and Alice said goodbye there. There was a big family gathering, her brothers all taking time off from work to come home for however short a time. Her father and Maud saw her off from Victoria Station with the other nurses on 25 November and (wrote Alice of that day) – 'not 5 minutes was she out of my thoughts'.

During the time of waiting and preparing, Alice had not failed to keep her causes and charities going and on the Monday after Hester's departure, she writes simply that 'We are very busy preparing for the work of this week which is no small matter. I find it difficult to think yet of anything but Hester'.

Hester wrote many letters from India and her mother had extracts from twenty-two of them privately printed for family and friends, the first written at the beginning of December 1897 during Hester's voyage out and the last dated 20 April 1898 – a period of less than five months but the magnitude of the tragedy for India and of the impact on Alice's family acts as a magnifier of time and makes it seem much longer.

Lying loose in Alice's diary are a large number of press cuttings about the plague in Bombay, from Reuters and *Central News* for January, February, March and April. She used the information in these to add statistics of deaths from the plague during the months covered by the letters, and to include extracts from newspaper accounts and Government statements about the riots which followed the measures taken by the authorities to contain the disease. The peak of the disease was in the week ending 18 March 1898, when the deaths from plague in Bombay alone totalled 1,194, an appalling number out of its population of just over 800,000.

Since these letters have more than a family interest, I have deposited my copy – the only one so far as I know – with the India Office Library in London. They say that they are the only eye-witness account of the Bombay plague in their collection. So the picture they give is a unique one of this sad but heroic moment in the history of the British in India.

Hester joined the S.S. *Himalaya* at Brindisi on the 28 November. It happened that her young cousin, Oscar, the son of Ben's brother Enfield, was also on the ship, on his way to Australia. This description of her at that time is from a letter he wrote me many years later, probably at the time of her death:

> I remember her vividly sitting on a deck chair in very hot weather. She really was a sight to remember – her wonderful red hair and her eager purposeful way of talking even though the heat made her feel ill and she was on her way to what was a very dangerous task. She impressed me then as a wonderful character.

Though the nurses were called 'lady nurses' they were given poor accommodation on the ship, while doctors and army officers travelled first class.

Everyone on board is very angry at the accommodation the nurses
have been given on both boats [Hester wrote]. We are down at the
bottom of the ship where they say the charge is less than 2nd class. It
is almost impossible to sleep: there are no port-holes ... My cabin
thermometer is 89, three of us in it and the vibration of the screw
shakes us in bed the whole time.

In these conditions, Hester developed some species of heat- or
sun-stroke. Two army officers, learning how ill she was, gave up
their cabin to her and here she was devotedly cared for by Miss
McDougall, one of the other nurses with whom she had already
become friendly.

Not only did the nurses have to travel rough, they found when
they arrived in India, that no arrangements had been made to meet
them and that they had to find their own accommodation for the
first four days until they were moved to their permanent quarters in
the grounds of the old Government House.

They reached Bombay on 11 December when, according to
Alice's account, deaths from plague in Bombay city were under a
hundred a week, but the disease gained ground with terrifying
speed – by the end of January, the weekly death toll had risen to
834. 'The plague is getting worse & worse & the work is much
harder than I expected', Hester wrote on 16 January.

In our hospital there are about 150 plague beds and 48 in each of two
acute wards, each of which has only two English nurses in the morning and one only thereafter. Most of the acute cases would, if in
England, have two special nurses each, so you may imagine how
frantic one feels with the nursing here! It is especially hard for the
most highly trained of the nurses, like my friend Miss McDougall,
who is a gold medallist at Barts.

There was a shortage of all necessities like clean sheets and
blankets and because the European nurses were so few, all the real
nursing had to be done by Indian ward boys who were largely
untrained and difficult to discipline and who 'having become

199

familiar with death and disease are often I am afraid far from kind to the poor suffering creatures'. The hours in the crowded wards were long and she felt the heat very much, though the hospital itself kept reasonably cool – being made of rush and bamboo, with a space of about six feet below a thatched roof.

Their routine on day duty was to get up at six a.m., have breakfast and drive a mile and a half to the hospital. Lunch was at twelve, after which on alternate days they went back to the ward until four, or else to their quarters until three-thirty and then back to the ward until eight-thirty. 'The work is very hard and trying' she wrote in an early letter.

> All the people are so ill and delirious, and so difficult to feed and manage. There is such a rush to get even the larger part of one's work done. We have lunch in a tent which is like an oven, as the sun pours on it all day. The native 'ward boys' have to do the actual nursing mostly, as we have only time to take Doctor's orders, give medicines (which are all 2 hourly and some every half hour), take temperatures; give feeds; and see that the boys do their work. We have all sorts of castes and religions in the hospital. Some of them don't like us to touch them, and most refuse to take food at our hands. We have to try to get hold of the ward boy of the same caste before they will take it, unless they are delirious.

A fortnight later she describes the scene on night duty:

> We often have as many as nine new cases in the day, and sometimes we find we have lost nearly as many during the night. Nearly every one of them is off his head, and has to be tied in bed, or they would be out of the Hospital in no time. The wards are just a long low shed, with flat four-legged bedsteads made of cane, like a cane-bottomed chair, about a foot from the floor. Over the cane is laid a cotton blanket, then the patient, and over him again a cotton blanket (white) and a dark warmer rug which he pulls over him when cold. There is no mattress or bedding. We find it a great business to get enough clean blankets, and it is a continual struggle to get fresh ones from the office on the premises and to see that the dhobi-wallah does not steal any. It is so

200

cold at night now, that we have little tiny things like saucepans on legs, filled with charcoal in the wards.

Language was a serious problem. She and her friend had started learning Hindustani on the voyage out and they tried to go on with this while at work, but the authorities gave no help or encouragement and it was difficult to get teachers to go out to the nurses' quarters outside Bombay. So communication between doctors and nurses and their patients had to be conducted almost entirely through the ward boys. Hester felt deeply her inability to understand the pathetic pleas of the patients and their relatives –

> I feel dreadfully for the poor patients here taken by force, by an alien race, out of their homes, and obliged to enter our hospitals and be treated and drugged by any young English doctor who may have come out ... The poor things are forced, every two hours, to take nauseous medicines which they genuinely believe to be poison, to drink milk whether they like it or not and generally to be made miserable for the little time the majority of them have left to live.

She had always felt strongly antipathetic to the attitude of those Europeans who looked on the native Indians and their religion as inferior. 'It sometimes makes my blood boil,' she wrote,

> to see how the personal feelings and caste and religious prejudices of the people are despised and trodden on, especially by these young men fresh from England. The people who have been out here longer are more tolerant.

Again and again she wrote of her admiration for the devotion shown by the patients' relatives –

> They will stop, squatted on the floor behind the bed night and day, taking hardly any sleep or food. Every movement of their sick they will watch and tend and when we go to give medicines or milk, up they are in a minute trying to persuade and coax them to do what we want in hopes of preventing our having recourse to force or nasal feed.

201

The measures taken to combat the disease and force the sufferers into hospital inevitably resulted in the nurses having to face the added unpleasantness of being disliked and misunderstood, a result increased in Hester's view, by misunderstandings due to language: 'I fear a good many of the natives hate us,' she wrote. 'One of the nurses was stoned when she tried to catch a patient that was running away from the hospital.'

Among the Europeans who knew India well and respected its people and its customs, Alice especially mentions Dr Dimmock, the plague doctor in charge in Bombay, and one of the army officers whom Hester had met on the boat on the way out; he was returning to his regiment after spending a year studying Hindustani. I suspect it was he who first encouraged Hester to try to learn the language –

> Though only 27, he knows 9 languages & in a land where most English men & women 'run down' the natives, it is a treat to come across one like him who really seems to know them & yet to like & admire them; he is very anxious that we should not get to despise them.

In the fashion of the time no Christian names were used even for these friends, and her close woman friend is always Miss McDougall.

During the first two months, there had been a happy side to Hester's life. She and Miss McDougall shared a bungalow and became as inseparable as their hospital duties allowed. They enjoyed making their bungalow into a home with the help of 'Peter' their Indian servant, who slept on their veranda.

> He wakes us at 5.45 with hot water for our baths, then goes and cooks our breakfast (an egg poached or otherwise); it is ready in our sitting room by 6.30 and we eat it sitting in luxurious lounge chairs. Then we go on duty driving to the hospital. The country round here, with palm trees and heaps of foliage, looks lovely at that time of the morning, a kind of blue mist hanging about between the trees. When we get back

off duty, Peter has our baths ready for us, and makes our tea, cutting us elegant ham sandwiches and thin bread and butter. We lie in our chairs and he pours out the tea and hands it to us, so we don't have to exert ourselves much, which is a good thing as we are always very tired. We read aloud to each other a good deal and generally seem to like the same books. Peter is an excellent housemaid, keeps flowers in our rooms and on the table at meals, buys our food and keeps beautiful accounts which always begin with 'Miss Sab Gaving' and end up 'Boy balance'.

The charm of this picture was reduced by Hester's frequent headaches and the fact that her 'hands and feet are in a chronic state of being swollen and aching from mosquito bites,' and on one occasion when she came in exhausted from the hospital and flung herself down to rest, she woke to find her face so covered with bites that she looked as if she had smallpox.

In spite of the gruelling work and the time necessarily given to rest and to the fun of setting up house together, the two young women had time for some social life. Mostly this revolved round an army friend who appears in the letters as 'Mr. P' but they also met some naval officers who took them sailing, including 'Dr. K' – Dr Kilroy whom Hester would later marry.

As early as January, the measures taken by the authorities to try to control the epidemic had led to serious riots in the Bombay Presidency, though not in Bombay itself. Hester wrote that they had been sparked off by the government's attempts to contain the disease through house-to-house searches (so as to get people treated as quickly as possible), by the segregation of sufferers and by compulsory examination of corpses to find out whether death had been from plague. (My mother told me herself of one of the house searches where a man, already dead from the plague, had been propped up so as to appear alive and playing cards with his friends.)

On 28 January, *Central News* had reported that – 'At Nasik the mob broke into the buildings connected with the medical administration, attacked officials with ruthless fury and murdered the doctor in charge.' And at Sinnar, the Plague Committee chairman was murdered.

According to Alice's press cuttings, the situation was met at first by increased military intervention: on 1 February, *Central News* reported that the Shropshire and Durham regiments had been 'told off for the purpose of assisting in the inspection of houses'; and a Reuter's report for 4 February, mentioning that a quarantine barrier had been set up round Bombay, was all about military preparations to deal with panic.

And then, in the middle of February, only two months after Hester's arrival in India, came the tragedy of Miss McDougall's death from the disease. Starting one day with a sore eye, it spread to her throat, and in less than a week she was dead.

One of the Reuter's reports purported to explain how she came to catch the plague:

> a patient was seized with a fit of coughing as the nurse bent over the bed, and some particles of the contagious sputum entered the eye.

Hester nursed her friend as long as she was able, but she became ill herself and it was believed for a time that she also had the plague: 'It seems so strange,' she wrote, 'that all I have been living through this last week was unknown to you and that I might be dead and buried from the plague before you could know I was ill.'

This might almost have been the case. The news that Miss McDougall was one of the nurses who had caught the plague was released in the English press only just about the time that she died.

News of the death a week earlier of Miss Florence Morgan (the acting superintendent of the general plague hospital) had reached England on the 14 February and on the 21st Alice wrote that they 'saw in paper that two other nurses have got the plague in Bombay & this makes us very anxious'. Given the news that was coming from India, the surprising thing is that Alice was as calm as she was. A newspaper cutting for the 17 February had described 'Plague-stricken Bombay' as a 'City of Horror' –

> Fires of sulphur are burning in the streets and our nights are lit up with lurid flames arising from the funeral pyres heaped with burning bodies.

Alice wrote at once to the India Office to enquire who the two nurses were. Their reply came on 23 February, but this was the day on which the news of Miss McDougall's death was released by Reuters and on which, also, *Central News* had reported that 'the Queen Empress had expressed her sympathy' over the death of both Miss Morgan and Miss McDougall –

> We saw 1st thing in paper that poor Miss McDougall, Hester's friend, who has lived with her, has died yesterday of the plague!! Later a letter from the India Office wrote us that Hester also is ill of fever not plague, last Saturday, but is 'better'. We were of course greatly upset.

The next day came another letter from the India Office saying that 'as Hester is recovering, he doesn't suppose the Bombay Govt will telegraph again'. It seems that the India Office must have been remiss in not writing sooner to tell Hester's parents that she was ill but Alice does not suggest that she felt this.

Inevitably, they remained very anxious – 'We seem to be living on a mine as far as regards Hester and everything else seems trivial,' Alice wrote.

An extract from *The Times*, included amongst Alice's cuttings, records the answer to a question in Parliament on 26 February. It asks for news about the progress of the plague in Bombay and the Bombay Presidency and the measures taken to deal with it. The answer takes up almost a whole column and gives, amongst other things, the information that: so far, fifty-nine doctors and sixty-one nurses had been sent from England; 16,600 houses had been inspected, discovering 600 plague cases; persons leaving infected cities were being examined and detained if necessary; and things were improving in the Bombay Presidency, deaths a week having decreased from 2,000 in November 1887 to 747 during the week ended 18 February 1888.

In Bombay city, however, the situation had got no better and there were strikes and riots – this time in Bombay city itself – due to feeling caused by the measures taken by the Plague Committee, especially – it appears – the attempt to isolate Bombay from the rest of the country thus interfering with established trades and to the house-to-house searches by or with the assistance of European soldiers. On 10 March, Alice wrote in her diary that –

> The papers tell of dreadful plague riots & bloodshed at Bombay, the plague measures are resented. I feel more & more anxious for news of Hester.

While on 14 March, Reuter's reported that –

> All plague parties are now escorted by troops ... Numerous arrests of rioters have been made, including the assailants of the two Shropshire men, who were murdered.

However, on the same day, a question in Parliament asking whether British soldiers had been employed in the enforcement of plague regulations in Bombay city, received the reply that 'British soldiers had ceased to be employed a few days before the beginning of the recent disturbances'.

Indeed, the situation had become so serious that the authorities had to give way. Hester wrote that, on 15 March, the Governor of Bombay issued a Proclamation in four languages announcing the abandonment of the official searches and the inspection of corpses, leaving it to the people to report cases of plague to the local headman. 'Government do not wish to make the cure of the plague a cause of suffering for the people. They desire the greatest kindness and sympathy to be shown to all.' A press cutting, headed 'Bombay itself again' and dated the 16 March, tells the same tale –

The position of affairs in Bombay is more hopeful today ... The Government have issued a circular which practically abolishes plague search parties and leaves the heads of the various communities to do the work themselves. This step appears to have satisfied all classes.

Hester wholly approved the change of policy. She wrote that it 'has very greatly appeased the anger of the people but some of the English are very angry as it is giving in to the natives because of rioting'.

One of Alice's cuttings is from *The Standard* for 29 March, reporting a question in Parliament which reflects the attitude of the English community: it asked 'why the Governor of Bombay had cancelled the orders complained of after the riot had taken place' and whether the regulations were issued 'in pursuance of orders from home'. The reply makes it clear that the decisions were being taken in Bombay not in London –

I was aware of their general tendency and have throughout supported the governments of India and Bombay. I have not received any information concerning the riots except by telegram but I understand a Despatch may be expected shortly.

After a period of convalescence following her illness, Hester had been offered a choice of three other hospitals where the work would be less hard, but she insisted on returning to Bombay to carry on her friend's work – an act of special courage now that she had had personal experience of death from the plague which was then still at its height in Bombay, with 1,259 deaths in the week ending 24 March. But the numbers declined rapidly thereafter from 678 (8 April) and 442 (29 April) to 138 by the middle of May.

In the increasing heat, and depressed as she was by her friend's death, Hester found it difficult to fight irritability – 'a most common disease out here that we all suffer from. I don't think I have ever lost my temper so much,' she wrote in April. 'People seem to have lost interest now the rush is over and I shall be glad to leave'. In fact, as Alice's cuttings show, the plague continued much at the rate in May right through the summer and autumn and Hester stayed until the end of the year and through January arriving in England on the 1 March 1899.

Unfortunately none of Hester's letters from India after that May survive and thereafter almost nothing is known about Hester's life there for, though Alice's diary records the regular arrival of letters, she does not mention their contents. Both Alice and Ben must have been comforted by having her friend Dr Dimmock to stay at Broughton and for a trip on the yacht in the summer. Mrs Dimmock also paid them a visit just before she returned to India in November. Of course, too, they continued to watch for news of the plague in the press: Alice's newspaper cuttings survive for August, September and October but none do much more than give the weekly statistics of deaths.

During the year of anxiety with Hester in Bombay, Alice had not failed to report in her diary, both the political happenings and the family doings in England – there had been the usual L.V.R.S., C.O.S. and Women's Suffrage meetings and, in particular, an important anti-vivisection meeting at which she was a delegate when, as she writes with obvious approval, 'it was *just* carried to go in for $\frac{1}{2}$ the loaf, sooner than total abolition and no compromise' (9 February). She had gone to a lecture on theosophy by Mrs Besant who was staying, while in Nottingham, with son Will and his wife Nellie (23 February).

Mrs Besant lectured on theosophy all over the world but she is known chiefly for her influence in India where she founded the Indian Home Rule League, was elected President of the Indian National Congress in 1917 and had an important influence on education in India. There is no information about how she came to include Nottingham in her lecture tour, or to meet Alice's son and daughter-in-law but I know from my own experience that both my uncle and aunt and my twin uncles became interested in theosophy at that time; the twin uncles kept a faith in it for the rest of their lives and I remember that my uncle Will and aunt Nellie had a 'Mahatma' staying in their house on one occasion in the early 1920s, so they were still interested up to that time.

On the 3 March, in the midst of the anxieties following Miss McDougall's death, Alice wrote that she went to a bazaar Committee and 'I ought to have gone to two other meetings today but could not manage it'. Next day she was writing to condole with Miss McDougall's relations.

She had gone with Maud and four of her sons, to hear a concert by Paderewski – the great Polish pianist and patriot who would one day become his country's prime minister and die in exile in 1941. Alice's only diary comment at this time, however, was 'v delightful' (14 March).

Also in March, she took a major part in organising a meeting on the State Regulation of Vice ('Vice' of course meaning 'prostitution'), for which there had been a preparatory meeting in February. They had sent out 200 cards and 2,000 leaflets for the meeting to which seventy-five people came. Alice provided the tea, Emily and maids helping. 'Rather a business' was Alice's comment (17 March). A week later, a former maid came to stay for a few days 'being out of a situation again poor girl' and – recorded by Alice as a matter of course – she joined in family doings during that time, such as going to tea with Nellie (26 March).

She and Maud went to see Mrs Patrick Campbell in *Mrs Tanqueray* – 'a wonderful piece of acting but a dreadful, haunting play' (23 July). Amongst the letters of this period, there is a packet from Mrs Patrick Campbell to Maud who, clearly, was quite as much an admirer of the actress as Hester was.

In October, they packed up the Broughton house (as had apparently become the custom) and went back to Nottingham 'with our 14 packages' – '*Very* sorry to leave & Mrs Allsop [a local helper] in tears but nice to feel we were all together again at home' (14 October). Next day, Saturday, 'Maud and I plunged into full work at once, she for the new Social Group, I for L.V.R.S.'

On Christmas Day that year, she wrote that Will gave a magic lantern show and a few days later, that they went, 'nine of us in two cabs, to dine at the RE's [Richard Enfields]'; and on New Year's Eve that 'the sisters' (her unmarried sister's who lived at Bollington) are settled in Italy for the winter – apparently as much a matter of course as Alice's move back from Broughton to Nottingham in October.

However, undoubtedly the most important public happening of that year and for Alice too – other than the riots and plague in India – had been the death of Gladstone on 19 May. On this date Alice told her diary that 'all the papers [are] in mourning, flags half mast high, and nothing else spoken of,' and the following day that 'the papers are full of Gladstone and a wonderful feeling of sympathy and admiration is thrilling, all over the world'.

On subsequent days, she detailed with loyal satisfaction the national and world-wide recognition of the statesman who has been for her *the man* – '*Hundreds* of churches and chapels had sermons about Gladstone – all with one voice!' (22 May); 'Gladstone's coffin lies in State in Westminster Hall all today and tomorrow when 100s of 1000s of people pass thro' to pay their respects' (26 May); and 'funeral of Gladstone in Westminster Abbey. A tremendous function but very bare and simple as he wished. No flowers ... I went to the memorial service at St Mary's church' (28 May).

It may be that her personal sorrow at Gladstone's death was muted both by his losing favour with her for having voted against Women's Suffrage, and by the fact that at this date she was at last feeling relieved about Hester's welfare in Bombay.

CHAPTER 13

Turn of the Century

'I was struck dumb with horror when she [Hester] said –
"I must have my smoke".'

THE LAST year of the century saw important happenings, both in
the family and nationally. Hester's return from India, basically so
welcome, was a time of unhappiness both for her and for her mother, who also had to part with her 'dear Rob' leaving for South
Africa to take a job in Johannesburg. And in the international
sphere, there was the outbreak of the Boer War.

Alice had gone to London to meet Hester on her return from
India and had found her much altered. 'I think', she wrote in her
letter to me 'that in her mischief she rather enjoyed shocking us
after the rather free life she had been leading'. They stayed the
night with the Martineau relations in Esher before travelling on to
Nottingham and –

> when we went to bed, sitting over the fire together, I was struck dumb
> with horror when she said 'I must have my smoke!' In those days the
> idea of ladies smoking was unheard of in our sort of society at any rate;
> & to think of Constance & Carry smelling it!!

Alice had always disliked the fact that her two eldest sons smoked
– 'though they know I do not like it' – and she had had many
tussles with them. And now not only was her daughter indulging
in the habit but also publicising it to relatives.

From all that is said and not said, my reading of the situation is
rather different from the one my grandmother tried to present in
her letter to me of June 1925. I think that both she and my mother
had some very unhappy months at this time and that my mother
had probably lost her heart in India to a married man, or anyhow
someone who could not or did not want to marry her. I and my
youngest sister certainly gained that impression – and children so

often gather more of what goes on than is realised. There is, too, the fact that Hester's letters tell of her being very unhappy at the time she left India; and that in spite of her searing experiences with the plague, she kept a romantic love of India all her life, which her children could not fail to notice.

Hester applied to go out to South Africa to nurse the Boer War wounded and, when she was not accepted, went back to nursing in London, first in a hospital for epileptics, then in a fever hospital. Two years later 'after', Alice wrote, 'much hesitation and indecision' she became engaged to Dr Kilroy and was married in December 1900 at the age of thirty-two.

Judging from the one piece of her Commonplace Book which has survived, Alice too had been going through a difficult time in the closing months of the century. All her children were now grown-up and she was going through the painful realisation that they no longer necessarily followed or even wanted her advice: 'I love to plan for them, it is so interesting' she wrote.

> But sometimes it seems as if my suggestions were never taken and were always ridiculed or worse in their eyes ... I can control myself not to answer back but my *heart* is often in such a boil.

She was still very full of her causes and charities and her zeal for knowledge was as keen as ever. With her daughters, she was *beginning* a course of lessons in Italian – 'the Italian lady came for our first Italian lesson' (3 March) – and, even on the same afternoon, she would attend lectures on Dante and Shakespeare. Her continued wide interest in knowledge of all kinds is shown by a press cutting of a letter she wrote on 12 November 1899 to the *Nottingham Daily Guardian*, suggesting that because 'a star shower' of meteors was expected, 'the street lamps should not be lighted on Tuesday & Wednesday nights, as they interfere seriously with any star gazing in the town'.

She was, however, relying increasingly on Maud for the routine work connected with the most demanding of her causes and she was spending more time at 'dear peaceful Bro'ton'. There she took pleasure in everything rural, going for walks with Ben, visiting the needy or sick in the village, rearing chickens, growing and bottling fruit, working in the garden with Ben and, again and again, trying (usually without success) to persuade him to sleep out of doors.

The earlier part of the nineteenth century had seen the railways transform distance and Ben, in his professional capacity, has been reported as having to do with their development and finding it very interesting. The last quarter of the century saw first the bicycle, then the motor car begin their sway. The frequent references to cycling in the diaries at this time concur with the view that this period was the high watermark of cycling before the motor car took over. I have already mentioned the big birthday party at Broughton in August 1897, to which the guests came by bicycle from Nottingham; and cycling to and fro between Bro'ton and Nottingham was as usual for the children as the train was for their parents.

An invitation card shows an unusual kind of joint party in June 1899, split both between hosts and venue: 'afternoon tea, 5.0 to 6.0' with Mr and Mrs W. E. Dowson in Nottingham and 'supper at 8.0'clock' at Broughton with Mr and Mrs Dowson, a space being left at the top of the card for the names of guests coming by bicycle. Then there was a Thursday afternoon spent at Bro'ton – 'All had tea in the garden, so pretty innocent & happy. Then home by cycle & B & I stayed alone till last train.' (21 April 1900)

Alice did learn to cycle herself and was proud of it – 'I cycled nearly all the way to the station' she wrote but this was at Broughton, only about a mile away. She had always been prepared to drive the pony-cart, though not really with pleasure; she was apt to be a little frightened that the pony might shy or slip and it some- times did. When the motor car arrived, the pony was at first kept on. When it went, Alice's independence at Bro'ton must have been taken away, for there is no suggestion that she ever cycled far or learned to drive the 'motor' as she called it. Will did buy a small 'motor' for Nellie and taught her and Maud to drive. It was a French car called a Zedal with the accelerator on the steering wheel. This I know because later aunt Nellie taught me to drive on it.

Will was the first in all Nottingham to own a car – with the number AU1 – and Alice describes being taken out for drives by him and once going 'so fast that it was rather frightening'. (I have a childhood memory of sitting beside my uncle while he forced the car up to sixty mph along a straight piece of the road between Broughton and Nottingham, with my aunt protesting in the back.)

At this period Will and Nellie had rented a bungalow on the Trent, where they spent summer days and nights and, as an alternative to Broughton, Alice, and sometimes Ben, would go for an evening and even stay for a night. On 8 July 1904, for example, Alice wrote that Ben had been worried and harassed but that, at Will and Nellie's –

> he seemed another man, so happy in the boat & bungalow. We had a grand supper & I slept out of doors; Will too. So lovely & warm & ideal! Will & I woke up under the ash tree soon after 5 am & went a heavenly walk across fields & spinneys & dew & early sunshine ...

Alice had her fill there of the outdoor life she so craved at this period and it included evening parties, music, reading aloud – George Meredith's *Egoist* is mentiond – interestng company and conversation. This account is full of happiness –

> to the bungalow, where they had Mr Ellenberger & his string quintett playing Brahms all evening on the balcony ... Maud, Nellie & I slept out of doors on our mattresses. Woke early & went up the hill in dressing gown to meet the morning. Then an early walk with my dear Will. Then a bathe all four together in river, so lovely! And with a pair of blown up 'wings' I could swim quite safely!! (19 and 20 July 1905)

About this time too, Alice mentions that Mrs Weekley (the

PORTRAIT OF BEN BY ARNSBY BROWN, C. 1907

future Mrs Frieda Lawrence) came to dinner and that it was a pleasant but not especially interesting evening (9 March 1905). She can have had no inkling of Will's affair with Mrs Weekley, which I learned of for the first time in Janet Byrne's *A Genius for Living*. (My eldest sister and I certainly used to play with the Weekley children and, wishing to test the authenticity of the story, I have recently had the pleasure of talking once again – after some ninety years – to the youngest and only survivor of the Weekley children over the telephone from Italy where she now lives.

Photography was another great interest at the time. Will and

215

Bernard were devotees and members of the Nottingham photographic club and Hester, too, took it up. All three produced beautiful pictures and some survive to demonstrate as much. A newspaper cutting from the *Daily Mail*, dated 25 September 1899, describes an exhibition of the 'photographic salon at the Dudley Gallery [in London?] which ends: 'A birch glade in Sherwood Forest' by Mr W.E. Dowson has almost the quality and delicacy of refinement of a Corot.'

In those days, developing and printing was done in ones own dark room and I can remember the thrill of seeing the picture gradually appear on the glass plate under the developing liquid.

The first mention of Switzerland for winter holidaying was, I think, in 1901 when a family party of Will and Nellie, Maud, Tom and the twins went to Grindelwald for skiing. After this, Alice mentions their going out several years running but, tantalisingly, though she refers to letters from them, says nothing of what they may have said about the pleasures and problems of the new sport of skiing.

How did the women manage to ski with those long skirts right down to the ground? Contemporary photographs show that they did continue to wear them. Reading the diaries, one realises that women's dress in those days hampered them in all physical activities; its interference with quick movement may well, for example, have been one of the reasons why Alice did not feel quite at home driving the pony or – as she admitted – on the yacht, without a man.

On 20 February 1902 the sale of the yacht for £640 was reported without comment either of regret or approval. They had been considering for some weeks whether to sell and Alice had noted that Maud would feel it most. No doubt the continuation of the Boer War which depressed Ben even more than Alice would have produced a ready climate for the sale of the yacht but, in any case, the times when it could be used must have decreased a good deal with Rob and Hester both away and the younger sons perhaps keener on cricket and tennis: Bernard and his partner won the

Nottingham tennis tournament about this time and I notice the first mention on 8 May 1901 of ping-pong – 'Bernard brought Madge Bradley in for ping-pong'. Ping-pong is recorded as having been very popular from 1899 to 1904.

The telephone, first mentioned in Alice's diary in 1901, must still have been an expensive item since Hubert and Lina (recently married and well off) had a telephone and Alice did not: she wrote that in order to call the doctor, 'I cycled up to Hubt's to telephone' (29 November 1901).

When Rob had left to take up his first job in South Africa, Maud had gone with him to help him settle in. Though she had only a short time there, the journey by sea each way meant an absence of more than two months and according to Alice, both she and Maud had dreaded this. When Maud returned, Alice wrote – 'Oh what a joyful moment it was. All so excited ... we quite forgot the 1st April!' (4 April 1899). But was it? Can it have been such a joyful moment for Maud, young, pretty and very ready to join in the normal activities and pleasures of youth? What a thrill the whole expedition must have been for her, going out to South Africa with her brother and having the fun of the voyage to and fro. Indeed, in a letter written from the boat on the way home, she says – 'I really don't know when I have enjoyed myself so much'. How is it that Alice did not see it that way? I find the answer in her 'Commonplace Book' in which she says how much she disliked Rob's decision to go and work in South Africa – 'a horrible wicked place' – and that she believed that Maud felt the same way but would not confide in her mother about it –

> Our sweet precious fierce Maud goes with him. She feels it so much but indulges in no expression or sentiment with *me*. This silence between us is v hard for me. Sometimes I have dreadful seizures of jealousy and longings that tear my heart.

But for this outpouring of feeling, I should have felt critical of Alice for not realising that Maud might be expected to see her return as the regretted end to a splendid holiday, rather than as a happy home-coming.

Dependent as Alice had become on Maud, she had been accustomed to be 'in the driving seat'. But Maud was now in her 30th year. It was inevitable that tensions and misunderstandings should develop between these two generations bound together so closely both at work and at home.

I think that Maud has to be seen as the tragic figure in Alice's family, an example of the nineteenth century sacrifice of the daughter to her parents' needs which is idealised by Victorian novelists. She had the satisfactions of being a second mother to her sister's children and she was a much loved aunt to her other nieces, but she was undoubtedly a person of very considerable intellectual potential who was never given the chance to flower.

In her Commonplace Book, Alice shows that she is well aware of Maud's intellect and feels the gulf between them but not its inevitability – 'I don't know how to say how I wonder at and worship her. She thinks so much and such beautiful thoughts when I get a peep at them'. But –

> She is hard to please. ... There is such an element of artistic and strange wandering into new fields I cannot follow. ... It seems to upset so much I have always thought good. If Maud could find someone to fill her life, how thankful (I think) I should be!

In that 'I think' – so typically honest of Alice – lies the rub. To what extent is it fair to say that she took Maud for granted as the daughter-at-home? Certainly she must not take all the blame. Partly, there was the accepted social tradition; partly, the care of daughters for mother was also a firm family tradition – in the diaries, this responsibility is one of the most strongly emphasised duties, appearing sometimes even to outweigh, for Alice, the temporary claims of children and husband. But quite as much, I think, it was Maud's own readiness for self-sacrifice which invited and decided the course she took.

There had been a sad family blow in July 1899 when it was learnt that 'the dear sisters are going to leave the old home. Herbert [their eldest brother, now married] wants to live there'; and when Alice left Bollington, she wrote (21 October 1899) that – 'it was as lovely as ever, rooks cawing etc. Too sad to think we shall know it no more.'

Abroad, too, there were depressing happenings at the turn of the century. Ben's letter condemning Russian treatment of Jews has already shown the family attitude to anti-semitism so Alice's sympathy for Dreyfus was to be expected. In 1898 she had noted 'the great excitement in France about the Dreyfus affair, all sorts of forgeries having been committed' (3 September 1898) and in the last days of the century she wrote of 'the shameful decision on the Dreyfus case', that – 'All the world is on his side, except France.' (9 September 1899)

But her chief interest abroad had to be in the threat, and then the actuality, of war in South Africa. England's fortunes were at their lowest ebb at the end of 1899, with three main towns, Kimberley, Ladysmith and Mafeking, under siege; and 'B was very low-spirited about the war.'

No doubt because they now had a family interest in the Transvaal, the shadow of the coming Boer War had fallen upon Alice and Ben months before it broke out. As early as 27 March 1899, Alice had gone to a 'peace' meeting called by the Mayor of Nottingham, where both Mr Ellis and Mr Stead had spoken but Alice had to report that – 'to our disgrace, there were hardly any of the gentry there'. She doesn't say what peace was being discussed but a later entry (8 June) makes this clear – 'Alas the Kruger-Milner conference, which tried to settle the Transvaal differences, has failed – what will follow now!' Sir Alfred Milner was then Governor of Cape Colony and High Commissioner for South Africa.

In August, they were on holiday with the yacht in Torquay and she refers to 'a little domestic fracas which was rather upsetting'. Again, we learn from an entry on the 29th that this was a difference of opinion with Ben about the coming war – 'B & I are very anxious about the war, but luckily agree now about it. We wrote to several people & the paper to protest against Chamberlain's speech of Saturday.'

One of the letters had been to their MP, Mr Ellis (husband of Alice's friend, Maria Ellis). In a reply to Ben, marked 'private' and dated 30 August 1899, he wrote that 'too much importance should not be attributed to Mr Chamberlain's utterances', that what was needed is for 'old Kruger's mind' to move more quickly and 'I agree with all you say as to the unpolicy – nay wickedness – of war.' (A single petal stuck on the blotting paper opposite this diary entry, against which she has written – 'from a rose given to me at breakfast by B.D' – shows, I think, how deep were their feelings over this difference of opinion.)

Their anxiety about their son Rob was relieved by a telegram on the 3 October telling them that he had reached Capetown. He arrived home after midnight on the 21 October – 'escorted by the 5 brothers & sisters' and 'we talked & talked till nearly 4.0'c.'

In a long account to the local paper and enclosed in Alice's diary, Rob described his uncomfortable experiences in the flight of British subjects from Johannesburg on 29 September. This was well before the actual outbreak of war but the Boers had already taken over the railway and most of the rolling stock for transporting their troops, leaving only four carriages for passengers on the night train for the Cape; these were fully occupied by women and children and everyone else had to travel in open coal trucks – Rob counted between fifty and sixty in his; there was no food or drink and early in the journey 'a tremendous thunderstorm, accompanied by torrents of rain, broke over us'. He seems to have been more or less ill for some months after this ordeal and he did not return to South Africa until September 1900.

Alice reported almost daily on the war during the autumn of 1899 and, as always, her chief concern was with the suffering: 'the news of battles & wounds is very dreadful' and 'the war news very sad & harrowing' (23 and 25 October) 'the war news overshadows all else' (3 November), and, on 21 November, 'our troops hemmed in ... there has been a lot of slaughter'.

Not unnaturally, Rob was 'very anti-Boer', which must have produced some awkward discussions with his parents, though nothing is said of this in the diary. On his return to South Africa, he enlisted as a lieutenant in the Cape Volunteers.

At the relief of Ladysmith, reported on 1 March 1900, Alice wrote that – 'with her father's permission, Maud bought a big Union Jack & Hester & Alex hung it out. All the town is decorated with flags.' The implication of the reference to 'her father's permission' clearly is that, had the decision been hers, she would not have given it. Her revealing comment as to her own feelings is – 'Oh this war! What questions it raises!' (It is 'family knowledge' that my grandparents were considered to be 'pro-Boer' and I learned from my cousin Oscar that the same was true of his father, my grandfather's brother Enfield, and his family: cycling in France at the time, he had been shouted at for being anti-Boer and had been able to put himself right with the strongly pro-Boer French.)

It was not until the end of May 1902, that: 'The news of PEACE came – Hurrah, Hurrah! We put up some flags' (2 June). A newspaper cutting is enclosed opposite this page of the diary which must have given Alice very special pleasure; it gives an account of Kitchener's visit to the Boer camp, following the conclusion of peace when –

> he congratulated them on the good fight they had made and said it was no disgrace to be defeated by overwhelming force. [He] ... welcomed them as citizens of the great empire and hoped they would do their duty to it loyally as they had to the old State ...'

In the early 1900s, Alice did not fail to note in her diary the attack on the Peking Legation and the assassination of the King of Italy, both in 1900, nor the 'horrible massacre of the King and Queen of Serbia' in 1903. But normally her feelings were personally engaged only where family were involved, as in South Africa, or she found

221

something to praise or condemn in the actions of governments. Thus, she joined with others in pressing for a meeting 'to protest against the Balkan massacres, which are truly awful' (September 1903), was 'v. excited by Japan's generous terms for peace' with defeated Russia (30 August 1905) and was instinctively on the side of the Russian people and against the Czar, in the revolutionary rumblings of 1905 – 'Dreadful news of a massacre in St. Petersburg, the military firing on the unarmed peaceful crowds of strikers – the cowardly Czar in hiding' (23 January), and 'the Grand Duke Sergius is assassinated! and a good thing too!' (17 February). But, after the defeat of the Russian fleet in May, doubts crept in for a time – perhaps because she could not help feeling that revolution and mutiny were unpatriotic? 'News fr Russia is very bad (or good?) a sort of revolution (& massacres) at Odessa & a big battleship has mutinied' (5 July).

By November, however, her sympathies are very firmly back with the workers –

> Martial law proclaimed in Poland tho' there is no excuse for it (15 November). The Russian affairs are worse than ever! The Govt having declared martial law (to provoke excesses) St Petersburg has struck work & everything is in an awful state!

Her niece, Ethel (Ronalds) was in St Petersburg at this time, as governess to some of the young aristocrats. This would have given Alice a personal interest in what was happening and she reported having one of Ethel's letters from St Petersburg 'abt the revolt' sent to her to read. Unfortunately, she says nothing of its contents.

Illnesses due to the common cold and to migraine (though not so-called) were unchanging and quite as bad and frequent at the turn of the century as they had been in earlier years. It was by no means unusual for most of the household to be ill or ailing at the same time – 'Bernard in bed all day and v. shaky. B at the office again but not right. I am also a poor thing & M too' (3 May 1898).

Toothache too was a continuing scourge, for which the treatment seems to have been to take the teeth out rather than to save them. Felix had all his teeth out in 1898 when he was twenty 'because it seemed the only thing to do', though he was a healthy young man who had recently got a 'blue' for football at Oxford; and Maud paid three or four visits to the doctor in quick succession having two or three teeth out each time. No reasons are given in either case. Dental skills, as well as patient expectation, were less in those days. In particular, the only form of anaesthetic normally available until early in the twentieth century, at any rate outside London, was to render the patient unconscious with gas and this must have meant that stopping teeth was less often acceptable because of the pain. In any case, dental patients in those days seem to have been readier to accept pain than we are now. Maud was not the only one to have her teeth out without gas. Alice reports (9 February, 1910) that their maid Fanny 'had 18 stumps out, w'out gas! & did not seem much the worse!'

In the 1890s influenza epidemics had been added to the list of frequent illnesses. On New Year's Eve 1899, Alice had Hubert ill in bed with influenza with a temperature of 104 and wrote that – 'The Medleys have influenza & Esher & Starston & the Pooles & the E. Enfields and $^1/_2$ the people we know ...'

But at Christmas she had been able to report her grown up family unchanged and as united as ever – 'A good muster. All ten children together once more! ... for 2.0'c dinner and presents which were v numerous and successful'.

223

CHAPTER 14

Grandmother Alice

'Hester, Bimbi & Bay came ... to keep the old grandparents company into the New Year.'

IN THE year that began with the death of Queen Victoria, little Alice, married at just nineteen and now the mother of ten grown-up children, became a grandmother with the birth of her eldest daughter's first child.

She recorded the 'general anxiety' about the Queen (20 January 1901) and the precise date and time of death – 6.20 p.m. – and of the news arriving in the papers – about 9.30 (22 January) and, the following day, that 'all felt very full of the dear Queen of course, everyone goes into mourning'.

In 1910, she would report quite enthusiastically on the splendid funeral of Edward VII –

> The grt day of the King's funeral. I suppose there never was such a pageant before in all the world ... Ben & I & the servants went to church here ... processions everywhere today ... Maud & the other 3 eventually got good places for the procession [in London].

There is no sign in either case of the very personal feeling for royalty that she had had as a young woman – in which she had been by no means alone.

There had been two family weddings in 1900, Hubert's to Lina Bourne on 17 July and Hester's on 5 December. It must have pleased Alice that Hubert's wedding was at High Pavement Chapel, since this was the Unitarian chapel supported and attended by her and Ben. She describes how –

> Maud, Felix & B came early from Bro'ton bringing heaps of flowers & most of us were all morning at chapel decorating till it

looked *ex*quisite ... Tom was best man ... Hubert looked so happy ... Maud & Hilda [Greg niece who would later marry Gerard] very pretty bridesmaids.

Hester's wedding had to be in Malta because her husband was a Royal Navy surgeon on his ship there and he was refused leave to come to England. His father – an Irish Protestant would have nothing to do with a son who insisted on marrying a Roman Catholic. So no one from the Kilroy side of the family went to the wedding.

The voyage out to Malta by sea – parents, Maud, and Alice's two sisters, Katie and Isobel – was very rough, all except Ben being prostrate in their berths practically the whole way. The party arrived much shaken on 2 December and the wedding, arranged for 4 December had to be postponed for a day to allow them time to recover. Inevitably, it was a small affair as they knew no one in Malta, 'a reception of about 35, mostly naval men in uniform & their wives, such a nice set' & they left again on the following day – 'of course we had left our hearts behind us'.

Earlier in the year, there had been a sorrow for Alice in the sudden and quite unexpected death of her much loved eldest sister, Amy, who had died in London at the house of a relative, nursed by her two sisters. Alice reached her the day before her death and she wrote that 'our dear Amy fell asleep while all we sisters were with her'. As usual, she marked an emotional occasion by pressing a flower in her diary – in this case a still well-preserved freesia, against which she has written – 'a bit of the fresia we had put in Amy's bedroom, March 14, her last visit to us. She loved the scent of it. Emily kept it for me.' (25 March 1900)

At the beginning of 1901, in her summary of her family, Alice records that only Maud and Bernard were now living at home – 'such a reduced little party'; that 'Hubert & Lina are a *very* happy thought, they come to us every 3rd Sunday & otherwise on Saturday evenings', and that there are frequent letters from 'poor little Hester' who had been ill in Naples on her honeymoon.

So it cannot have been quite a surprise when a letter, and then a telegram, came from Lancelot to say Hester was ill and depressed and – 'it would be a great relief if mother could come'. She left at once, of course, this time travelling overland to Marseilles and thence by ship to Valletta, taking only five days. She had to stay six weeks.

It became very hot in Malta during May and it seems, in any case, to have been taken for granted by Lancelot that his wife would go home to England during the heat of the summer – (it was I believe the expected thing for all naval wives then). But she was so weak and ill that Alice was much relieved when Lancelot got leave to travel with them as far as Marseilles; Alice describes Hester being 'carried on board like a corpse, in an invalid cot by 8 soldiers'. They were met at Calais by Ben, in London by Maud and by Bernard, Nellie and Will in Nottingham. 'Oh how happy we were'.

The heat, the always attendant headaches, and the sheer hard work of nursing all those weeks and then packing up for departure, plus the overall worry about Hester's health, including some disagreements about treatment with her doctor husband, took their toll on Alice's health. She developed an unidentified illness with a high temperature that might, they thought, have been Malta fever, and was so ill that their doctor (Miss Gray) came every day and the order went out that Alice was not to be allowed to be worried about anything. For a time, she wasn't even allowed to write letters and was prevented from seeing her two sisters because the arrangements for them to leave Bollington and find somewhere else to live had caused a family quarrel with their brother Herbert and Alice found this upsetting: 'Herbert's attitude is very sad ... I felt very shaken'. 'We are full of pity for them and indignation elsewhere' (17 and 20 July 1901).

The family quarrel took time to heal and it would be some years before Alice went back to Bollington in happiness. When she went next she was received by Herbert's wife, Herbert happening to be away. But in May 1910, Alice paid a two-day visit to The Mount when she was received more kindly. While there, she went to see a number of people she knew in the village. Being the rememberer that she was, of people, birthdays and places, it could not but have been a sad occasion. 'I wandered in garden,' she wrote, 'first alone, & then w Herbert ... Oh the ghosts that hang around'.

She took time to recover from her illness. She had planned a resolution about district nursing which was clearly important to her but it had to be arranged for someone else to look after it – 'I can't do even what I used to could', she writes charmingly (30 October 1901).

However, in these early years of the century, she continued to work for the L.V.R.S. and to visit many poor homes at Broughton. And another 'cause' is mentioned in 1901 that has not appeared in the diaries before but ties in very naturally with Alice's other interests – 'Nellie & I in morning to Police court as requested by the temperance people. We looked after some of the cases till dinner time' (25 February 1901).

The first grandchild was born at 'Felixstowe' on 24 November 1901. She was given a string of names – Winifrede (for unknown reasons) Maud (for Hester's much loved sister) Greg (for Alice) Mary (for religion) – but she was always called 'Bimbi'. My mother must have thought this was Maltese for baby. Alice's diary entries about the arrival are not of delight but of staff worries; a day or two before she had written that 'Cook & parlourmaid are both leaving us middle of December, too bad of them & v worrying to find new ones!' On the day of the birth, there is only the comment that 'Hester became ill as soon as Miss Hendrie [Hester's friend who came as monthly nurse] & two maids were off to church'. The household was fairly large in any case, so with the addition of Hester, the new baby and nurse, it is not surprising that they all felt 'pretty tired' and that 'poor Emily had to succumb & go to bed, for once!' They sent a wire twice a day to Lancelot in Malta, overseas telephone of course not yet being available.

In contrast to her own elaborate celebrations for the first of her children, Alice found Bimbi's christening very unsatisfactory –

Hester and I took baby to the Cathedral to be christened. Mrs D acted godmother for Maud. It was a cheerless service. (30 December)

The second grandchild, Hubert's son, was born on 25 July 1902: 'B bro't news that Lina has a son. Hurrah!' and next day, 'just saw Baby & Lina for a minute & dear old Hubert, who says Baby's name is to be Benjamin!' Given Ben's pride in being the fourth Benjamin, it is surprising that none of his eight sons was given that name.

Anti-vivisection Committees and functions appear as frequently in the early 1900s as in the last years of the nineteenth century. They were more often attended by Ben than by Alice though she remained as involved as ever. On 19 November 1903, she wrote –

Oh dear the vivisection trial is given against Mr Coleridge, w. £2000 damages! How disgraceful! I did feel dashed abt it, & Ben & Bernard were also horrified.

Coleridge was the secretary of the Anti-Vivisection Society involved in a libel action in what became known as The Brown Dog Affair. Two Swedish girls who were medical students in London had published a book, *The Shambles of Science*, in 1903, about the sufferings of a brown terrier dog in the laboratories of London University Hospital – the same place, of course, that Hester's letter had complained of – and Coleridge had made a public statement about the case, naming two scientists. No wonder Alice and Ben were horrified. Even now, I cannot bring myself to read the detail of what was being done to dogs in England in the year of my birth.

The treatment of animals had also always been a major concern of sister Isobel (Sibbie), who later, despite a heart-attack, would

228

relax 'none of her work & efforts for animals' (Alice's summary report of their family 1910).

In this year of 1903, however Alice had a new cause – anti-vaccination. She had noted (19 March 1902) that Bimbi had been vaccinated 'as Lancelot wished', attended a two-day conference in London on the subject in March 1903 and then, in October, was very upset when Bernard was forced by his insurance company to be vaccinated –

> The silly Insurance Co. won't insure him unless, except at a cost of £3.10.0. a yr extra!!! What tyranny! So B has decided after v.m. deliberation, to be done, alas!

As usual, her diary gives no reasons for her views but fortunately there is a copy of a letter she wrote to the press about it. Signed 'A.D.' and undated but included in the September section of the 1905 diary, it is written in support of the '35 brave men who are to be imprisoned in Derby for following their honest consciences' and argues that 'many feel that medical attention is too much concentrated on vaccination in place of, as we think, far cleaner & safer methods' and 'the recent "scares" about smallpox appear to many of us as [being] as trivial & paltry as they are misleading'.

The 35 men had been arrested for refusing to have their children vaccinated against smallpox and they served seven days in prison.

In May 1904 Alice became very agitated because Albert (her old flame) was in hospital and 'might have to have an operation'. It was thought to be serious and he was moved to Watford where Alice, who happened to be in London, planned to visit him but got a wire advising her not to go. She clearly expected the worst for she writes that – 'I had *v.m.* wished to see Albert once more. I felt quite collapsed! 'The same evening however, she learnt that he was out of hospital and had had no operation.

This is the first mention that I have found anywhere in the diary of any member of Alice or Ben's families going to hospital, except for Hester, who of course was already a practising nurse in hospital when she became ill. One or two cases appear in the diary of people going to hospital for surgery (e.g. cancer of the tongue) but there is no example in Alice's or Ben's extended families of anyone going for illness or for birth or death. So far as I can gather, this attitude to the use of hospitals also applied in the previous generation; it certainly extended forward to my generation, in so far that my sister's and my adenoids were operated on in our bathroom. Of this occasion Alice wrote only that –'Maud went "to help Hester thro" the operation for adenoids. At $^1/_4$ to 1, I got a wire that it was well over, poor dears!' This happening is one of my earliest memories – I see myself walking along the passage to our bathroom and finding it made strange by a table covered with a sheet on which something is to be done to me and my sister. I don't remember feeling any fear. The presence of my mother and aunt must have made me confident.

The problems involved in finding, organising and keeping staff had not got any less as the years passed. Though Alice moved some of the maids about between her two houses, she had to maintain a skeleton staff at each and there was a housekeeper for Broughton, Emily being housekeeper at 'Felixstowe'. As always, day-to-day household problems could be intrusive and embarassing when, as so often now, there were guests. Alice mentions one occasion when they had a little-known guest and – 'our drains being up are a dreadful smell & bother. I am also worried looking for a successor cook and p'md and – 'I *can not* get a cook!'. I take 'p'md' to be 'parlourmaid'. Over the years, Alice developed a very personal brand of shorthand for her diary, which grew shorter and shorter. For example, 'I p.m.t'd w M.E.' translates as 'I to afternoon tea with Mary Enfield'.

Spring-cleaning which took place regularly each year in May or early June was a good deal more complete than would be at all likely nowadays. I have already mentioned that it included 'white-washing' which, judging from the following, must have been for

ENVELOPE FROM 1905 DIARY

on which Alice has jotted down her time-table and food for Christmas. The children staying in the house were Hester's four, the youngest (Angela) only a month old.

the kitchen and scullery walls – 'V. busy in kitchen depts white-washing and cleaning – *such* a mess! but all good tempered' (22 March 1904). Indeed Alice explains an extended visit in London as 'They are re-papering & cleaning ... & are glad for me to stay away a bit longer' (11 May 1904).

The diary entries for the 1905 spring-cleaning show what a great amount of work must have been involved: 'Began spring cleaning' (4 May), 'Spring cleaning still going on in full force (15 May), 'We have lunch in town just now for the servants spring cleaning convenience' (17 May), 'Spring cleaning drawing to an end at last!' (22 May), and 'our servants all had a holiday & picnic together to Belvoir' (30 May).

Relations with her staff were not invariably happy and, as always, Alice was made unhappy when they were not. She still did not hesitate to correct when she found a fault which – to her surprise – could still lead to the corrected one giving notice; and there could, too, be a general malaise. The following quotes for the years 1900 to 1906 encapsulate through Alice the situation between mistress and staff at this time: the health and resilience of the mistress, her general attitude to her staff and her organising ability and the help of the daughter left at home –

A dinner party for 12, including the Kitcheners went off v.w. we thought in spite of the dinner being hardly cooked! (13 February 1900)
My new cook gave notice. (17 February) [I expect she got told off.]
The servants seem depressed, tired & sullen, which weighs on me. (9 January 1903) [Hester and monthly nurse in expectation of another baby had been added to the usual household.]
Got some domestic talk done satisfactorily. A great relief. (16 March)
We had Mrs C (charwoman). This poor old cook can't get thro' the work a bit. I am rather in despair, can hear of noone at all suitable. (4 April 1903)
I am cook hunting again! But I am so well it does not matter. (20 May)
Cooks and servants make me v busy. (24 April 1904)
My domestic affairs have gone wonderfully but needed some management!! (11 July)
All are drefful busy ... Maud seeming like 3 people instead of one. (21 & 22 December 1906)

For a year or two, staff problems appear less often in the diaries but in 1910 they are again very troublesome, the difficulty being not in keeping those she has but in finding replacements: almost every other day in August and early September, she refers to writing high and low, and interviewing in Melton Mowbray, Nottingham and

Salcombe in her search for a cook to replace one who is leaving, after seven years, to get married and also in her attempt to find a servant and a governess for Hester's household.

In 1910 (and again in 1912) Alice mentions 'our old servants' party' as though referring to an established annual occasion. But it is not clear when the practice began.

> In afternoon we had our old servants' party, Lizzie Beckett, Hannah & Nellie, Tacy Milne (McAig that was), & Sally Mrs. Davis. Ada Ede & Mrs. Amy Peacock & Mrs Clayton must come another time. It went off v well from 4 to 8.30 & all enjoyed it. The 5 children & Hester were a great help & pleasure. (26 July)

In November 1904, Alice became, for a short time, what I call an active grandmother. This was because Hester went to Bermuda to set up house for her husband while his ship was there and felt able to take with her only Bimbi and baby Robin who had been born only four months before, on 27 June. So I had to be left behind in my grandmother's charge – as always of course in my aunt's and Emily's as well. I was my mother's second child, born on 2 February 1903 and christened Alix, for my grandmother, and Hester, for my mother, but called 'Bay' in the family.

Hester and her two babies left for Bermuda on 9 November, Ben going with them to support them during the voyage – 'Little Bay settles down happily,' Alice wrote but 'Poor Maud, parting with Bimbi'. So Maud was already beginning her role of being second mother to her sister's children. In fact, this period of grandmotherly responsibility lasted only four months because, within weeks of Hester's arrival in Bermuda, Lancelot's ship was ordered home and the little family arrived back in England on 7 April 1905. 'Maud and I took Bay down to station to meet Hester and two children. Such a happy meeting ... Bimbi looked prettier and sweeter than ever.'

For the time being, the Broughton house was handed over to

Hester so she now became the hostess and Alice the visitor there – 'The children bewitching and Hester such a clever natty hostess and housekeeper,' Alice wrote (4 May) and, a month later, she described 'a beautiful Sunday, so peaceful and sunny, Hester and the dear chicks, Ben and me,' and enclosed a pressed flower – a clover head – 'from my dear little Bay at Broughton' (4 June).

Alice's opening summary for the year 1905 ends with the statement that 'Ben is in pretty fair case & I also, considering our age' (Alice was now sixty). But, though that year also contains the statement that 'the glamour of cricket is over for me' (31 May) – a remarkable statement for this cricket-mad family – she has not lost her enthusiasm for trying to put right what she thinks is wrong, or for the enjoyment of life.

She is excited by the election of Campbell-Bannerman's Liberal Government in December 1905, especially since her friend Mrs Medley's brother, Austin Birrell, was made president of the Board of Education. He was a famous wit and would be chief secretary for Ireland from 1908 to 1916.In 1906, Alice wrote –

> Mr Birrell bro't his Education Bill into the H of C before a brilliant & distinguished audience; a great excitement for Emily Medley who was there. A very good speech. (9 April)

I have perhaps not said enough about Alice's friends; she had only four important ones outside the family, two school friends – Fanny Bibby (who had died in middle age) and Sarah Courtauld – and two friends acquired through her political interests and activities – Emily Medley and Maria Ellis. In her early married life, Alice's numerous family supplied most of her social life in Nottingham – her sisters who so often came to stay, her aunts and a cousin of her own age, Mary Enfield, who lived at Lenton. But as time went on, her two political friends took on increased importance; quite often they came to stay a few days with her and when she could get away from her family responsibilities, she went for relaxed luxurious short holidays with them.

Mary Ellis's husband died suddenly on 1 December 1910, only a day or two after he had unexpectedly announced his retirement from Parliament. He came of a Quaker family and had been a Nottingham MP and a supporter of the suffrage cause for many years. Alice was fond of him too and she was clearly hurt when she reported, on 30 December, that 'Maria Ellis has now written to Emily Medley & me, for the 1st time since her husband's death.'

Sarah Courtauld had died in 1906 – 'the true friend of 47 years' Alice wrote (10 April). At the time, little Bimbi was at 'Felixstowe' with an attack of whooping cough, which may explain why Alice did not go either to the cremation in London or to the memorial service in Braintree. She was comforted by the letters of sympathy she received especially by one from Sarah's daughter, Renee, telling her that her mother 'was very peaceful at the last, after long waiting'.

Fortunately, Alice still had her two political friends and in this same year 1907, when so much else was happening, she joined them in London for the memorial meeting for Mrs Josephine Butler, following it with a happy day together – 'I lunched at the Ellis's. Only Maria there & Emily Medley who was staying there. We did have a delightful cosy day! We talked on end for five hours.'

The two years, 1906 and 1907, were years of great change and great activity for Alice and Ben: they went on a long holiday abroad which they called their second honeymoon; they handed over their Nottingham house to Will and Nellie and retired to Broughton; and they acquired a house at Salcombe in South Devon which, a hundred years later, is still owned by a member of the family and has been a joy to generation after generation of its children. The Salcombe house, Tourelle, was later bought but at first it was rented at £120 a year and the cost shared amongst the family in £10 shares: Alice took five, the twins two each, and Ben, Maud and Felix one each – but the work of getting the house ready fell almost entirely on Ben and Maud.

The first occupation was an occasion of real excitement for Alice. There was nothing in the house except beds when they arrived, so they stayed the first few days in an hotel. When finally they moved into the house, Alice's enthusiasm is patent –

> We had a carriage & brot all our traps up to settle there! Oh how exciting and delightful ... luckily the table came in time! A lovely nearly full moon, a sunset, & birds, & *rooks* about! What riches & beauty!' (27 March 1907)

While they are still enjoying this first Tourelle holiday, Alice wrote that – 'Alex & Bernard have bought a little motor car! B & Will are to fetch it from London this week – great excitement thereat of course' (3 April). The twins still lived at home and, apart from the natural excitement of owning a motor car – which I note had to be fetched from London – may have had the move to Broughton in mind.

So large a move naturally took several days and for most of their belongings (including Rollie, their dog) it came a day or two later. Last of all came Emily and the cat. The move was especially painful for Emily who had always been based in Nottingham – 'Poor Emily finds it hard to settle down in a new home, but is trying her best & we do all we can to smooth it for her' (22 June 1907). Alice needed comfort herself. The Broughton house had come to mean peace and rural delight but, for Alice, the move meant also some degree of retirement and loss of her established social life. In the daily diary she wrote bravely of – 'the great day of our move to Bro'ton' – but confessed to her Commonplace Book that 'it was a very great wrench' and the following year, that – 'I can't help feeling that we did not sufficiently realise what it would mean for ourselves & others, and that we ought to have considered it more before deciding to make the move'. Alice-like, she looked at once for the bright flip-side – 'the thing is to make the most of life in this beautiful home'.

The Josephine Butler meeting had set up a committee to consider what could be done to carry on her work. Alice was a

SULNEY FIELDS
the house at Broughton

member and this involved her in going to London for the day during the move from Nottingham to Broughton. She does not say what happened at the meeting. Two years later (1909), however, she reported going with Mrs Medley, to a 'State Regn' committee meeting at the Caxton Hall in London and again, in 1910, she went with Emily Medley to 'our "Ladies National" committee which was a long & interesting one' (5 April). In the absence of any other such national body having been referred to, I think it likely that these were other names for the 1907 committee and must be linked to the active Josephine Butler Society of today, which traces its origins back to 1870.

Now that the permanent numbers in the household had shrunk to the two of them, Maud and the twins, Alice continued very much to keep open house and invite many to stay. In 1905, the count was thirty-one, in addition to occasional overnight stays by the 'marrieds' (Will and Nellie and Gerard and Hilda – Hubert and Lina less often) and, of course, Hester and her five children.

It is clear from many entries in the diaries that Hester and her children were a special concern and charge on the grandparents in these early years of the twentieth century. This was partly because they had no settled home, their father being usually away on his ship and a naval surgeon's salary being small; and partly because Hester had some serious illnesses when her husband was away and Alice had to go and look after her. Lancelot was able to provide a family home when had a shore job, as at Sheerness or Plymouth, but mostly they lived at Tourelle or at the Broughton house or at a rented house in or near Broughton village or in Nottingham. So, they came to regard their grandparents' home as more home than anywhere else.

Little Ben too, was a frequent and enthusiastic visitor to Broughton after the grandparents moved from Nottingham but they were short stays of a night or two, since he had a settled home of his own. 'He is a charming & happy boy,' Alice wrote (8 March 1910) and she described his grandfather having 'a fine bonfire for the children to their huge delight!'

Alice and Ben spent Easter 1910 with Hester and her family at Tourelle and they both joined the children on their quite strenuous expeditions; by then Ben was seventy-three and Alice sixty-five. In August, they and Maud had a holiday at Salcombe with Hubert and Lina and their little Ben and Molly. 'Ben was greatly in love with his grandchildren,' Alice wrote in her Commonplace Book.

During this same year 1910, Alice went often to Nottingham for the committees of her various causes, including women's suffrage, and is a conscientious visitor amongst the sick or poor in Broughton village. She was also arguing for a Sunday post – and got it – and they were planning to get a hot-water supply upstairs. (I can remember hip baths and hot water brought up to the bedrooms in containers like outdoor watering cans.)

BEN AND ALICE
with the eight grandchildren born before the Golden Wedding

Much as Alice enjoyed the frequent visits from the grandchildren and the many adult tennis and other parties, she found that 'the constant large parties & comings & goings tho' very *nice*, are *rather* hard work' (4 August 1910) and when they are alone she finds that 'B & I are very cosy in our Derby & Joan condition!' New Year's Eve, however, was an occasion for a large party and she reported that 'every bed was occupied! 14 sleeping here. We sat up to let the New Year in.' Opening the front door to let in the New Year was a family tradition which I, for one, still follow.

CHAPTER 15

Mainly Women's Suffrage

'The Women's Suffrage Bill was "talked out" again! We do feel angry – furious – with our craven MPs'

THE WOMEN'S Suffrage cause occurs again and again in Alice's diaries from the 1870s onwards. In a sense it was the background to all her political activity but she does not say what her position was in relation to the local Women's Suffrage Society until, in February 1894, she is appointed secretary of the Nottingham branch.

Before this, she clearly occupied a prominent position locally, since she mentions being about to give a paper on Women's Suffrage to 'their' W.L.A. in April 1892, and that it was cancelled following the debate in the House of Commons on Women's Suffrage on 27 April when she considered that 'Mr Gladstone and "the party" have behaved very ill in opposing it'; there followed her shock on hearing next day (29 April) that 'the majority (anti-suffrage) of the W.L. Federation have resigned!!! What will be done now!' The debate was on the second reading of the Parliamentary Franchise (Extension to Women) Bill. Gladstone had voted against Women's Suffrage as early as 1870 but on this occasion, he had gone further and sent an open letter supporting the arguments of one of the opposing MPs.

Alice's local importance in the movement was made still clearer in June next year, by her being the only delegate to the local W.L.A., to hear a report on the meetings of the Women's Liberal Federation in London.

The anti-movement had begun some years earlier with the publication of an article in the prestigious *Nineteenth Century* Review, in June 1889, entitled 'An appeal against female suffrage'. It was signed by 104 influential women, many of them titled. There were several pages of argument, followed by a request from the Editor that more women would come forward, 'who entirely object to

240

mixing themselves up in the coarsening struggles of party political life' and claiming that 'the deliberate opinion of the women readers of the Nineteenth Century might certainly be taken as a fair sample of the educated women of the country'. It ended with the following shortest of short statements of what signatories were being asked to support:

FEMALE SUFFRAGE

The undersigned protest strongly against the proposed Extension of the Parliamentary Franchise to Women, which they believe would be a measure distasteful to the great majority of the women of the country – unnecessary – and mischievous both to themselves and to the State.

In November of the same year, the Central Committee of the National Society for Women's Suffrage issued a one-page, very-much-to-the-point, statement of eight 'Reasons for supporting the Proposed Extension of the Parliamentary Franchise'.

Both these documents are reproduced in Appendixes 2 and 3. The Anti-Suffragist women formed themselves into the 'Women's National Anti Suffrage League' in 1908 and joined with the men in the 'National League for Opposing Woman Suffrage' in 1909.

Alice does not mention the 'anti' statement so there is no means of knowing when she became aware of it; she would have found it additionally objectionable on family grounds, since it is signed by a member of her family, Mrs William Rathbone (Wilson) Greg, the second wife of her father's youngest brother.

After only a year and a half, Alice handed over the secretaryship to her daughter-in-law, Nellie. Partly, no doubt, her reason was ill-health – on the day she announced her decision to go, she wrote that, 'I have been better but today I feel quite poorly and done again'. But it must also have been because she had many other claims on her time and Nellie was ready, willing, enthusiastic and young.'

Apart from her other causes and charities, there were extra

demands on her from her mother's ill health at this particular time:
by a curious chance, her mother had been very ill on the day of
Alice's first annual meeting as secretary – resulting in her having to
go to help her sisters with night nursing – and on the day of the
next (1895), her mother was again ill, in fact died on the very day
of the annual meeting.

Alice's interest and willingness to help the movement remained,
of course, as strong as ever. Though it was Nellie and Maud, not
Alice, who went to Birmingham as delegates at a Suffrage meeting
the following year, she herself went to Mansfield in January 1897 'to
arrange the coming Campaign'. She seems always thereafter to
have retained more responsibility for the organisation of the
Society than would an ordinary member; two years after she ceased
to be secretary, she is having upsetting arguments about the
finances of the Society, 'met Mrs K.W. in town & had another
round with her (sequel to yesterday) re the Suffrage Committee &
paying the bills – v upsetting!'

She had never been one to put herself forward into positions of
public power or performance – although she now had grown-up
daughters, she has confessed to her diary that she is still shy and
unsure of herself in public – and even with the L.V.R.S. of which
she was the inventor and chief implementer, she gets another
woman to take the chair. But at the Nottingham Women's Suffrage
annual meeting in 1900, Nellie did, at last, get her mother-in-law to
take the chair – though how much her thoughts were concentrated
on the business of that meeting may be doubted, for that day a 'dis-
turbing' letter from Hester had been followed by a telegram from
Lancelot saying that they were engaged.

In 1905 and 1906, the movement had had the disappointment of
having pro-suffrage resolutions and Bills 'talked out' in the House
of Commons in spite of the election in 1906 of a Liberal
government, with Austin Birrell in the Cabinet. Alice made no
comment on either event but she had been very much involved
with important family matters in these years – Gerard's wedding,
the eldest grandchild ill with whooping cough, and plans to take

over the Salcombe house and to retire from Nottingham – but she did not cease to concern herself with the suffrage cause and her frustration at the lack of progress under a Liberal Government is expressed in her reference to 'our craven MPs' in the diary entry from March 1907 quoted at the head of this chapter. 'I had v blk specs on' she wrote next day but black spectacles and disappointment notwithstanding, her efforts and those of supporters generally, seem to have been redoubled in 1908: On the 26 February, there was a drawing-room meeting at 'Felixstowe' attended by some 30 ladies, at which Alice proudly boasts that – 'I was in the chair & all my five daughters were there!' This is the first time she has claimed five daughters; it must mean that for once Hester was able to leave her children to be there.

In April, there were two large suffrage meetings in Nottingham – one on the 6th at Circus Hall, 'a great success for which Nellie, Maud & Hilda have been working so hard for long past' and one on the 11th, addressed by Christobel Pankhurst, 'we had 5 sons & 4 daughters there'. And on 7 May, Alice reports that Maud went to Nottingham for an evening meeting addressed by Mrs Pankhurst.

In February (the day after the meeting at which Alice was in the chair) there had been a second reading debate in the House which had been passed by a majority of 179 but, as usual, it had got no further. So it is perhaps not surprising that Alice showed a rare cynicism at Asquith's reply to the deputation of MPs on 23 May 1908, 'Mr Asquith has had a deputation of MPs re suffrage & given a most clever but deceitful reply re'.

Apparently, he had implied that the government would act if it was clear that Women's Suffrage had the strong support of the women of the country. A local newspaper account suggests that the deputation was from MPs who were opposed to women's suffrage and certainly the views of the Anti-Women's Suffrage League which included many Liberals, must have influenced his attitude.

Whether as an answer, or by coincidence, the deputation was followed next month by a great gathering of women in London from all over the country, in support of the extension of the suffrage to women and 30 went from Nottingham. This is Alice's account –

> The grt suffrage day in London. Special trains from all parts of the country. Abt 30 went from Nottingham, including Nellie, Maud, Lina & Hilda. Alex walked in the procession with them helping to carry a banner. It was a memorable affair, 10,000 women, with beautiful banners etc. ... Bertha went [it is presumed from Hereford where she lived] & heaps of other friends ... M sent a wire 'splendid day'. (13 June 1908)

An article in the *Daily Chronicle* dated Monday, 15 June, was lyrical. Treating the gathering as a response to Asquith's reply to the MPs, it says that –

> No answer could be more impressive ... than this imposing pageant of womanhood. It was a microcosm of the womanhood of the nation. ... Distinctions of rank & class were obliterated ... No Statesman can ignore a demand so widely diffused ... It is highly probable that women's suffrage will be submitted to the country at the next General Election ...

But no action followed from the Liberal Government. Alice added – 'SNAKE!' – to her mention of Asquith in her summary of events at the end of that year.

Alice and Maud's suffrage activities in this busy year had also included going to London to be at the great meeting in the Albert Hall on 20 March, to welcome the suffragettes from prison – 'v interesting & inspiring', Alice wrote, 'they collected over £5,000!!! & Mrs Pankhurst & the other released prisoners were present; the speaking was good.' (20 March 1908).

I think it likely that Alice had been invited by Mrs Pankhurst. As already mentioned, she and her daughter both addressed meetings in Nottingham in April and May of this very year.

Militancy is not reckoned to have begun until 1905 and the name 'suffragette' was first coined by the *Daily Mail* in 1906 with the object of belittling them. Their organisation, called the Women's

Social and Political Union, had been set up in Manchester in 1903 with close links with the Independent Labour Party. The W.S.P.U. moved its headquarters from Manchester to London in 1906 and the actions of the militants were most visible in London.

There is no suggestion in Alice's diary that the militants were active in Nottingham and Alice was profoundly shocked over their treatment in prison: 'Our blood was set on fire this morning on seeing in the papers that the suffragettes in prison are being forcibly fed!' Alice wrote. 'Words will not express our bitter indignation. M. wrote at once to the papers' (28 September 1909).

She soon found, however, that everyone did not agree with her and that her friend, Emily Medley, was one of those who took a different view –

the forcible feeding of suffragists is causing a gt deal of indignation, & the papers are pretty well full of it, for or against. Emily Medley does not agree with us about it, & all her indignation is against the militants.

The Medleys now lived in London and, of course, Mrs Medley's brother was in the Cabinet.

Maud's letter to the paper had expressed her sense of shame that 'methods which remind one of Russian doings' should be introduced in Britain –

that women who in no sense can be called criminal ... should be seized upon by men ... gagged and made to submit to what amounts to torture, and this should arouse laughter in the House of Commons, is a disgrace and a blot upon our country. Whatever we may think of the methods of warfare employed by the suffragettes, surely we have by this time evolved some ordinary human sense of compassion. (29 September 1909)

The reference to cruelties in Russia is explained by a diary entry that August – 'Our King & government are actually receiving the

Czar officially, at Cowes, this week, after all the cruelties and butcheries he keeps rewarding!'

Maud's letter had warned that such behaviour 'is likely to arouse the sex warfare which is so much dreaded' and she was particularly aware of the possible spread of violence because, earlier that summer, she had been among those attacked at a public meeting in Nottingham Market Place.

On that occasion, a Mass Meeting in Nottingham to be held by the National Union of Women's Suffrage Societies had been advertised, with Mrs Henry Fawcett, Miss Eleanor Rathbone and Mr Edward Carpenter among the named speakers. The police were informed in advance and promised to be present, but when the time for the meeting arrived, no police were there. Alice would have attended but for a cold. She wrote that –

> the mass meeting, open air in Market Place, was disgraceful riot, owing to want of the police promised us! The ladies were badly hustled, Maud being struck! (5 July 1909)

As hon. sec, Nellie sent a letter to the local paper protesting about the absence of the police. It is not clear how many people managed to speak in the hostile and unruly atmosphere but Alice mentions that Eleanor Rathbone was not able to speak and that Edward Carpenter had been discouraged from being present because, 'some bad accusation against our dear Edward was made'. Presumably this was to do with his suspected homosexuality; he never married but had a male companion, George Merrill, who lived with him for 30 years until he died. Mr Carpenter was probably more of a socialist than Alice would have approved but he was a man of great personal charm and wrote pamphlets on vivisection and other subjects that would have appealed to her.

Alice reports that there were meetings next day (no doubt not open air) at which Mrs Fawcett and Eleanor Rathbone both spoke. No doubt Edward Carpenter too; he and Eleanor Rathbone were Will and Nellie's guests at Felixstowe.

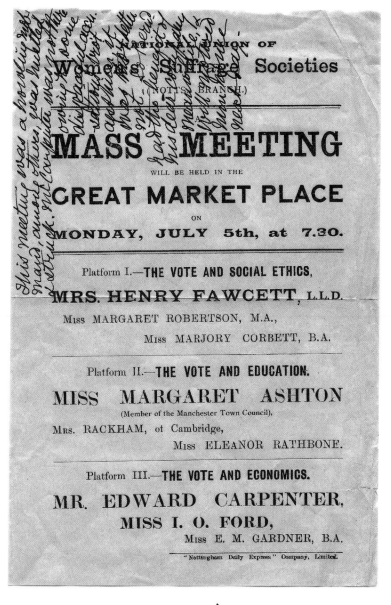

BILL POSTER FOR THE WOMEN'S SUFFRAGE MEETING
in Nottingham in July, 1909

Alice's diary in the early years of the twentieth century gives us a good picture of the many kinds of activities entered into for the cause of Women's Suffrage – from routine committee meetings, drawing-room meetings, 'At Homes', garden parties and public meetings in Nottingham, to national and international meetings in London. The 1909 diary provides a good example –

> January – 'At home' at which 'Nellie made a splendid speech' (28 January)
> February – Alice takes the chair at a suffrage 'At Home' (25 February)
> March – 'M, Nellie & Hilda are always at work on suff affairs' (4 March) & 'crammed' suffrage meeting at Circus Hall at which Mr Forbes Roberson made 'a splendid speech'. (18 March)
> April – Alice attends big reception of W. S. International in London 'with my 3 daughters' (28 April)
> May – Special effort week with a suffrage market stall which Maud helped to run, a concert run by Lina, a play in which Hilda had a part & a lunch (at 2/6 a ticket) run by Nellie.
> June – W.S. Committee (14 June) & much business for Maud preparing for public meeting in July (25 June)
> July – Mass meeting in Nottingham Market Place (5 July) (see above)
> September – Suffrage 'At Home' (23 September) Maud's letter about treatment of suffragettes in prison (28 September)
> October – Maud, Nellie & Hilda doing suffrage work (12, 20, 21 and 23 October)
> November – Maud running suffrage stall (3 November)
> December – Alice & Nellie at Caxton Hall meeting (6 December). Suffrage shop (20 December).

Since she had given up the secretaryship, and more so since moving from Nottingham, Alice is more often reporting what others are doing than what she is doing herself. Partly, as already suggested, this was the natural handing over from age to youth – Alice was 65 in 1909 – but also she had a very great deal of minor illness. In this year, 1909, for example, she appears literally to have spent half her days in bed. This was not due to a definite illness – only once was she so unwell that the doctor was sent for – it simply was that she was 'but poorly' and continually suffering from, or in fear of, the common cold (which could cause a quite painful throat). And for this, she stayed in bed.

This was not from lack of courage or stamina: she longed for health – 'I stayed in bed till aftn v tired again & low spirited. What to do to get better?!' she wrote in October. She got her desire that time for it was mid-March before she had a cold of any sort and it was not until October, 1910, that she was confined to bed with a cold and wrote triumphantly that – 'it is nearly a year since I had a real bad one!' (13 October)

Over the years, it has been seen that the state of Alice's spirits (especially in her relations with her staff) has tended to affect her health and there were examples of other reasons in 1909: her summary at the beginning of that year opens with a statement of difficulties which she does not identify but was no doubt connected with the move frrom Nottingham –

> We are getting through our 2nd winter in this house, & things are apparently much as usual, but there are many ups & downs beneath the surface....

And a row of some sort had developed amongst the Unitarians about which she wrote that – 'I am not v w being a good deal upset abt a unitn dispute involving the Warrens & Thomas's, in wh we have joined on the W's side & m sore feeling ensues!' (1 June 1909); and the next day 'I did a bit of gardening but it tired me too m & shewd me that I am old & have no strength in reserve.'

Notwithstanding which, she did not take what might have seemed ordinary precautions for someone of her age and risk of cold – 'I slept out on the balcony' she had written on 22 May. (The balcony was outside her bedroom window.) When she felt well, she could undertake a schedule that a much younger woman might have thought punishing: in the *winter*, between the four days 5 to 8 December in this year 1909, for example: she travelled to London from Salcombe; attended a public meeting on Women's Suffrage in

London; travelled to Nottingham to lunch with Hubert and Lina and see their children; travelled that day back to Broughton; left the next day to go to Wilmslow to see her sisters; and was surprised that she could not carry out her plan to return to Broughton on the 10th, because on the late evening of the 9th, she 'was unaccountably seized with violent sickness'.

After an exhausting December, she wrote this clear summary at the opening of her diary for the year 1910, of the national and international matters that interested her:

> This year opens in prospect of the Ge. Election, wh this time is a v. crucial one. The Liberals hope to win again, if by again, if by a reduced majority, their cry is 'Down w. the veto of the Lords' – Lloyd George's (rather revolutionary and socialistic) 'Budget', & Free Trade. The tories are for Tariff Reform, wh they say wd make more employment, & anti-budget & anti-socialism, & the right of veto for the Lords. We women are doing all we can for suffrage – non-party & non militant. Maud, Nellie & Hilda are working v hard at it but have to contend w so m apathy! ... The dreadful King Leopold is dead at last, but there are many other terrible influences still at work in the world, & make one feel pessimistic at times.

She does not allow her interest in the suffrage movement to blind her to everything else; she had noted what she called 'the Congo atrocities' the year before – which would explain her reference to King Leopold – and, in 1911, it would be the treatment of the Arabs by Italy that aroused her angry sympathy:

> 'The accounts of the terrible atrocities & slaughtering of Arabs by the Italians in Tripoli are really too awful', she tells her diary. 'Our Govt only "deprecates any questions likely to be offensive to a friendly power."...B is writing to the paper about it.' (3 November 1911)

She wrote herself to the *Manchester Guardian* and a copy of that letter is included in her diary – 'Where', she asks, 'is the spirit that prevailed when we had a Gladstone with us in the days of the Bulgarian atrocities? Where are the noble traditions of the great

Italian patriots?' She would have felt that last point particularly keenly.

There were, in fact, two General Elections in 1910. The first was in January and the diary entries show that Maud, Hilda and Nellie worked hard every day to promote the Suffrage cause, going to work almost as regularly for the cause as anyone in full employment for a wage. Meetings were held in the larger villages in the rural areas as well as in the towns and amongst these was a non-party one at Hickling (near Broughton) that is reported in the local paper, at which Nellie and Ben both spoke.

There had always been some Tories who were in favour of women's suffrage and Ben was now one of them. He had voted Tory for the first time back in July 1895 – 'rather sad to differ' – Alice had written but she was clearly comforted that their difference was not on a matter that was important to her. Now, in 1910, she explains that Ben voted Tory 'because anti budget & tariff reform'.

It was by no means only the apathy mentioned by Alice that the women had to contend with. Maud's warning that the treatment of the suffragettes was likely to arouse 'sex warfare' had been only too foresightful. Alice mentions, with surprising calm, that at a suffrage meeting in Newark, 'they got pelted with rotten pears' (5 January 1910) but things got worse: 'Maud is busy every day now on suffrage work, helping at open air meetings, sometimes rather rowdy' Alice writes. On actual polling days (which were then different for different towns) the suffragists who went to the booths to plead the cause, had often to contend with a good deal of unpleasantness. The 19 January was polling day in Nottingham and Alice writes that –

> Maud, Nellie, Hilda & abt 10 others, manned the polling booths mostly for all day! to get voters petitions signed. M had friendly officials who let her sit in shelter, but H & others had to stand all day in the street and met w some rudeness! Poor dears, it was horrid for them! ... and in other towns, ladies have been still worse treated! ...

I helped to keep the shop & went running abt to visit H & Nellie & other ladies. B saw Maud ... (19 January 1910)

And on polling day in Rushcliffe, where Mr Ellis was standing as a Liberal –

Maud & Hilda had a terrible day, so did Nellie & others, outside the polling booths all day, w screaming children & unfriendly populace & police. They were more dead than alive at the end! I took chge of the shop for a while ... (26 January 1910)

After the physical violence that Maud and others had suffered at the meeting in Nottingham two years earlier, their persistence now must have called for considerable courage from these non-militant women.

The two Liberals were 'thrown out, alas' in Nottingham but Mr Ellis got in at Rushcliffe. It is to be noted that Alice herself had been active on election day in Nottingham and she reports that she continued, the day after it was over, collecting subscriptions in the *rain*, while her daughters were presenting signed petitions to Mr Ellis, the newly elected MP.

At the outset, Alice had mentioned that the first polling day would be for sixty-seven seats and would be held on 15 January and that 'our young ones all stayed to sleep at Felixstowe & hear the result of the first day in this very crucial election'.

The family were split about 50-50 politically (though not of course on women's suffrage) but their differences do not appear to have caused any family ill feeling: Alice writes on 20 January that –

B & I were busy filling up the election map; the tories are gaining the day more than expected. B & Bd [Bernard] are glad and Hubt. Will, Felix, Maud & I are more or less radical.

As the elections were on different days, the national result, of course, could not be announced immediately and Alice did not trouble to record it in her diary until the opening of Parliament –

The King opened Parlt, Asquith & the Govt are in a v awkward box just now, the elections having thrown the casting vote to Labour & the Irish. (21 February 1910)

Campaigning for the cause was naturally less hectic after the election but much activity continued. The Women's Suffrage shop was regularly manned and as early as March, a meeting was arranged in the Mechanics Hall, addressed by Mrs Snowdon with Mrs Ellis in the chair, to which 'we all went'. The hall was two-thirds full and 'Mrs. Snowdon's speech was good but not so inspired or uplifting as last time ... and so disappointing to us'. But clearly the supporters were not discouraged for Alice goes on to say that – 'We sat up v late talking – the young ones went on at it till 1.30!'

That summer they organised a big garden fête in The Park held partly at 'Felixstowe' and partly at another large house, with a play on the subject of women's suffrage arranged by Hilda, fairy lights in the evening and a play – *Titania & Oberon* – in which eighty children took part. Alice was on holiday in Switzerland with her sisters at the time but she writes that 'Of course my thoughts have been with them all day'.

This day-long occasion must have involved a great deal of work and yet they also managed to arrange for a contingent to go from Nottingham on 9 July – 'Maud, Nellie, Hilda & 4 servants & 25 more' – to join a demonstration in London in support of the second reading of a suffrage Bill. And in the same month, Alice and Maud attended a suffrage committee meeting and Maud went to Nottingham 'for several open air meetings'. The Bill for which the demonstration was organised was the first Conciliation Bill, so called because it was hoped it was so drafted that it would bring together supporters of all parties.

By this time in her life, political activity largely ceased for Alice in the summer months and she does not refer to suffrage meetings again in 1910 until October, when she reports being hostess for the tea at a suffrage 'At Home' and attending a Women Workers executive committee (one of her more active causes) which was 'rather important abt the suffge' (21 October). It can be guessed that this was to do with some of the women workers being anti the suffrage cause.

The second General Election had very similar results and the diary for 1911 opens with a depressing view of suffrage chances –

> This year opens w a lately-elected Parliament, the 2nd in one year, the result being nearly the same as before. Mr Asquith & the Libls remain in power, but the Irish hold the balance. Suffrage I fear stands a poor chance; Nellie Hilda & Maud are indefatigable.

In spite of her previous disappointments with Asquith and the Lliberals, she still felt that their election was crucial to the suffrage cause but her mistrust and dislike of Asquith himself was undimmed. On 22 November, she wrote that it was 'a critical day for suffragists at Westminster; this Government tries to play with them'. And the next day that: 'I was furious to hear how Mr Asquith has again disappointed us w his false & empty promises! & the Militants made a great riot in Westr y'day. Quite justified *I* think!' (23 November 1910).

Her comment on the militants' action was typical but, as will be seen, it was not long before she began to feel that they might now be doing more harm than good to the cause.

In the summer of 1911, there was an even more splendid Suffrage march and gathering in London than the one in 1908 and, this time, Alice walked in it herself, joining it in London. 'A great day!' she wrote –

> M & the others had brought 100 people fr Nottingham & a great business it was for them! ... The great suffrage procession was a wonderful experience, so interesting, though tiring. Lancelot joined us & was most kind & helpful ... Luckily it kept quite fine & not too hot. (17 June 1911)

She would be sixty-seven that August.

The Times printed a whole column account (reproduced as Appendix 3) in which it describes 'the procession of 40,000 persons' as being 5 miles long and taking 2¹/₂ hours to pass a given point. The article includes the following descriptive phrases –

> the women suffragists, constitutional and militant made high festival in London for their cause ... the surprise was the unexpected strength of the constitutionalists ... women of every class of society seemed to be united in the demonstration ...

It is in March next year that Alice first mentions the militants with underlying anxiety that they may be going too far: 'They made another raid & broke windows to the damage of £5,000. Oh what times we live in!' (2 March 1912)

And she calls March 28th 'Black Thursday' because a pro-suffrage bill 'on which we had confidently expected a good majority', was defeated:

> to our dismay, the 2nd reading was defeated & a majority of 14 against it, wh was received in the H of C w loud huzzas! A v crushing blow & one feels furious at the broken pledges – after all the poor women's work!' (29 March 1912)

The Bill being debated was the third Conciliaton Bill. Whereas there had been a majority of 167 in favour of the 2nd reading of the second Conciliation Bill in 1911 – so Alice's expectation was not unreasonable – that majority turned into a majority of 14 against for the third Conciliation Bill in 1912. Alice does not say that she blames the militants but some of the loss of support is put down by historians to 'reaction to the suffragette disturbances'.

Propaganda for the cause continued in Nottingham (and no doubt elsewhere); Alice mentions a 'big suffrage bazaar' in Nottingham in November 1912. But in January 1913 their hopes were again dashed, this time to the point that Alice feels the cause is lost, perhaps for years to come –

Maud went to London to join Nellie (& Will) as the 'Grey Amendmt' suffge comes on today. The speaker however ruled it would be out of order if passed, which took all the heart out of it & Mr Asquith then withdrew the whole bill, & dashed our hopes for proby years to come! Gt indignation & despair prevailed.' (27 January 1913)

And then, in June, came Miss Davison's heroic act in throwing herself in front of the Derby horse –

Miss Davison, the suffragette who threw herself in front of the Derby race horse, has died. [Alice wrote] She *was* a heroine! having gone thro many imprisonments & forcible feeding, yet people don't seem to see it & many say such horrid things about her. (11 June 1913)

Her concern, as always, was about the feelings – the suffering and courage – of an individual. She encloses in the diary newspaper cuttings of letters from a number of people who also took her view.

There was another Suffrage march to London in July, 1913 and Maud and Nellie joined it – 'Maud starts her "march" with the suffrage pilgrims at Chesterfield, she and Nellie staying at the Vallances at Mansfield' Alice reports. (7 July 1913) and 'Maud wires they are having big meetings & doing v well' (9 July).

At this time, Alice was at Salcombe with Hester and the grandchildren. Hester had been quite ill at Plymouth where Lancelot was a doctor at the Naval hospital. Now he was posted abroad and his family had to be moved from Plymouth to Salcombe. With Hester ill, Alice had to pack the family up and take charge of our move –

Chaos reigned at 9 The Square ... I never saw such a scramble or so many toys & things to be disposed of, to burn, give away, store or go to Salcombe ... (4 July 1913)

Maud left the suffrage march before it got to London 'to help and support her father who is very disturbed about Hester's affairs' Alice wrote. She too is worried about what to do about Hester and the grandchildren – should she take them all back to Broughton or is Hester now well enough to be left to cope alone at Salcombe? She decides to leave them.

The worry about Hester and the grandchildren, whom Alice invariably refers to with unclouded affection, usually as 'the sweet chicks', was always first about Hester's health and next about where and at what cost we could be housed and provided for. Lancelot's salary was never enough.

In her opening summary for 1914, Alice wrote that –

poor Suffrage is in a bad way, the militants turn so many people against it & prospects are not good at present. Nellie has (nominally) resigned the secretaryship ....

It looks as if Alice's depressed view was general.

There was a Second Reading debate on a Women's Enfranchise- ment Bill introduced in the House of Lords on 5 May and defeated, but Alice makes no mention of it; at the time, she was on holiday in Norfolk with Ben 'looking up all his old haunts' while, at Broughton, 'the whitewashers & painters are in for our spring cleaning, wh is on in full force' (6 May).

A measure of Women's Suffrage was at last conceded during the war, in the Coalition Government's Representation of the People Act, which received the Royal Assent on 6 February 1918. It was limited to women over 30 who were – householders or wives of househholders, occupiers of property of £5 annual value or gradu- ates of a British University, including those who had fulfilled the qualifications but were not allowed to graduate. Cambridge did not grant degrees to women on the same terms as men until 1948.

Peering forward to see what Alice felt when she first exercised her vote, I found that the diary for 1918 is missing but that she wrote an extended summary about the events of 1918 in her diary for 1919. Tucked away in that are the words –

Women's Suffrage has become an accomplished fact! The result of so many years labour.

It tends nowadays to be assumed that it was what women did in the war that got them the vote, and not the long campaign of the Suffra*gists* starting in the 1860s, or the actions of the Suffra*gettes* in the 1900s. The Suffragists of Nottingham were in no doubt about the importance of their contribution and presented Nellie (Helena B. Dowson) with an illuminated address –

> in token of affection and as a memento of Victory by Friends and Fellow-Workers, in recognition of her splendid Services in the Cause of the Enfranchisement of Womanhood, through years of Struggle for Freedom and for Justice for the Claims of her own Sex and the Uplifting of the Race.

It will never be possible to say whether, as Alice clearly thought, the militants were now doing more harm than good. But the evidence of the diaries suggests, I think, that the great marches and gatherings in London, which were joined by all classes and by Suffragists and Suffragettes alike, must have played a major part in changing public opinion, notwithstanding the undoubted influence of the important anti organisation or the reaction of opinion one way or the other to the militants.

Another view, of which Alice was unlikely to have known anything, is that the Act of February 1918 extended the suffrage to all men over 21 and many of the new voters were of a class who were thought likely to vote for the growing Labour party; the Tories hoped that a good number of the women voters over 30 would vote for them.

Poor Miss Davison! Will history conclude that her last horrifying sacrifice was unnecessary or even damaging to the cause? Whether or no, it may still influence how the vote is used – even today, eighty years and more later, I have heard a mother say to her young daughter who wasn't going to vote, 'You jolly well will vote. I am not going to have that woman throwing herself under a horse for nothing!'

Epilogue

THE INTEREST of Alice's story lies in the fact that it is Victorian, but I am closing it in 1913 because that year and not 1900, marks the natural historical break between the centuries. It was also the year of Alice and Ben's Golden Wedding, so it makes a neat family climax too.

The day of The Golden Wedding began with an early serenade of our grandparents by us, Hester's five children, from the balcony outside their bedroom, where, in the not distant past, Alice had reported herself as sleeping out. It was organised – of course – by my aunt Maud who had smuggled a harmonium on to the balcony the night before.

'Awake! awake! and greet the happy morn' we sang. I remember it vividly: our grandparents were sitting up in their four-poster bed holding out welcoming arms; Ben had a patriarchal white beard and friendly pink cheeks; Alice had grey hair plaited in a circle on top of her head like a crown and her face was seamed all over with smile wrinkles.

Alice wrote of this early waking that 'B had been up early writing a letter to his children & then back to bed and at 7 o clock a wonderful & lovely serenade from the children & others ...'

He must indeed have been up early to write it and still be back in bed by seven. He honoured his older grandchildren by writing the same letter to them and I have mine still, duplicated in purple ink in its small matching envelope, addressed to 'Alix'.

A great deal was made of that day: there was the presentation of a beautiful silver art-nouveau loving-cup, produced at Liberty's and engraved with our grandparents' motto – 'Experience Worketh Hope' – followed by their marriage dates, 1863–1913, and the names of the designers, 'Omar Ramsden et Alwyn Carr me fecerunt MCMXIII'; there was also the presentation of a pianola, which would become a great delight to us grandchildren who could imagine ourselves playing Beethoven on it with our own idea of speed and expression; there was a concert in which Maud, Hilda and Will all took part; we children performed *The Mad Hatter's Tea Party*, coached by aunt Hilda, and Bimbi organised us into a girls' scout play in the garden. And, of course, there was a special lunch with delicious puddings, of which three helpings were allowed to the grandchildren because it was a Red Letter Day.

This is Alice's account:

> Our hearts were indeed too full, of thankful joy. We had H's 5 childn to lunch – & then came Hubert's Lina & their 2 eldest & G & Hilda & Mary Enfield, (Lizzie Beckett was ill) & Will & Nellie – & they sang & played & acted for us – & at 7 we sat down 18 for dinner – after wh Will made a thoughtful speech; & the 5 elder grandchildren came in to dessert & gave us the lovely cup w. inscriptions.

The five elder grandchildren would have been Hubert's two eldest and Hester's three eldest.

The Golden Wedding photograph, arranged and taken by Will, is of the immediate family only; it excluded Alice's sisters and cousin but included Emily. The one absentee was my father who had been there for the weekend but had had to go back to London on Monday.

The account of the occasion in the Press emphasised that, though Mr Dowson came from Norfolk, he had been a resident of Nottingham since 1853. It also mentioned that he had retired some years before. Though Alice doesn't say specifically when, I assume it was in the very active year 1907, when they moved to Broughton, by which time, Hubert and Bernard were both partners in the family firm. This still occupies the same offices, and is now called, simply, 'Dowson's', but there are no longer any Dowson partners in it.

At the time of the Golden Wedding, we (Hester and family) were living in a house in Broughton village belonging to our grandparents, and we were still there when the war broke out. I remember the placard 'War!' on that day.

In her 1914 summary, Alice shows no sign of foreseeing the

THE FAMILY ON THE GOLDEN WEDDING
Back row standing: Will and Nellie, Rob, Felix, Maud, Gerard and
Hilda; middle row sitting or kneeling: Hubert, Bimbi, Hester, Ben and
Alice, Angela, Tom, Lina, Emily (and on her knee, Susanna, then the
youngest grandchild); Bottom row: Robin, Ina, Bernard, Bay, little
Ben, Molly, Alex, Mona.

coming war; on national and international matters, she refers only
to 'v bloody & disastrous' wars in the Balkans and Mexico and –
interestingly to today's readers – to 'the Ulster party, in Ireland
arming & drilling to resist the Home Rule Bill'.

The coming world war seems, indeed, to have thrown no
shadows before it, at least that Alice's family recognised, since
there was a family holiday in Switzerland in June that included two
children – my sister and me – and Alice's sisters were holidaying in
the Tyrol till 21 July. Staggeringly, the first hint in the diary that we
might be involved in war appears on 1 August when Alice wrote
that 'Russia & Germany [are] mobilising ... we fear we may be

drawn in.'

On 4 August she wrote – 'V interesting & dreadful to read Sir E.G's [Edward Grey] fine & convincing speech – But alas we have to join in the war, & everyone is agog'. This was followed next day with 'England has *declared war* agst Germany. It cd not be avoided! G seemed determined to fight but tho't England never would. B v anxious, of course. Robin offered his car & services till he sails.'

No more than she anticipated its coming, could Alice foresee its horrors, but I do remember my uncle Will saying that, by the end of it, we might all be living in caves.

There were no deaths in the war in the immediate family: my father was at risk on his ship but survived; my uncles were all too old to be called up and Robin and Tom were the only ones who volunteered.

After the war, Alice and Ben's family all prospered more or less: Will had a successful lace and embroidery factory in Nottingham; Tom was a stockbroker in Manchester but his interest was in antiques and pictures (he was one of those responsible for establishing the Whitworth Gallery) and he was also, surprisingly, a member of the Jockey Club; Robin built a prestigious engineering and consultancy firm in Johannesburg and raised his family there until retiring and settling at Geldeston; Alex (the younger twin) was a director of W. R. Greg, cotton manufacturers in Stockport, living with Alice's sisters in Wilmslow during the week, but returning to Broughton at weekends where he and Bernard continued to share a bedroom until their deaths. (Though neither married, I was aware that both had ambitions that way at one time or another.) Gerard became an estate agent in Nottingham and was influential in local government, and Felix was first a master at Sedbergh and then set up his own very successful preparatory school – Cressbrook – at Kirkby Lonsdale. He married late (the matron at the school) but had no children.

And Maud: she remained the relied-upon daughter-at-home and the second mother to her sister's children. I believe she trained

BEN AND ALICE IN 1913

as a nurse in the war and considered going abroad with the Red Cross but gave it up because she thought her parents could not do without her.

Hester continued to struggle against ill-health from which she was constantly rescued by her parents and sister, but, as Alice's 1919 summary discloses, in 1918 at any rate, it was Hester who was helping to nurse first Maud, for 'a long illness, sciatica & genl break down', followed by an operation for breast cancer; secondly, her father Ben in his last illness (he died on 9 October); and lastly,

Felix, when all thirty boys in his new school were simultaneously ill with what Alice describes as 'the fearful epidemic called Influenza [which] swept over the whole world'.

I have wondered how the 1918 diary came to be missing. Did it just happen to get lost when all the other 53 survived? Or did Alice destroy it, either because there was so much sadness in it – Maud's two illnesses and Ben's death – or for some other reason? About this time, Maud had a suitor. What an upset it would have been in her parents' lives for their daughter-at-home to marry. Could this have been mentioned in the 1918 diary and been a reason for its withdrawal by Alice, or even Maud?

The first of Alice and Ben's children to die was Will, in 1934, the second Maud in 1936 and the third Hester, in 1941. The last was Alex (the youngest twin) in 1967. The house at Broughton is now occupied by Hubert's descendants and the Salcombe house by Rhona, Gerard's only surviving child, who continues to make all members of the family welcome there.

And Alice. What kind of adult woman grew from the young girl of Chapter One? In the course of writing this book, my 'Granny' has become a different person – ALICE – from whom, in a way, I am more remote than before, but whom, inevitably, I know more intimately than the Granny I thought I knew so well.

A similar transformation, of course, has overtaken my grand-father who died when I was a schoolgirl of fifteen and for whom I remember squeezing out what I felt to be an adequate quantity of tears. Sadly, I have no childhood memories of him, good and loving as the diaries show him to have been to his little grand-children. He emerges now, as a man of high intelligence and wide political and literary interests, and also as an astute businessman, building up his own law practice after his uncle's rejection and supporting his family of ten so well that they were never in want of what Alice might have called 'a v comfortable sufficiency'.

He was a 'modern' rather than 'Victorian' father to his children and he continued to be their concerned and caring adviser in the difficulties of young adult life, worrying with them and helping them over their early difficulties. In the few surviving letters to his daughters, he showed a touching love and understanding. And he remained throughout his life a loving, considerate and understanding husband.

Ben appears from his writings and Alice's diaries to have had no other attachment of the kind believed to be so common among Victorian men. His work often took him away from home but when he had to stay away, it was almost always for a night only and with relatives.

Before I return to *Alice*, I must go back to a few memories of my *grandmother* at the time I knew her best when, for some months – two school terms I think – I lived at Broughton with her and my aunt Maud. It was 1920/21, so 'Granny' would have been seventy-six years old – very old in those days – and she was leading a very quiet, protected and inactive widowhood, breakfasting in bed and resting on the sofa in her bedroom after lunch, doing a reduced amount of visiting the poor of the village, and in the evenings reading aloud, to my aunt and old Emily and me, the poetry of Tennyson or Wordsworth, or from the works of Scott. On Sundays, when the twin uncles were usually at home, she would preside over the tea-table in the dining-room and uncle Will and aunt Nellie almost always came over to join us. Sometimes on a Sunday she accompanied herself on the piano in the drawing room, singing her favourite hymns. She was never asked to join a game of bridge or chess or croquet which now I know she used to enjoy and seemed to show no interest in public affairs. It was clear that she had strong opinions, though keeping a refreshing tolerance of the opinions of others.

Did she chafe at this life? How could she not? She was no more ill than she had ever been, and that her mind was as clear as ever is demonstrated by the long letter she wrote to me about my mother in 1925. And then, inevitably, my aunt – her devoted carer – turned, at times, into a bit of a tyrant; a fact that became so obvious that at last my mother felt constrained to write to her asking her 'to let the little mother' have the freedom to decide some things for herself. Robin also spoke to Maud asking her to give her mother more freedom. My aunt reacted by not speaking to him for several days. While even I felt critical of my aunt at the time, knowing what I know now of how much she had given up for her mother, I can understand her anger better. I can also understand Alice's compliance with the 'tyranny', for she was always aware of how much she owed to Maud. Alice discussed this clash of wills earlier in her Commonplace Book – 'Maud is the right hand of all,' she wrote in 1906. 'It is inevitable she takes the direction and decides most things.'

I return to ALICE of the daily diaries and find her, above all, a loving mother but also a very commanding one. Very early in her marriage, she gratefully took advice once or twice from her own mother and her Nanny, Bar, about her staff; and she was quite humble over sister Katie's criticism of the way she was bringing up her children. But that *she* will organise her household and plan and decide her children's routine and education (only rarely in consultation with her husband) is never in doubt.

She was always concerned to see that the children had a lot of fun, and, long before they were grown up, she gave dances for them. But she was also a quite severe, though always kind, critic. This to Maud in Bonn is typical –

> I am sorry my poor little dear ... but if you *will* laugh & play tricks during the prep time, you can't wonder that people think you lazy, you know. It is the price you have to pay for the fun!

Her letters to her daughters in Bonn show a remarkable care to find topics that would interest them, whether an interest in their everyday lives there and the family's in Nottingham, or news of politics she knew would please Hester. Other letters have not survived but we know she also wrote twice a week to her boys at school.

There is no sign that Alice had favourites or that jealousy or competition for her favour developed among her children. They appear to have been a quite remarkably loving, happy and unquarrelsome family. In one of her letters, Alice quotes Felix (aged seven) as saying – 'we are a specially happy family, aren't we Mama?' But she confesses to her Commonplace Book that things were not always so smooth and happy – 'We are so critical in this family' she writes in 1900 –

> so hard to please. Whose fault is it? We have tried to be wise with our family; Ben is a most indulgent father. I am indulgent but I am afraid I am carping and anxious as well and oh I do think the children are! They don't give one their confidence or sympathy ...

Though she showed no favouritism, her relations with her first and last born had a special quality. She found Felix's growing up painful in a way not mentioned of the other children, the reason for which might partly be that she planned to have no more children. With Will, it was the other way about: I have felt critical of her off-hand treatment of him as a child when he clearly needed her expressed love and seemed seldom to get it, but when he was forty and she sixty, they developed a close companionship which could only have been based on a strong love on both sides.

Alice's next outstanding quality is her warmth and instant sympathy for any suffering she met or heard of, whether in the mass, as with the Bulgarian and Armenian atrocities and oppression in Russia and the Congo, or in individuals: when she hears that her friend's son has shot himself at Cambridge, her first thought is – 'poor boy, how he must have suffered first!' and only second – 'the poor parents'; she befriends a former governess because she has no home to go to; and employs 'old Lydia' who is not much use and they 'don't much like, because she needs the money'; and, in the bitter winter of 1895, she takes the rather original view that, 'it is delightful how everyone's hearts are softened by this hard winter! Everywhere relief funds are being worked & so m voluntary help given to the poor!'

Religion was very important to Alice but she always retained her individual judgement of its dogmas. She tried to find good in everything. Young Maud hit the nail on the head when she wrote from Bonn – 'You would like Amy ... she always finds out the nice parts in everything ... and says 'Oh how lovely is this or that ...' And when the girls were homesick, she coupled sympathy with the argument that the pain of parting was the 'shady side' of love. There are a number of references in the diaries to members of the family attending theosophy meetings following Mrs Besant's visit to Nottingham and Alice herself attended the first. There is no mention of her going to any other but she does record in her Commonplace Book that, 'my theosophical children have influenced me' and she wonders – 'shall I be able to sing in the next reincarnation that Will and Maud talk about?'

The flip-side, as it were, of Alice's sympathy for others was a need for sympathy for herself, a lack of self-assurance, a thin-skinnedness and shyness; she was all too easily hurt by other people's roughness or rudeness. Till quite late in life, she remained unsure of herself and shy in public and very ready to criticise herself. In her Commonplace Book, she writes endlessly about her 'shortcomings and littleness'. She longed for the comforting reassurance of her daughters' love and support and for their return from Bonn when they would do 'little pottering things' for her and enjoy reading together the poetry she loves. In almost her first criticism ever of Ben (either in letters or diaries) she writes that, 'Papa does not generally care for the same things and, if he does, he likes better to read it himself'. She delighted in reading aloud, even when she had to collect her servants for an audience. Her choice of book was usually serious but she also found amusing ones. And she read aloud beautifully – I can vouch for that. Basically very serious she knew how to enjoy herself and there are many references to evenings full of laughter. In her fiftieth year, when she had lost her shyness, she was writing – 'I danced away like anything'.

The differing needs of her large and growing family often became almost more than Alice could bear. Even when Will was grown up, his high spirits meant that, 'chaos reigned' when he arrived; happy as she was to have them all together, 'it is impossible to please everyone' she confided in her diary and, in October 1904 – 'between Hester's affairs' – she had three little babies & nowhere obvious to live – '& Rob's ditto & Gerard's ditto & my own domestics, I feel rather upset & worried & it is so difficult to keep calm'. Even after they were grown up they would still go, *en masse*, to the station to see family members off or greet their return to or from an important journey. In the 1900s, all ten might meet together for Christmas.

On the rare occasions when she and Ben could get away alone, they were very happy: Alice describes 'a heavenly walk' they took together in Norfolk which 'I hope I shall always remember'.

That both were feminists and supporters of the causes that mattered most to Alice must have contributed a great deal to their lifelong harmony. Alice's ancestry was feminist on both sides: her father had been a noted socialist and his mother Hannah was a remarkable woman, while Alice's mother Mary had attended Mrs Turner's unusual school and was one of the first to take up the Contagious Diseases cause. Young Alice was an active feminist from the moment she learned about the Married Women's Property Bill in March 1869.

She was, however, a feminist in the widest sense. She never took the view that the support of political causes – or charities – should have a gender: she encouraged her boys to help by turning the sewing machine handle and making petticoats for the poor and helping her run her Christmas parties for poor children; and it was a matter of course to her that her adult sons supported the suffrage cause, being only sometimes disappointed when, as she put it, 'none of the "he's" cared to go' to a particular meeting. But she certainly accepted that most of the political agitation would be done by women – no doubt because the men had a job to go to.

One last revealing comment typifies Alice's philosophy of life. Included in the 1912 diary, there is a letter written by Alice to the local paper, which shows that though by now in her sixty-ninth year, her mind was as up-to-date and as keen as ever. In this letter, she enters the new debate about eugenics with comments on a lecture on 'Heredity in Morals' given by a council member of the recently founded Eugenics Education Society; she is criticising the suggestion that power should be given to the medical profession to decide on the segregation of the feeble minded – 'The profession are splendid friends and advisers', she writes, 'but to be our masters, no!' – 'Character – the only thing we can take with us into the unseen – surely this is the most important of all,' she concludes, 'and it does not run on all fours with physical fitness nor even with mental capacity ... I myself know of cases where the feeble-minded child becomes the educator and blessing of the whole family ...'

When I first began to write this book I thought how surprisingly alike Alice's life had been to ours of the late twentieth century – her days were clearly full of interest and activity, their love of outdoor games was similar to ours, and even the language seemed to have changed little. But the more I have read of her diaries, the more the differences have become apparent.

The most obvious differences are those caused by large families: the numerous deaths amongst young mothers from having too many children; Alice herself would probably have died but for her considerate husband and the help she had from her extended family. The very size of the family, too, often separated the parents. And people died, gave birth and were ill (even of infectious or life-threatening diseases) at home without any resort to hospital – there was a more natural acceptance of death, though people of Alice's class were also very ready to consult London specialists.

Nor was a staff of servants an unmixed blessing. Their recruitment, their deployment, their disagreements and entertainment were a big task and worry to the head of the household. Alice treated her servants' jobs with consideration and with the respect – as a career – that they would rarely get now. Some stayed in their employment for years and became, if not quite social equals, old

270

friends about whom Alice remained concerned after they had left her employ and whose weddings she might celebrate at Felixstowe or Broughton.

The number of public discussion Societies and weekly public lectures in Nottingham and the amount of intellectual activity that Alice and Ben found time for was remarkable. Women, as yet without the vote, were prepared to work long hours for political causes, with the result that they probably did a good deal more political work than the women of today who have the vote. Alice's diaries provide a valuable everyday picture of the long campaign for Women's Suffrage and highlight the contribution made to it by the Constitutionalists, now so often overlooked. They show that men supported the cause as well as women, though active propaganda was almost entirely done by women.

Ben's comments show an acceptance of colonial acquisitions that is shocking today, but an example of the 'giving' side of Empire is the fact that the *local* Government of Bombay felt it had the right to request that doctors and nurses be sent out from England to help with the plague.

The social influence of Unitarian families in certain parts of England underlies the whole story. Hannah (Lightbody) Greg and her daughter, are special examples of it: Hannah's influence caused her husband's young workers to be taught to read and write in the 1780s; her daughter had a big influence on the public education Act of 1870. Unitarians were prominent in early days of the University of London, in founding their own University Hall.

There was certainly more snobbery then and none of the sense of shame about showing it felt nowadays – Alice complains to her daughters that a friend 'who might have been a duchess' is marrying a *journalist*, a new cook arrives who is 'very common ... we can't keep her' and a possible governess is rejected because she is 'no lady'. Social customs that no longer exist took up a lot of Alice's time: since there were no telephones, letter-writing dominated the day (and letters were, interestingly, relied on to arrive next day!) 'Calling' might take half a day; entertaining at home demanded a certain style, including waiting at table – Alice describes one 'smart dinner' that went on till four-thirty as having – 'peaked up napkins and pink glasses. Jenny & Annie managed the waiting v nicely. We had a goose & a beef steak pie.' There were also some surprising taboos: Alice could not ask her male host where to take little Felix when he needed to pee; and when she was middle aged, she still didn't like to go to a concert alone.

Where charity today can mean only signing a cheque, it was more personal for Alice's generation, often it involved inviting 'the poor' into your own home as well as spending much time providing for needs nowadays the responsibility of the State.

What I have found myself most moved by have been those differences I knew about but only *realised* the *significance* of from Alice's words or experience: that women had no access to universities or to most professional careers, and the waste in the life of the daughter-at-home. Alice had married young and had been unable to indulge her zest for knowledge. She never referred to the fact that, in any case, no university was open to her. For people like her this was a terrible deprivation – and it was, for her generation, an additional sadness that her lack of knowledge about higher education resulted in her also depriving her own daughters, who were just of the generation who could have benefitted.

In his Golden Wedding letter my grandfather wrote –

> Times have enormously changed in the last hundred years. In both families from which you have descended, there are notable men and women whose blood runs also in your veins; keeping alive in your hearts those who have gone before should be a real assistance in the difficulties and duties of life.

Those words are quite as fitting today. But now women have all the advantages and opportunities so long denied them. If, like men, all the learned professions had been open to women and they had had the precious advantage of three years at university, surrounded and taught by like minds, what more might Hannah Lightbody or Maud or even Harriet Martineau have achieved – or Alice?

272

Notes and Sources

The following notes and sources, listed under Chapters, have no numerical references in the text and, where necessary, are given under subject.

Preface

Description of Unitarians: Claire Tomalin, *The Life and Death of Mary Wollstonecraft* (Penguin, 1992).

1. Alice

Coach journey from Nottingham to Norwich: recorded in *Memoirs and Reminiscences of Lenton* (Arden Press, 1910).

Mary Needham's education: *Ibid.*

Quarry Bank Mill: Quarry Bank Mill is now owned by the National Trust and is run on their behalf as an example of enlightened industrial management of the period.

Hannah (née Lightbody): Mary B. Rose, *The Gregs of Quarry Bank Mill* (Cambridge University Press, 1986); Mary B. Rose, *The Gregs of Styal* (Quarry Bank Mill Development Trust/National Trust 1978).

Lajos Kossuth (1802-94): Hungarian patriot and a leader of the 1848 revolution. Once president of the newly formed Hungarian republic, after which he was forced into exile where he remained for the rest of his life.

Bollington as a Utopia: Margaret Ingram, *Portrait of a Village – Happy Valley* (Festival Publication, n.d.).

£32,000: In his *Gladstone*, Roy Jenkins calculates that a multiplier of 50 should be used to equalise the value of the pound sterling at the beginning of the nineteenth century with the present day. He has told me that the same figure can reasonably be used when comparing the second half of the century with today, and this calculation has been used throughout this book.

Engels and Robert Hyde Greg: Frederick Engels spent some time in England in 1842 visiting the Manchester cotton factory where his father was a partner, and made a study of factory conditions for his book *The Condition of the Working Class in England* (1844).

Samuel Greg: *A Layman's Legacy: selections from the papers of Samuel Greg, with a brief memoir* (Book Room, 1883).

Mary B. Rose, *The Gregs of Styal*

2. Ben

The details in this chapter are taken from Benjamin Dowson's Family Record, a copy of which is deposited in Nottingham Archive.

3. The Engagement

Details are based on Alice's private diaries and Ben's Family Record.

4. The Wedding

Based on Alice's private diary and Ben's Family Record.

5. Young Marrieds

'That afternoon before his birth ...': Family Record.

'how lovely she looked...': Ben's Golden Wedding letter to his children and grandchildren.

Garibaldi's London visit: Jasper Ridley, *Garibaldi* (Constable, 1974).

Information on tea: Mr S. H. G. Twining, a director of Twinings.

'The larger bulk of English people ...': Family Record.

6. Political Awakening

'The Acts were opposed from the first ...': *Chambers' Encyclopedia* (1888).

The Contagious Diseases Acts: Fawcett Society Library.

Harriet Martineau: Anonymous, *The Contagious Diseases Acts as applied to Garrison Towns and Naval Stations, Being a series of leading articles from the 'Daily News' of 1863* (T. Brakell, 1870); Vera Wheatley, *The Life and Work of Harriet Martineau* (Secker and Warburg, 1957).

In 1870 Harriet Martineau's leader articles on the Contagious Diseases Acts were published in book form, though anonymously. In them she had wanted prostitution abolished, not regulated (as the Acts had made provision for); she had advocated 'establishing hospitals at the expense of the State' to treat venereal disease *before* allowing the police to take draconian measures. She had looked forward to the 'provision of comfort, the tenderness of treatment and the prospect of cure' for these fallen women. She had examined why venereal disease was so rife in the army, and had felt that much could be done to counteract the boredom of barrack-room life: soldiers should be provided with 'reading rooms, innocent games, music etc., as well as muscular and intellectual exercise' and 'trades' which they could work at. 'Dens of infamy' should be abolished and 'a habit of temperance' restored. Most importantly, soldiers should have their wives with them at public expense (at the time only six in every hundred soldiers were entitled to this).

Information on Josephine Butler: L. Hay Cooper, *Josephine Butler and her work for Social Purity* (1922)

Number of petitions signed: Journal Office of the House of Commons.

'I spy strangers': Erskine May.

'Grass roots' attitude to Parliament: Paul McHugh, *Prostitution and Victorian Social Reform* (Croom, Helm, 1980).

7. Difficult Times

Arm-to-arm vaccination: information from books deposited with The Wellcome Institute for the History of Medicine Library.

Eulogy of uncle William: Family Record.

Dissolution of law practice: Family Record.

8. Coping with a Large Family

The 'common itch': *The Family Physician*, vol. 4 (Caxton Publishing Co, 1930).

9. Middle Age

Inaugural meeting of the National Liberal Federation: Roy Jenkins, *Gladstone* (Macmillan, 1995).

House of Commons resolution April 1883: Office of the Journal of the House of Commons.

'The Maiden Tribute of Modern Babylon': information supplied by The Fawcett Society Library.

Deaths from scarlet fever: information from books deposited with the Wellcome Institute for The History of Medicine Library.

10. Her Daughters' Education

Most of the sources in this chapter are family letters in possession of the author: Martha Westwater, *The Wilson Sisters* (Ohio University Press, 1984) and *The New Girl* by Sally Mitchell (published 1895 by Columbia University Press).

Alice's letter to Hester about her visit to the House of Commons (8 June 1886):

'Dear Little Hester, I must write a letter to let you know how *very* interesting it was, in the House last night, or rather this morning. [We] heard the latter part of Goschen's speech and Parnell's, which created a great sensation, by revealing how the tories had it in their minds to have done even more for Ireland if they had come into power. Sir M. H. Beach entirely denied it, when he came to speak, & you will read the little altercation between him & Parnell ... Mr J. Cowen was having his innings when we got there ... his speech was most eloquent in supporting the Bill. Then Sir M. Beach was very long winded and dull, & we went at last to get some tea in the back room. We had hardly begun it when somebody said Gladstone was up, so we left our tea and tore back to the gallery, & got there before the cheers had subsided, that greeted his rising. It was a wonderful sight, to see that old man so powerful, & energetic in mind still. He spoke with much gesticulation & very earnestly – part of it was rather dull but all the latter part was *fine*. At last he sat down at 1.10, having spoken an hour & a half or more. Deafening cheers from the Irish – & then they divided, *all* the members going out, to be counted outside in the division lobbies ... At last they reassembled, & the excitement was so intense that one felt as if one could hardly breathe & the numbers were read out. Deafening cheers broke from the tories, & defiant ones from the Irish for quite a long time, & then they called for cheers for the G.O.M. & for Parnell, & groans for Chamberlain, which he received with a cheerful smile. He & Mr Gladstone & Lord Randolph Ch. all had swell flowers in their buttonholes but the other MP's none of them seemed to. The Prince of Wales was not there, nor any royalty.

'Then we drove home in a cab ... & I woke up the others & they got up & we had some supper & talked it all over &d then went to bed about 3 in daylight! So ended the great &d wonderful adventure! ...

'Please send these letters to Granny to read but keep them in their own envelopes. Will would like to see this too.

'From your mother.'

11. Her Family Almost Flown

Epidemic of typhoid 1889/90: *Everymans Encyclopedia*.

12. A Daughter in India

Letters from Hester (published privately) and now deposited with the India Office Library, London.

Deaths in India from the plague: The population of Bombay, recorded by the 1891 Census was 806,144.

13. Turn of the Century

Will's affair with Mrs Weekley: Janet Byrne, *A Genius for Living* (Bloomsbury, 1995).

14. Grandmother Alice

Coleridge and Anti-Vivisection Society: Richard D. Ryder, *Victims of Science* (Davis-Poynter, 1975).

15. Mainly Women's Suffrage

Fawcett Society Library, *passim. Women's Suffrage & Party Politics in Britain 1866–1914*, by Constance Rover, Routledge & Kegan Paul and University of Toronto Press 1967.

Re Edward Carpenter: O.U.P 1895. Dictionary of National Biography 1922-1930.

Appendixes

Petition of February 1871 against the Contagious Diseases Acts

PETITION

Your Petitioners pray for the total repeal of the Contagious Diseases Acts 1866 to 1869:

First. Because the said Acts are unjust as applying to one sex only; they are cruel in operation, and although professedly designed for the mitigation of disease, they ultimately tend to increase it by encouragement they give to vice.

Second. Because although unchastity is no legal offence, they treat women accused of it worse than suspected criminals, inasmuch as they are condemned upon the mere statement of police spies, deprived of trial by jury, and the benefits of the Habeas Corpus Act, and the said Acts in so doing violate the fundamental principle of English jurisprudence, which is, that every British-born subject is equal before the law.

Third, Because these Acts confide to the police a power not only dangerous, but one inconsistent with personal freedom and perfectly intolerable in a free country, and they place all women at their mercy by enabling the police to force any and all women to register themselves as prostitutes, or to defend their chastity in open court, and there is no adequate security against the abuse of power.

Fourth. Because the police employed for these Acts and entrusted with this power are appointed by central authority, and not subject to local control, thus making a vast stride towards centralization, and striking a fatal blow at municipal government.

Fifth. Because these Acts recognise and legalise prostitution. Your Petitioners are utterly opposed to any legislation having for its object or necessarily involving the legal recognition, superintendence, or regulation of prostitution, inasmuch as such laws are contrary to the traditions, the principles and the feeling of this country, and will have a most debasing effect on the youth of both sexes, who with such laws in operation cannot be expected to distinguish between what is legally allowable and what is normally reprehensible.

Sixth. Because the experience of other countries does not show such laws to have been attended with beneficial results in the suppression of disease; but, even if such were the case, your Petitioners cannot accept any amount of material good as an equivalent for the sacrifice of constitutional safeguards, the perpetration of cruelty and injustice, the banishing of morality and religion from our legislation, and the degradation of national character which such legislation involves.

And your Petitioners will ever pray, &c.

John Manning, Mayor.

Anti Women's Suffrage Article (published in 'The Nineteenth Century', No. CXLVIII – June 1889)

AN APPEAL AGAINST FEMALE SUFFRAGE – JUNE 1889

WE, the undersigned, wish to appeal to the common sense and the educated thought of the men and women of England against the proposed extension of the Parliamentary suffrage to women.

1. While desiring the fullest possible development of the powers, energies, and education of women, we believe that their work for the State, and their responsibilities towards it, must always differ essentially from those of men, and that therefore their share in the working of the State machinery should be different from that assigned to men. Certain large departments of the national life are of necessity worked exclusively by men. To men belong the struggle of debate and legislation in Parliament; the hard and exhausting labour implied in the administration of the national resources and powers; the conduct of England's relations towards the external world; the working of the army and navy; all the heavy, laborious, fundamental industries of the State, such as those of mines, metals, and railways; the lead and supervision of English commerce, the management of our vast English finance, the service of that merchant fleet on which our food supply depends. In all these spheres women's direct participation is made impossible either by the disabilities of sex, or by strong formations of custom and habit resting ultimately upon physical difference, against which it is useless to contend. They are affected indeed, in some degree to have an influence on them all. This influence they already have, and will have more and more as the education of women advances. But their direct interest in these matters can never equal that of men, whose whole energy of mind and body is daily and hourly risked in them. Therefore it is not just to give to women direct power of deciding questions of Parliamentary policy, of war, of foreign or colonial affairs, of commerce and finance equal to that possessed by men. We hold that they already possess an

influence on political matters fully proportioned to the possible share of women in the political activities of England.

At the same time we are heartily in sympathy with all the recent efforts which have been made to give women a more important part in those affairs of the community where their interests and those of men are equally concerned; where it is possible for them not only to decide but to help in carrying out, and where, therefore, judgement is weighed by a true responsibility, and can be guided by experience and the practical information which comes from it. As voters for or members of School Boards, Boards of Guardians, and other important public bodies, women have now opportunities for public usefulness which must promote the growth of character, and at the same time strengthen among them the social sense and habit. All these changes of recent years, together with the great improvements in women's education which have accompanied them, we cordially welcome. But we believe that the emancipating process has now reached the limits fixed by the physical constitution of women, and by the fundamental difference which must always exist between their main occupations and those of men. The care of the sick and the insane; the treatment of the poor; the education of children: in all these matters, and others besides, they have made good their claim to larger and more extended powers. We rejoice in it. But when it comes to questions of foreign or colonial policy, or of grave constitutional change, then we maintain that the necessary and normal experience of women – speaking generally and in the mass – does not and can never provide them with such materials for sound judgment as are open to men.

To sum up: we would give them their full share in the State of social effort and social mechanism; we look for their increasing activity in that higher State which rests on thought, conscience, and moral influence; but we protest against their admission to direct power in that State which *does* rest upon force – the State in its administrative, military and financial aspects – where the physical capacity, the accumulated experience and inherited training of men ought to prevail without the harassing interference of those who, though they may be partners with men in debate, can in these matters never be partners with them in action.

2. If we turn from the *right* of women to the suffrage – a right which

on the grounds just given we deny – to the effect which the possession of
the suffrage may be expected to have on their character and position and
on family life, we find ourselves no less in doubt. It is urged that the
influence of women in politics would tell upon the side of morality. We
believe that it does so tell already, and will do so with greater force as
women by improved education fit themselves to exert it more widely and
efficiently. But it may be asked, On what does this moral influence
depend? We believe that it depends largely on qualities which the
natural position and functions of women as they are at present tend to
develop, and which might be seriously impaired by their admission to
the turmoil of active political life. These qualities are, above all,
sympathy and disinterestedness. Any disposition of things which threat-
ens to lessen the national reserve of such forces as these we hold to be a
misfortune. It is notoriously difficult to maintain them in the presence of
party necessities and in the heat of party struggle. Were women admitted
to this struggle, their natural eagerness and quickness of temper would
probably make them hotter partisans than men. As their political
relations stand at present, they tend to check in them the disposition to
partisanship, and to strengthen in them the qualities of sympathy and
disinterestedness. We believe that their admission to the suffrage would
precisely reverse this condition of things, and that the whole nation
would suffer in consequence. For whatever may be the duty and privilege
of the parliamentary vote for men, we hold that citizenship is not
dependent upon or identical with the possession of the
suffrage.Citizenship lies in the participation of each individual in effort
for the good of the community. And we believe that women will be more
valuable citizens, will contribute more precious elements to the national
life without the vote than with it. The quickness to feel, the willingness
to lay aside prudential considerations in a right cause, which are amongst
the peculiar excellencies of women, are in their right place when they are
used to influence the more highly trained and developed judgment of
men. But if this quickness of feeling could be immediately and directly
translated into public action, in matters of vast and complicated political
import, the risks of politics would be enormously increased, and what is
now a national blessing might easily become a national calamity. On
the one hand, then, we believe that to admit women to the ordinary
machinery of political life would inflame the partisanship and increase
the evils, already so conspicuous, of that life, would tend to blunt the

special moral qualities of women, and so to lessen the national reserve of moral force; and, on the other hand, we dread the political and practical effects which, in our belief, would follow on such a transformation as is proposed, of an influence which is now beneficient largely because it is indirect and gradual.

3. Proposals for the extension of the suffrage to women are beset with grave practical difficulties. If votes be given to unmarried women on the same terms as they are given to men, large numbers of women leading immoral lives will be enfranchised on the one hand, while married women, who, as a rule, have passed through more of the practical experiences of life than the unmarried, will be excluded. To remedy part of this difficulty it is proposed by a large section of those who advocate the extension of the suffrage to women, to admit married women with the requisite property qualification. This proposal – an obviously just one if the suffrage is to be extended to women at all – introduces changes in family life, and in the English conception of the household, of enormous importance, which have never been adequately considered. We are practically invited to embark upon them because a few women of property possessing already all the influence which belongs to property, and a full share of that public protection and safety which is the fruit of taxation, feel themselves aggrieved by the denial of the parliamentary vote. The grievance put forward seems to us wholly disproportionate to the claim based upon it.

4. A survey of the manner in which this proposal has won its way into practical politics leads us to think that it is by no means ripe for legislative solution. A solution change of momentous gravity has been proposed; the mass of those immediately concerned in it are notoriously indifferent; there has been no serious and general demand for it, as it always the case if a grievance is real and reform necessary; the amount of information collected is quite inadequate to the importance of the issue; and the public has gone through no sufficient discipline of discussion on the subject. Meanwhile pledges to support female suffrage have been hastily given in the hopes of strengthening existing political parties by the female vote. No doubt there are many conscientious supporters of female suffrage amongst members of Parliament; but it is hard to deny that the present prominence of the question is due to party consideration of a temporary nature. It is, we submit, altogether

unworthy of the intrinsic gravity of the question that it should be determined by reference to the passing needs of party organisation. Meanwhile we remember that great electoral changes have been carried out during recent years. Masses of new electors have been added to the constituency. These new elements have still to be assimilated; these new electors have still to be trained to take their part in the national work; and while such changes are still fresh, and their issues uncertain, we protest against any further alteration in our main political machinery, especially when it is an alteration which involves a new principle of extraordinary range and significance, closely connected with the complicated problems of sex and family life.

5. It is often urged that certain injustices of the law towards women would be easily and quickly remedied were the political power of the vote conceded to them; and that there are many wants, especially among working women, which are now neglected, but which the suffrage would enable them to press on public attention. We reply that during the past half century all the principal injustices of the law towards women have been amended by means of the existing constitutional machinery; and with regard to those that remain, we see no signs of any unwillingness on the part of Parliament to deal with them. On the contrary, we remark a growing sensitiveness to the claims of women, and the rise of a new spirit of justice and sympathy among men, answering to those advances made by women in education, and the best kind of social influence, which we have already noticed and welcomed. With regard to the business or trade interests of women, – here, again, we think it safer and wiser to trust to organisation and self-help on their own part, and to the growth of a better public opinion among the men workers, than to the exercise of a political right which may easily bring women into direct and hasty conflict with men.

In conclusion: nothing can be further from our minds than to seek to depreciate the position or the importance of women. It is because we are keenly alive to the enormous value of their special contribution to the community, that we oppose what seems to us likely to endanger that contribution. We are convinced that the pursuit of a mere outward equality with men is for women not only vain but demoralising. It leads to a total misconception of woman's true dignity and special mission. It tends to personal struggle and rivalry, where the only effort of both the great divisions of the human family should be to contribute the characteristic labour and the best gifts of each to the common stock.

Dowager Lady Stanley of Alderley, Dover Street
Lady Frederick Cavendish, Carlton House Terrace
Lady Wimborne, Arlington Street
Lady Randolph Churchill, Connaught Place
Lady Fanny Marjoribanks, Piccadilly
The Duchess of St Albans, Bestwood, Arnold, Notts.
Lady Alwyne Compton, The Palace, Ely
Lady Louisa Egerton, Piccadilly
Mrs. Goschen, Portland Place
Viscountess Halifax, Hickleton, Doncaster
Lady Revelstoke, Charles Street, Berkely Square
Hon. Mrs Meynell Ingram, Temple Newsam
Mrs. Knox-Little, The College, Worcester
Lady Wade, Cambridge
Mrs. Creighton, Cambridge, and The College, Worcester
Mrs. Westcott, Cambridge, and Abbey Gardens, Westminster
Mrs. Church, The Deanery, St Paul's
Mrs. Boyle, The Deanery, Salisbury
Mrs. Woods, Trinity College, Oxford
The Countess of Wharncliffe, Wharncliffe House, Curzon Street, W.
Mrs. Mundella, Elvaston Place, S.W.
Mrs. Osborne Morgan, Green Street, Grosvenor Square
The Countess of Morley, Prince's Gardens, S.W.
Mrs. Henry Broadhurst, Brixton
Lady Constance Shaw Lefevre, Bryanston Square, W.
Mrs. T. H. Green, Oxford
Mrs. Leslie Stephen, Hyde Park Gate, SW
Mrs. Humphry Ward, Russell Square, WC
Miss Beatrice Potter, The Argoed, Monmouth
Mrs. Holford, Dorchester House, Park Lane
Mrs. J. R. Green, Kensington Square, W.
Hon. Mrs. John Talbot, Great George Street, Westminster
Mrs. Loftie, Sheffield Terrace, Campden Hill
Viscountess Bury, Prince's Gate, W.

Mrs. Sutherland Orr, Kensington Park Gardens
Lady Layard
Mrs. Frederic Harrison, Westbourne Terrace, W.
Mrs. Huxley, Marlborough Place, W.
Mrs. Henry Hobhouse, Hadspen House, Somerset
Miss Lucy Garnett, Upper Bedford Place
Hon. Emily Lawless, Eaton Terrace, S.W.
Hon. Mrs. Chapman, Paul's Cray Hill, Kent
Mrs. Poynter, Albert Gate, S.W.
Mrs. Baldwin, Wilden House, Stourport
Miss Cureton, Matron, Aldenbrooke's Hospital, Cambridge
Miss Soulsby, High School, Oxford
Miss Ottley, High School, Worcester
Miss Topping, Superintendent, St John's House, Worcester
Mrs. Bell, The College, Marlborough
Mrs. Lynn Linton, Queen Anne's Mansions
Mrs. Beesly, Warrington Crescent, W.
Mrs. Courtenay Ilbert, Gloucester Place, W.
Hon. Mrs. Arthur Elliot, Cavendish Square
Mrs. Wynne Finch, Charles Street, Berkeley Square
Mrs. Simpson, Cornwall Gardens, S.W.
Mrs. Lathbury, Barkston Mansions
Mrs. Seeley, Cambridge
Mrs. Hort, Cambridge
Mrs. Bridges, Wimbledon
Mrs. Routh, Newnham Cottage, Cambridge
Mrs. Priestley, Hertford Street, Mayfair
Mrs. Kegan Paul, Ashburn Place, S.W.
Mrs. W. Bagehot, Hurd's Hill, Somerset
Mrs. Rathbone Greg, Melbury Road, W.
Mrs. Lilly, Michael's Grove, S.W.
Lady Bunbury, Mildenhall
Mrs. Russell Barrington, Melbury Road
Miss Edith Anderson, Brighton
Mrs. H. H. Asquith, Hampstead
Hon. Mrs. Ralph Dutton, Halkin Street, W.
Mrs. D. Carmichael, Sussex Gardens. W.
Mrs. Spencer Walpole, Onslow Gardens, S.W.

Mrs. Maxwell Lyte, Portman Square, W.
Mrs. Higford Burr, Eaton Place
Mrs. Alma-Tadema, Grove End Road, W.
Miss Frances Poynter, Brompton Crescent
Mrs. Sherlock Willis, Foulis Terrace, S.W.
Mrs. R. Ward, Onslow Square
Mrs. John Ball, Southwell Gardens, S,W.
Mrs. Bishop, Prince of Wales Terrace, S.W.
Mrs. Meredith Townsend, Harley Street
Mrs. Andrew Cross, Delamere Terrace, W.
Lady Wynford, Grosvenor Squre, W.
Mrs. Blumenthal, Hyde Park Gate
Hon. Frederica Spring-Rice, Sumner Place, S.W.
Hon. Catherine Spring-Rice, Sumner Place, S.W.
Lady Monteagle, Onslow Gardens, S.W.
Miss F. H. Chenevix Trench, Elm Park Gardens, S.W.
Hon. Mrs. J. R. Arthur, Queen's Gate Place
Mrs. Wm. Raikes, The Beeches, Farnborough
Mrs. Cecil Russell, Lowndes Square, S.W.
Mrs. Edward O'Brien, Cahirmoyle, Limerick
Mrs. T. Wells, Manchester Square
Mrs. W. E. Forster, Wharfeside, Burley
Mrs. Matthew Arnold, Cobham
Mrs. Arnold Toynbee, Oxford
Mrs. Max Müller, Oxford
Mrs. Agnew, Great Stanhope Street
Mrs. Buckle, Queen Square, W.C.
Mrs. James Knowles, St. Jame's Park
Lady Victoria Buxton, Grosvenor Crescent
Mrs. Charles Buxton, Fox Warren, Surrey
Hon. Mrs Edward Talbot, The Vicarage, Leeds
Mrs. J. R. Thursfield, Montague Place, W.C.

[In furtherance of the foregoing Appeal – which has hitherto been only shown privately to a few persons – the accompanying proposed protests is laid before the readers of the *Nineteenth Century*, with the request that such ladies among them as agree with it will be kind enough to sign the opposite page and return it, *when detached*, to the EDITOR of this Review.

The difficulty of obtaining a public expression, even of disapproval, about such a question from those who entirely object to mixing themselves up in the coarsening struggles of party political life, may easily become a public danger. Their silence will be misinterpreted into indifference or consent to designs they most dislike, and may thus help to bring them about.

It is submitted that for once, and in order to save the quiet of Home life from total disappearance, they should do violence to their natural reticence, and signify publicly and unmistakably their condemnation of the scheme now threatened.

The deliberate opinion of the women readers of the *Nineteenth Century* might certainly be taken as a fair sample of the judgment of the educated women of the country, and would probably receive the sympathy and support of the overwhelming majority of their fellow countrywomen.

EDITOR, Nineteenth Century.]

WOMEN'S SUFFRAGE

*Reasons for supporting the Proposed Extension
of the Parliamentary Franchise*

Because it is a recognised principle of the British Constitution that representation and taxation should go together.

Because it cannot be shown that Women who possess every qualification required by law for the exercise of the Franchise except that of sex, are naturally disqualified by sex alone.

Because the exclusion of women, solely on the ground of sex, from their fair share in the government of the country, inflicts upon them an unjust disability and tends to lower them in general estimation.

Because the anomaly that a woman, while herself unable to vote, may as a householder or employer of labour be the means of conferring the vote on men employed in her service, is to be seen, not in a few isolated cases only, but on a large scale and in all parts of the country.

Because exclusion from the Parliamentary Franchise is an authoritative expression of the view that women are not called upon to think and act as responsible citizens in public affairs.

Because this view is not now held by leading statesmen and other persons qualified to judge, and the law is therefore out of harmony with competent opinion.

Because while women are invited by all parties to take a prominent part in political agitation, those to whom such action is distasteful, being prevented by law from giving a quiet vote, are excluded from political influence.

Because the experiment of the exercise of voting power by women has been tried during a considerable period in municipal and School Board elections, and with such satisfactory results that the further concession of the vote for County Councils met with no opposition.

Because the measure is thus shown to be in accordance with justice, sound theory, and practical experience.

CENTRAL COMMITTEE OF THE NATIONAL SOCIETY FOR WOMEN'S
SUFFRAGE
10, Great College Street, Westminster, S.W.

The Times report of

THE WOMEN'S SUFFRAGE DEMONSTRATION

of 13 June 1911

A FIVE MILES PROCESSION OF 40,000 PERSONS

ALBERT HALL MEETING

THE woman suffragists, Constitutional and militant, on Saturday evening made high festival in London for their cause, transfiguring the West-end – through which they marched for four or five hours – with pageantry. The women have had triumphal processions before though not, as yet, so often as to blunt by familiarity the public sense of their beauty and uncommonness – but this was beyond them all in numbers and effect. At the gathering on the Embankment the marshalled lines, gleaming with banners, extended the entire length of the great promenade. Just as Big Ben was striking half past 5, Mrs Drummond, riding astride and dressed in a dark green habit with a broad-brimmed hat, came to the front, and the procession moved off, up the crowded Northumberland-avenue to the still more crowded Trafalgar-square.

THE PAGEANT

At the head of the procession there were two arresting figures which embodied and gave dramatic expression, each in its different way, to the spirit of the demonstration. The first was the standard-bearer, carrying the purple, white, and green colours of the Women's Social and Political Union – a slim fair girl in white who was given this post of high distinction because she had endured weeks of forcible feeding in prison. The other was a striking personation of Joan of Arc. Next came the martyrs of the cause, nearly a thousand strong led by their fighting leaders, Mrs Pankhurst, Mrs Pethick Lawrence, and Miss Christabel Pankhurst – the last in academic dress.

The artistic elements of the procession were many. Nothing could be better than the historical pageant illustrating the prominence and distinction of women in public life in the Middle Ages. Standing out of the throng was Abbess Hilda, founder of the Benedictine monastery of

Whitby, who presided over an Ecclesiastic synod in 664. In this contingent was also seen Queen Elizabeth, a tall, commanding figure in jewelled array. Interesting, too, was the group which immediately followed of great women of the 19th century. Here were Grace Darling, Jenny Lind, Florence Nightingale, and Charlotte Brontë – to mention just a few of a little company in poke bonnets and ringlets.

Next in point of attraction came the representatives of the Celtic fringe. Scotland led the way with a band of pipers playing 'Annie Laurie,' and a women wearing tartan. The Irish section had colleens in flowing red cloaks; but Wales had the most distinctive costume, the girls with the nation's high conical hat, kerchief apron, and striped gown. The Welsh women as they marched sang their national songs, and were led by a band with a circlet of oak-leaves binding his long grey locks. In the Colonial contingent all the Dominions were to be seen, the place of honour being given to New Zealand, the first country in the British Empire to give women the vote. There was also an international contingent in which the distinctiove dress of every nation in Europe was exhibited.

Classes and Professions

Women of every class of society seemed to be united in the demonstration. Mainly, however, they were women of assured circumstances. The representatives of the wives and daughters of the working classes were comparatively few. On the other hand, many indications of wealth were to be observed, not least in the number of motor-cars and smart carriages and pairs – festooned with flags and flowers – which brought the leading personages to the Embankment and fell in at the rear of the procession. The class, however, that loomed largest was what is usually known as the lower middle. Every profession, business, and calling followed by women was represented. A group of elegantly-gowned women carrying bamboo poles wreathed in carnations, roses, and smilax was composed of actresses. In contrast with them in modes was the University section – a long line of women in black gowns and caps. Politics of all shades had contingents. Even the Churches were represented by separate organizations. In this Church of England group were to be seen clergymen carrying banners. There was also a Catholic Women's Suffrage Society, and the contingent representative of the Free Churches was the largest of the three.

CONSTITUTIONALISTS AND MILITANTS

The surprise of the demonstration, however, was the unexpected strength of the Constitutionalists which it showed. The Women's Social and Political Union and the Women's Freedom League combined were outnumbered and overshadowed by the National Union of Women's Suffrage Society, led by the president, Mrs Henry Fawcett. Every part of the kingdom was represented in this immense section. It was brilliant also, such was the lavish display of its particularly vivid colours of red, white, and green.

The procession took two and a half hours to pass a given point. But it was interrupted frequently at several crossings on the way to allow the traffic – mainly motor-cars with people in evening dress – to pass. It was half-past eight o'clock before the last contingent turned from St. James's street into Piccadilly – that is, three hours after the head of the procession had left the Embankment – and in Piccadilly they had covered only a third of their journey to the various places of meeting. The procession was five miles long and about 40,000 women walked in it. The march, toilsome and trying though it must have been, was well maintained in spirit as well as in stateliness, showing a wonderful capacity to endure physical strain and discomfort. As for for spectators, they were deeply interested, but not demonstrative. Perhaps the only individual in the procession who got a cheer from the disinterested onlookers was Mrs Despard as she went by bare-headed, carrying a sheaf of yellow lilies. To many people, no doubt, it must have been a spectacle that troubled and provoked as well as fascinated.

Index

NOTE: Alice and Ben are not indexed and individuals are indexed only where they are the centre of the action.